Staff Studies for the World Economic Outlook

By the Research Department of the
International Monetary Fund

INTERNATIONAL MONETARY FUND
Washington, DC
September 1995

recycled paper

Contents

Changes in economic systems provide rare opportunities to redesign basic institutional structures in labor markets. This paper attempts to provide guidance for such institutional choice by drawing on the findings of recent labor market research in market economies on the links between institutional structure and labor market performance. After considering the suitability of research from market economies for the labor market problems faced by economies in transition from central planning, the paper considers the effects of alternative institutions for wage determination—collective bargaining structures and minimum wage and indexation legislation—employment security, income security, and active labor market policies.

The divergence between production and consumption indicators in Russia suggests that the magnitude of the output collapse in the course of the transition is overstated by the official statistics. Alternative estimates for real GDP are derived that reconcile the official production and consumption data. Based on cautious assumptions, real GDP appears to have declined cumulatively by no more than one third rather than by one half. The estimated drop in household welfare is much smaller still, as the output mix shifts and deadweight losses are sharply reduced.

A number of aspects of foreign direct investment and its role in the "globalized" economy are examined from both microeconomic and macroeconomic perspectives. Following an exploration of historic patterns of foreign direct investment, with emphasis on the large surge that took place after 1985, key characteristics of foreign direct investment and the multinational corporations that generate it are examined in detail. These include the determinants of foreign direct investment and the international expansion of firms. The relationships between foreign direct investment and capital formation, technology transfer, international trade, and economic growth in both host (recipient) and home (investor) countries are also analyzed. Policy issues surrounding the possible extension of multilateral trade rules to cover foreign direct investment are discussed.

Preface

Staff Studies for the World Economic Outlook contains background analyses for the World Economic Outlook exercise carried out by staff in the International Monetary Fund's Research Department and by visiting scholars. The *World Economic Outlook* project is directed by Flemming Larsen, Senior Advisor in the Research Department, together with David T. Coe, Chief of the World Economic Studies Division.

The papers have benefited from comments by colleagues throughout the Fund and, in some cases, by the Fund's Executive Directors. However, the views presented in the papers are those of the authors and should not be interpreted as representing the views of the International Monetary Fund. The authors would like to thank Claire Adams, Sheila Bassett, Sungcha H. Cha, and Toh Kuan for research assistance and Susan Duff and Margaret Dapaah for word processing. Thomas Walter of the External Relations Department edited the manuscripts and coordinated production of the publication.

The following symbols have been used throughout this paper:

... to indicate that data are not available;

—   to indicate that the figure is zero or less than half the final digit shown, or that the item does not exist;

–   between years or months (e.g., 1991–92 or January–June) to indicate the years or months covered, including the beginning and ending years or months;

/   between years (e.g., 1991/92) to indicate a crop or fiscal (financial) year.

"Billion" means a thousand million.

"Basis points" refer to hundredths of 1 percentage point (for example, 25 basis points are equivalent to ¼ of 1 percentage point).

Minor discrepancies between constituent figures and totals are due to rounding.

The term "country," as used in this paper, does not in all cases refer to a territorial entity that is a state as understood by international law and practice; the term also covers some territorial entities that are not states, but for which statistical data are maintained and provided internationally on a separate and independent basis.

I

Saving Behavior in Industrial and Developing Countries

Paul Masson, Tamim Bayoumi, and Hossein Samiei

Saving has always been an important issue in economics. It plays a central role in income determination, both in the short run through aggregate demand and in the long run through capital formation and wealth accumulation. The prospects for aggregate saving are a particularly relevant issue currently, as there are large potential future demands on world saving. In particular, the investment needs of transforming and newly industrializing economies may come at a time of significant government dissaving in many industrial countries, where aging populations are also likely to reduce private saving rates and raise government deficits in the coming decades. Understanding the determinants of saving is necessary in order to assess the resources that will be available to finance investment and the prospects for real interest rates.

Cross-country variations in saving rates are also of considerable interest. High-saving countries—for instance, Japan, Korea, and Singapore—have typically also experienced high growth rates, although the direction of causality is unclear. With limited capital mobility, increases in the stock of productive capital have to be financed mainly by higher national saving. When capital is mobile, differences in saving propensities may lead to large external imbalances, such as those of the United States and Japan.

There is already an extensive literature on saving behavior.[1] This paper extends that literature by looking at a broad set of possible determinants of private saving and applying them to saving data for a large number of industrial and developing countries. Both time-series and cross-section information is used, as the explanatory power of potential variables differs widely in those two dimensions.

The plan of the paper is as follows. The first section discusses measurement issues and presents an overview of data on saving. The next section briefly surveys the various theories of saving and gives a selective survey of previous empirical work. Following sections present empirical results, in the form of panel and cross-section estimates, for both industrial and developing countries

and use these estimates to project the effect of the more important explanatory variables. Finally, the paper offers some conclusions relating to policy issues.

The Evolution of National and Private Saving

Personal saving can be broadly defined to equal the increase in an individual's net worth. Because saving is also equal to income minus consumption, this definition would imply that income should be measured to include capital gains and losses on assets (including those related to depreciation, so that net, not gross, saving would be used), while consumption should include only the services of durable goods, not their purchase. In addition, accumulation of rights to future pensions would be included in a person's saving, whether or not that individual made related pension contributions. Such a broad definition would also include expenditures on research and development[2] and on education as part of saving and investment, rather than consumption. However, such adjustments to the national accounts definition of saving are not attempted in this paper, which, in line with most empirical work on saving, uses gross saving data from the national accounts because of their widespread availability. Even on a national income accounts basis, however, data are not strictly comparable across countries, as the treatment of particular items often differs.[3] In order to enhance comparability, data on private, not personal, saving are used, thus combining household and business saving.[4]

Charts 1–3 give a visual impression of gross national and private saving rates for selected industrial and developing countries since 1970. The ratio of private

---

[1]Aghevli and others (1990) provide a literature survey and discuss the evolution of saving in industrial and developing countries. See also the survey in Deaton (1992).

[2]The wages and salaries of those involved in doing research and development are typically excluded from investment in the national accounts.

[3]Measurement issues are discussed in the appendix.

[4]This is also the choice of Lipsey and Kravis (1987), who compare different measures of saving. Auerbach and Hassett (1991, p. 93), among others, find evidence that households "pierce the corporate veil" and take fully into account business saving when making their consumption decisions.

Chart 1. National and Private Saving
(In percent of GDP)

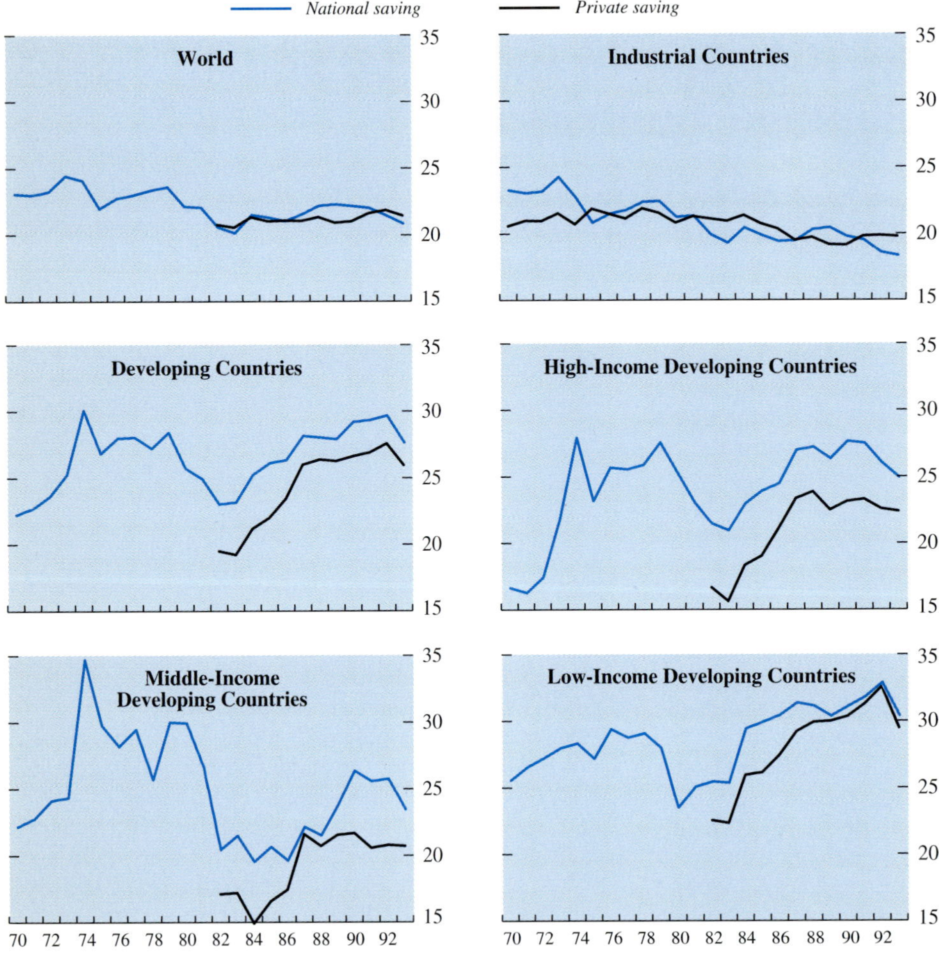

Source: World Economic Outlook database.

saving to GDP has remained relatively stable for the larger industrial countries, although there is a downward trend for Japan, the United States, and Italy. However, there is a much more pronounced decline in national saving rates for these countries over the past decade (except for Japan, where government saving has increased), as a result of an increase in government dissaving.[5] The ranking of private saving rates in some countries, such as Japan and Italy, has tended to remain high, while, in other countries, such as the United States and the United Kingdom, it has tended to remain low. Still other countries—for instance, Sweden—have seen substantial fluctuations in their private saving rates. As documented by Dean and others (1990), gross and net saving rates exhibit similar trends.

The data for developing countries suggest that, if anything, national saving rates may have seen a trend increase for developing countries taken together over the past 25 years—although it is not the case for the middle-income countries as a group.[6] Trends in national and private saving are similar, although countries' experiences vary considerably, both in terms of levels of saving and their variation over time, with, for instance, particularly dramatic declines in

---

[5]Maddison (1992) compares 11 territorial entities (8 countries now classified as industrial, plus India, Korea, and Taiwan Province of China) since 1870. His data suggest that national saving rates after World War II were unusually high from an historical perspective, and that the recent declines have to be interpreted in that context.

[6]The aggregation uses weights that change with movements in relative GDPs, which are converted to a common currency via exchange rates based on purchasing power parity. As fast-growing countries typically have had higher saving rates, the aggregate saving rate can show an upward trend because high-saving countries are becoming more important, even if saving rates in individual countries are unchanged.

saving rates in Venezuela and Egypt. Conclusions concern-ing cross-country differences and the evolution of saving over time should be tempered by a recognition that the quality of data is imperfect. In particular, the national accounts data may not fully capture all economic activities, and saving rates could therefore be unreliable. It may also be the case that, for high-inflation countries, measures of saving have a severe upward bias because nominal interest rates (and, hence, income) are high to compensate for the decline in the real value of financial assets.

The Analytics of Saving

Theoretical Considerations

Saving is properly viewed as resulting from a choice between present and future consumption, and Irving Fisher is at the origin of a rigorous development of its analytics.[7] A key element in the choice is the rate of time preference; if there are no constraints on shifting consumption intertemporally, optimal consumption for an individual in the absence of uncertainty will involve equating the rate of change of the marginal utility of consumption to the difference between the rate of time preference and the rate of interest. In this framework, consumption is independent of the timing of income; it depends instead on lifetime resources. Saving, by adding to financial assets, or dissaving, by running down assets or borrowing on future income, allows achievement of optimal consumption paths. Furthermore, the classical analysis of Fisher and others saw the interest rate as bringing about equality of saving and investment for the economy as a whole. Increased saving—for instance, owing to a decline in the rate of time preference—would lower real interest rates and stimulate investment.

Keynes changed the prevailing view about the role of saving in the economy by arguing that movements in income, as well as in interest rates, brought about ex post equality between saving and investment. The mechanism by which this process occurred depended on a close link between consumption and current income. Consumers were viewed not as intertemporally smoothing their consumption but rather as mech-anistically spending a fraction of their increases in income.

The discovery of the long-run stability of the saving rate in the United States by Kuznets and the immediate postwar experience of a consumption boom as households ran down assets highlighted the inadequacies of the simple Keynesian view, and interest in intertemporal approaches to saving revived. The theoretical literature since then has mainly involved, on the one hand, drawing out the implications of the intertemporal model in the context of demographic changes, government deficits and taxes, and stochastic fluctuations in income and, on the other hand, explaining how the Keynesian link between current income and consumption can be justified formally through liquidity constraints and other rigidities that prevent full intertemporal smoothing.

In the first category are the permanent income hypothesis (PIH) models of Friedman (1957) and Hall (1978), which for simplicity assume an infinite horizon, and the life cycle hypothesis (LCH) models of Modigliani and Brumberg (1954) and Modigliani and Ando (1957), which attempt to model a finite lifetime with successive stages of schooling, increasing earnings, and retirement. The existence of bequests raises the possibility that finite lifetimes are consistent with an infinite horizon, in which case government deficit changes could be offset entirely by private saving behavior (Barro (1974)). Other intertemporal models (Yaari (1965), Blanchard (1985), and Buiter (1988)) combine the infinite horizon approach with a constant probability of death (but no bequests) and a positive birthrate, thereby introducing a (small) wedge in equilibrium between rates of interest and rates of time preference and implying that government deficits are not offset one-for-one by private saving. However, all of these intertemporal models suggest a high degree of offsetting of expected future taxes by private saving and a small correlation of consumption with current income. In these models, lifetime resources, including financial wealth, are the determinants of consumption, rather than current incomes.

The second strand in the literature, which puts Keynesian consumption functions—perhaps augmented by intertemporal factors—on a sounder theoretical footing, has concentrated on elucidating the reasons why consumption smoothing might not be possible. The literature on liquidity constraints has been surveyed by Hayashi (1985); Deaton (1991) presents a model in which individuals engage in short-run buffering but do not optimize over their lifecycle. Another reason why households might not plan consumption on a lifetime basis is uncertainty. Nagatani (1972) argues that uncertainty on the part of individuals about their future income pros-pects explains why income and consumption might be more closely associated than in the LCH models.

The two paradigms have important implications for the response of saving to various factors, including fiscal variables, interest rates, demographics, and income growth. These and other explanations of private saving behavior are discussed in what follows.

---

[7]See, for instance, *The Theory of Interest* (Fisher (1930)), where optimal consumption in a two-period context is derived. Ramsey (1928) calculates optimal national saving behavior on the basis of an infinite horizon.

Chart 2. Selected Industrial Countries: National and Private Saving
(In percent of GDP)

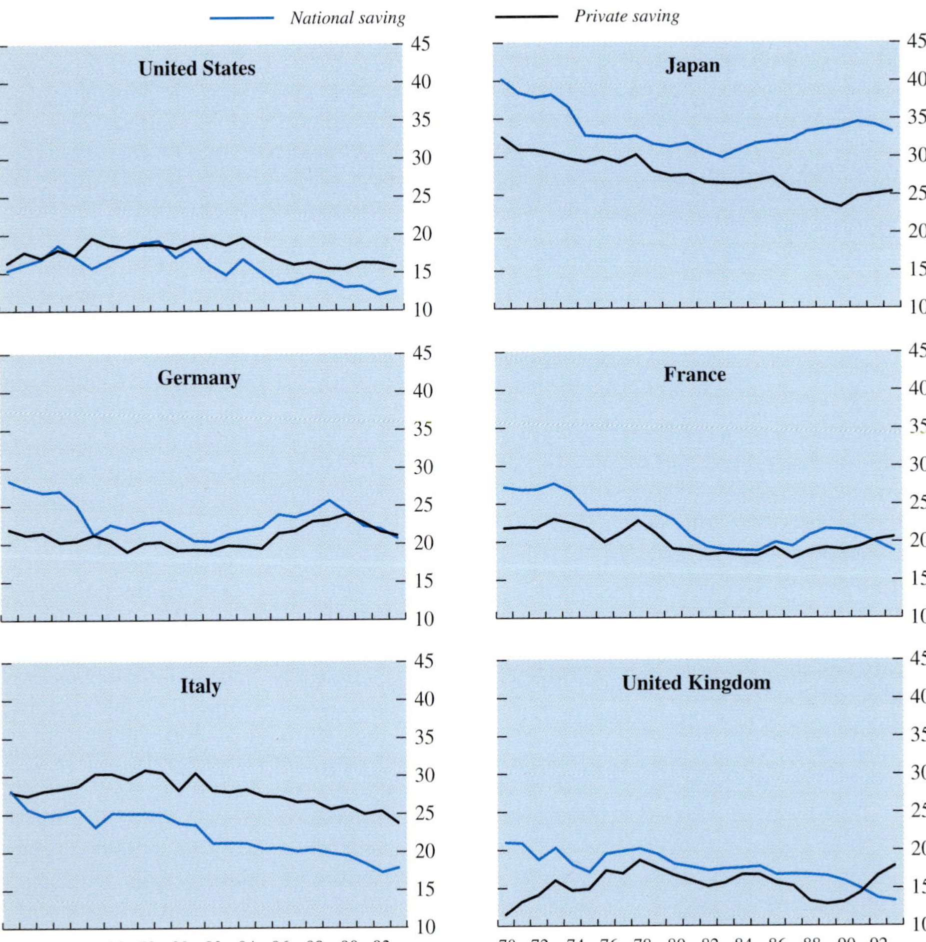

Outstanding Empirical Issues

Despite an extensive empirical literature, a number of issues remain unresolved. Although this paper will not attempt a comprehensive survey of that literature, it will nevertheless discuss the main hypotheses that have guided previous work and the tentative conclusions, if any, that have resulted. In this way, the empirical evidence presented in the following section can be placed in the appropriate context.

Does Consumption Follow Current Income or Fully Reflect Intertemporal Considerations?

A major theme of empirical work since the seminal article by Hall (1978) has been to test whether, in contradiction to the LCH and PIH models, variables (such as lagged income) help to predict consumption in addition to its lagged value. The evidence is mixed: Hall finds that income has no predictive power in addition to lagged consumption, while Flavin (1981) and oth-ers find that consumption is not sufficiently smooth but instead responds excessively to income. Carroll and Summers (1991) present evidence that consumption growth parallels income growth to a much greater extent than in fully intertemporal, optimizing models, although they support the idea (Deaton, 1991) that saving does buffer short-run income fluctuations and that some intertemporal smoothing does occur. Hence, the typical model of intertemporal consumption smoothing based on a representative agent not subject to borrowing and lending constraints does not appear to accord fully with the evidence. Hayashi (1985) and Flavin (1981) conclude that perhaps 20 percent of households in the United States are affected by liquidity constraints. Campbell and Mankiw (1989) find that roughly half of U.S. consumption can be attributed to forward-looking consumers, and half to those who consume a constant proportion of their income. Not surprisingly, liquidity constraints have also been found to exist in developing countries (see below).

Chart 2(concluded)

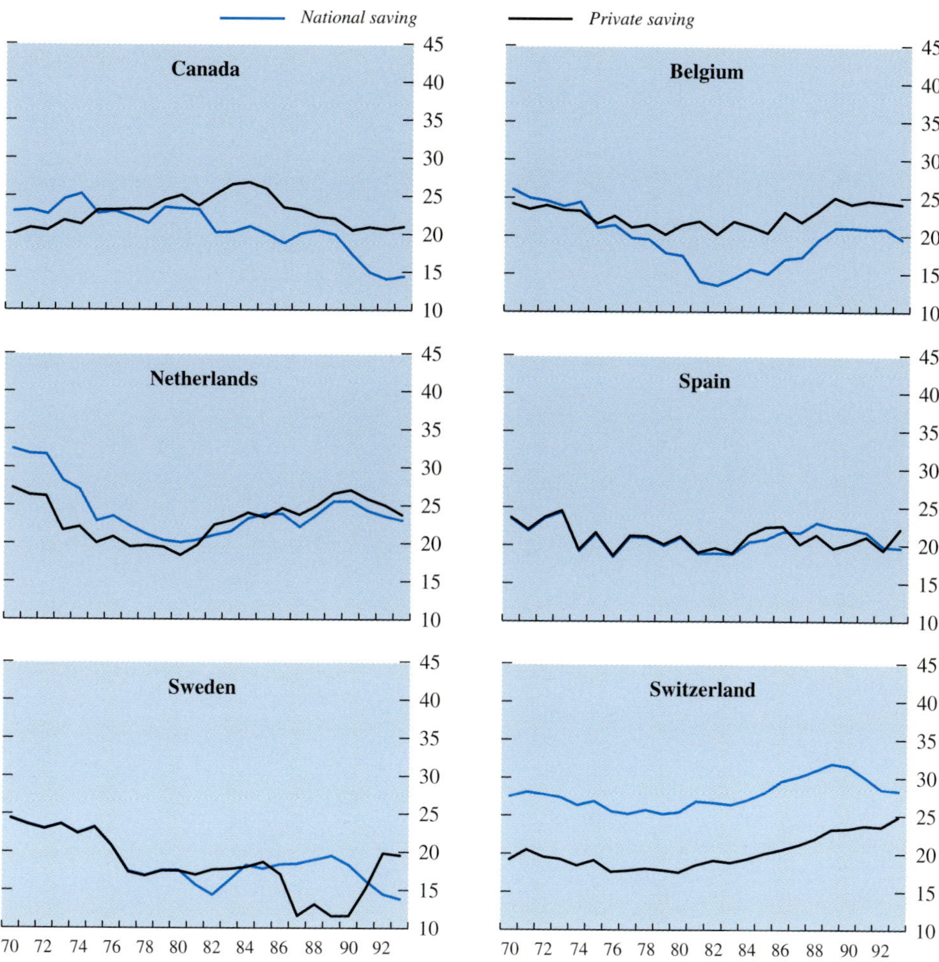

Source: World Economic Outlook database.

Does Private Sector Saving Offset Government Dissaving?

The empirical literature on the private saving offset to government deficits (or dissaving) has generally concluded that the hypothesis of a full offset (Ricardian equivalence) is rejected by the data.[8] Bernheim (1987) summarizes existing evidence for industrial countries, which indicates that a unit government deficit increase would be associated with a decrease in consumption of 0.5 to 0.6, and he presents new empirical results tending to confirm this range. Similar results have been obtained for developing countries, and Corbo and Schmidt-Hebbel (1991), in a typical estimate, also find a roughly 50 percent offset on private saving of changes in government saving. Haque and Montiel (1989) overwhelmingly reject Ricardian equivalence for their sample of 16 developing countries. They also test for the reason for non-equivalence—either short horizons or the presence of liquidity constraints affecting at least some households—and find that the latter cause is the reason for rejection, as liquidity constraints affect a proportion of households ranging from 0.182 for Korea to 0.713 for Thailand.

An increase in the government deficit can be expected to have different effects on private saving depending on whether it is due to lower taxes or higher government spending. Increased government spending may lower the resources available to the private sector and hence have a negative effect on private saving, whether or not it affects the deficit. The composition of government spending may also be important. Public investment, to the extent that it is viewed as productive, would not be expected to require further

---

[8]See, however, Evans (1988). Seater (1993) concludes that the evidence supports the hypothesis, although he recognizes that different government behavior could imply non-Ricardian equivalence in the future.

Chart 3. Selected Developing Countries: National and Private Saving
(In percent of GDP)

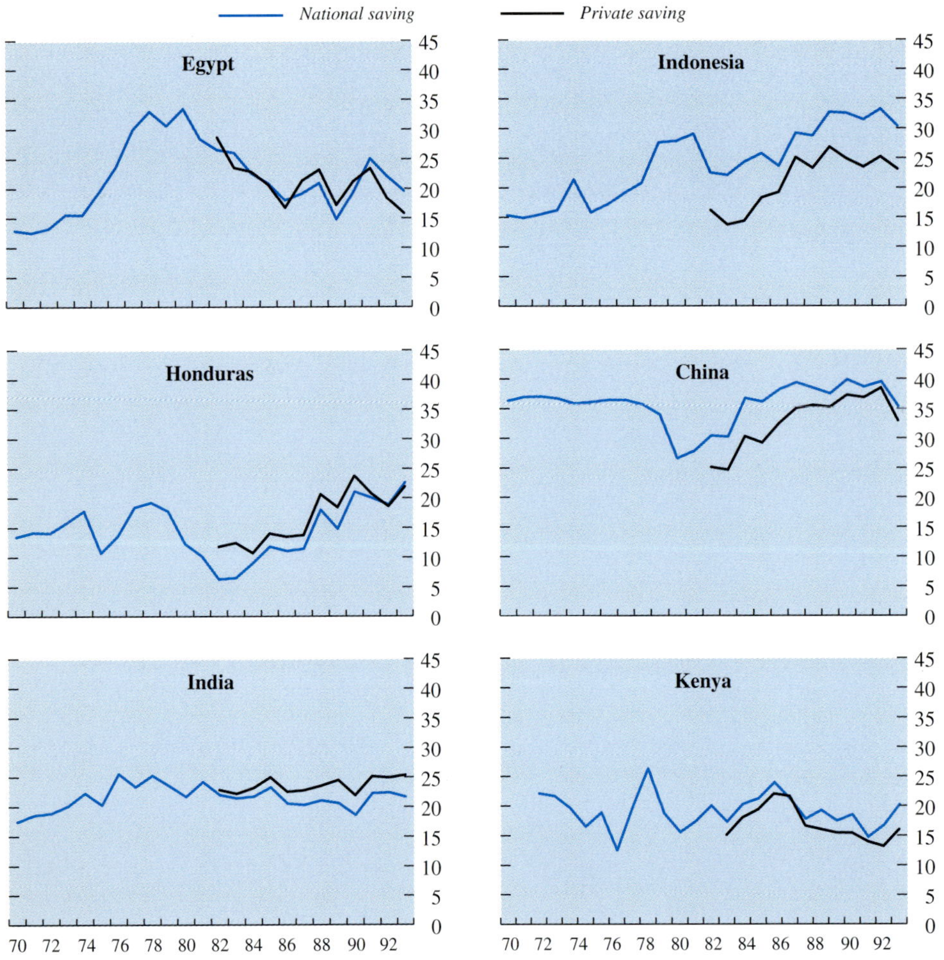

Source: World Economic Outlook database.

taxes and thus should not generate a private saving response. Its coefficient in a saving equation should be smaller than the coefficient of government consumption. In contrast, investment that does not generate revenues for the government (and hence is considered equivalent to government consumption) would involve future taxes and thus might induce a larger private saving offset.

Does Higher Income Growth Lead to Higher Saving?

A different issue concerns the relationship between income growth and the level of saving. Modigliani (1966) argued that a higher growth rate (whether owing to population or productivity growth) would, with unchanged saving rates by age groups, raise aggregate saving because it would increase the aggregate income of those working relative to those not earning labor income (including retired persons living off their accumulated assets). It is in fact the case that saving seems to be positively correlated with income growth (Modigliani (1970)), as high-growth countries such as Japan and Korea have also had high saving rates. However, Tobin (1967) pointed out that unchanged individual saving rates are consistent in this context only with myopic expectations of future income. If workers correctly expect that their income will grow in the future, they should, according to the LCH model, want to consume more today. It is thus possible that individual saving rates for those in work will fall by a sufficient amount to offset the aggregate effects of higher growth, a hypothesis confirmed by calculations based on the length of working lives relative to retirement. Thus, the empirical positive correlation of saving with income growth is not on the face of it consistent with the LCH model, unless the higher income growth is expected to be at least partly transitory. Carroll and Weil (1994) confirm that lagged values of increases in income growth seem to explain higher saving rates; they argue that the usual consumption models employing either uncertainty or liquidity constraints are not sufficient to explain this result and advance instead the hypothesis of habit persistence. If growth leads to higher saving, for whatever reason, there could be important implications for countries whose growth has slowed, such as Japan. However, another explanation for the correlation may be that a high growth rate is a proxy for a high rate of return on capital, which may be inadequately reflected in domestic interest rates (especially if financial markets are not liberalized).

Do Higher Interest Rates Lead to Higher Saving?

The effect of interest rates on consumption is ambiguous theoretically, being subject to potentially offsetting substitution and income effects, positive income effects of a rise in rates reflecting the fact that the private sector is a net creditor in financial assets. It is true that human wealth (that is, discounted future labor income) for a typical individual is much larger than financial wealth, and human wealth varies inversely with the rate of interest—suggesting that the negative substitution effect should dominate. However, consumers may not plan their lifetime consumption but respond primarily to current income. The empirical importance of the income effect is enhanced by pension plans' saving behavior: for defined benefit plans, higher interest rates increase the income available to pay pensions, allowing lower contributions (Bernheim and Shoven (1988)).

Empirical research has reported mixed results, paralleling the theoretical ambiguity surrounding the relationship between interest rates and consumption. For instance, using saving data for industrial countries, Bosworth (1993) finds a positive interest rate coefficient in time-series estimation for individual countries but a negative coefficient in panel (cross-country) estimation. For developing countries, Giovannini (1985) concludes that in most cases the real interest elasticity is zero, while Schmidt-Hebbel, Webb, and Corsetti (1992) also find no clear effects on saving. Ogaki, Ostry, and Reinhart (1995) find positive interest rate effects that vary with income but are still small.

Given that financial liberalization may have changed interest rate effects, it is not too surprising that results are not robust. The effect of liberalization on saving behavior can operate through at least two channels. First, financial development may provide outlets for financial saving, thereby raising saving rates (McKinnon (1973) and Shaw (1973)), a channel that has been emphasized in the development literature. The second aspect involves liberalization of consumer access to bank credit, as occurred in a number of industrial countries in the 1980s. Regulatory changes have allowed banks to lend more freely to individuals—for instance, for house pur-

chase or for consumption—which may lead, at least initially, to a significant decline in saving. Financial liberalization may involve one or another of these aspects, or both of them.[9]

The first channel, the McKinnon-Shaw hypothesis, focuses on the opportunities available to savers: financial liberalization leads to increases in interest rates, which should stimulate financial saving, add to total saving, and thus boost investment. However, it is important to distinguish between financial saving and saving that takes other forms, for example, house purchase, and it is not obvious that financial liberalization will increase aggregate saving. Furthermore, although liberalization should involve a wider menu of financial assets, it could be associated with a *decline* in some interest rates, as improved possibilities for diversification (including purchase of foreign assets) may lower risk premiums. A proxy for financial development that has been used is the money-income ratio, but evidence for a positive correlation with aggregate saving is weak. In any case, financial liberalization generally affects the form that saving takes and also the efficiency of investment; as a result, it may lead to improved growth performance, even if it does not raise the level of saving (De Gregorio and Guidotti (1994)).

A second aspect of financial liberalization, one that has been more prevalent in industrial than developing countries, involves an increase in households' access to credit. Without liberalization, some consumers may not be able to smooth their consumption intertemporally by going into debt. For instance, young consumers may want to borrow in anticipation of future increases in labor income but be unable to do so. Financial liberalization, either by easing regulations on borrowing or by stimulating greater competition among intermediaries, allows consumers more easily to use debt in order to smooth consumption and make their saving more sensitive to interest rates. Increased access to credit causes a temporary stimulus to consumption, as some previously credit-constrained households borrow in order to dissave, while the behavior of those who have already accumulated assets (for instance, the old) remains unaffected. Empirical evidence in countries that have liberalized access to consumer credit generally supports the above analysis (Jappelli and Pagano (1989), Bayoumi (1993), Lehmussaari (1990), and Ostry and Levy (1994)).

Does Saving Vary with a Country's Income Level?

Differences in per capita income may possibly explain the wide range of saving rates in developing

---

[9]Financial liberalization in a given country may also expand the international diversification possibilities of other countries, making their saving more responsive to foreign interest rates.

countries. At subsistence levels, the potential for significant saving is small. A rise in per capita income may therefore lead to higher saving rates. The size of this effect is likely to decline as per capita income rises and may even become negative for rich countries, where investment opportunities and growth are relatively lower. It seems to be a stylized fact that the process of development involves initially low saving rates, a period of high growth accompanied by high saving rates, and lower saving rates in more mature economies.

Ogaki, Ostry, and Reinhart (1995) show that the pattern of saving rates by average income tends to confirm that subsistence considerations are important for low-income countries, which also have low saving rates. They also find that the relationship between the two variables seems to be nonlinear, with the largest increases in saving occurring in the transition from low- to middle-income countries (see also Rebelo (1991)).

Is the Age Structure a Significant Influence on Saving?

An implication of the LCH model is that the age structure of the population is important. If a high proportion of the population is of working age—and especially if at peak earning years—the economy's private saving rate should be high, as the workers are providing for their retirement. Conversely, when this cohort reaches retirement age and dissaves (or, at least, consumes a greater fraction of its income), the aggregate saving rate should decline. An extensive literature attempts to link demographic variables to saving behavior. Studies using cross-country data (either as cross sections or panels) have been more successful than time-series studies for individual countries in finding significant demographic effects, probably because the variation over time of demographic variables is relatively small. In particular, Leff (1969), Modigliani (1970), Modigliani and Sterling (1983), Graham (1987), and Masson and Tryon (1990) have found that higher proportions of the young and elderly to those of working age—that is, higher dependency ratios—are associated with lower saving rates. These estimates, combined with the projections of population aging in coming decades, should produce quite large falls in private saving in many industrial countries, especially Japan.

Koskela and Viren (1989), however, question the robustness of the demographic effects identified by Graham (1987), and there remains a conflict between macroeconomic results (including across countries) and studies using microeconomic data for consumers by age cohort. Kennickell (1990) and Carroll and Summers (1991), for instance, argue that age-consumption profiles do not differ enough to explain why aggregate consumption should be very much affected by demographic factors. The discrepancy may, however, be explained by interactions between generations that are picked up by the macro-economic data

but ignored by the microeconomic data studies: bequests may lower the saving of the young and, hence, aggregate saving, even if the elderly do not themselves dissave (Weil (1994)). Therefore, the thought experiment of changing the age structure of the population while keeping age-specific saving profiles unchanged may not be legitimate. Nevertheless, it must be acknowledged that studies using macroeconomic data have also found diverse results.

A debate has also raged as to whether individuals actually dissave in their later years, and, if not, whether the absence of dissaving by the elderly contradicts the LCH model.[10] An alternative model, the dynastic model, postulates that individuals save to make bequests, in order to transfer wealth to their descendants. Interpretation of the data is complicated by various factors. One is that different cohorts may behave differently (or perceive the future differently), so that what is needed is longitudinal data for a given individual or household throughout its lifetime, not just age-saving profiles at a given point in time. Another is that the motive for bequests is important. As death is uncertain, bequests may not be planned. Alternatively, bequests may simply be part of a bargain made with children, in exchange for their taking care of their parents, and should properly be classified as purchases of services (Bernheim, Shleifer, and Summers (1985)). Hurd (1990) concludes from the evidence of longitudinal data for the United States that the elderly do dissave, a view also maintained for Japan by Hayashi (1992) and Horioka (1993). However, others have pointed to the size of inherited wealth as an a priori indication that life cycle considerations are not a very important factor in saving (for example, Kotlikoff (1988)).

Do Other Government Policies Affect Saving?

In addition to the possible offset of government deficit changes by changes in private saving, government policies can also be expected to affect private saving through tax distortions and through public pension and medical care policies.[11] The first effect may operate through taxes, subsidies, or other incentives applied to the rate of return to saving. For instance, many countries tax income from saving differently than labor income. Moreover, they try to influence the composition of saving—for instance, by allowing contributions to retirement plans to be deducted from taxable income or exempting bank interest from tax. Detailed knowledge of each country's tax code is required to assess whether this factor is important in explaining cross-country differences in saving rates (as opposed to differences in the form that saving takes—such as insurance contracts

---

[10]See Modigliani (1988) and Kotlikoff (1988), among others.
[11]The literature on this subject is surveyed by Smith (1990).

versus housing). Because a comprehensive source of such data is not available,[12] this important issue is largely ignored in the discussion that follows.

Public pensions can lower private saving because they may substitute for private pension contributions. The effect on national saving depends on the way that public pensions are financed. Feldstein has argued that the introduction of a pay-as-you-go system would lower national saving because the pensions would be paid by those still unborn (or at least not yet working), who therefore could not adjust their saving behavior, and because their parents are presumed not to do so, contrary to Ricardian equivalence. The empirical literature (Feldstein (1974) and Munnell (1974)) is mixed concerning the importance of this factor for saving behavior. Given current demographic trends, there may be some doubt as to whether benefit levels will in fact be maintained because the burden on those working in the future may be viewed as too great. More generally, the extent that governments provide services, such as education, health care, and unemployment insurance, may also affect the need for private saving. This area has so far been little explored, partly because of the difficulty in making comprehensive structural comparisons across countries.

Does the Availability of Foreign Saving Affect National Saving?

In the absence of constraints on foreign borrowing, foreign saving is determined by the difference between national saving and investment. However, when foreign borrowing is rationed, as is often the case in developing countries, the direction of causality changes, and foreign saving becomes a potential determinant of national saving. An exogenous increase in foreign saving is likely to replace national saving at least partially by raising domestic consumption; nevertheless, by increasing the total saving available for investment, foreign saving can also promote growth. Some empirical evidence also supports such a negative relationship between national and foreign saving (Fry (1978) and (1980) and Giovannini (1985)), and between household and foreign saving (Schmidt-Hebbel, Webb, and Corsetti (1992)).

An important source of external saving in the case of the poorer developing countries has been foreign aid. Empirical evidence suggests that foreign aid tends to have a negative effect on national saving but increases overall saving (Hadjimichael and others (1995)). Recent studies indicate that, on average, about 40 percent of foreign aid goes into consumption (Levy (1988) and World Bank (1994a)), reflecting the tendency of foreign aid to flow to countries where per capita income is low and subsistence considerations dominate saving decisions.

Is There a Terms of Trade Effect on Saving?

Another aspect of saving behavior that has appeared in the literature is the possible relationship between the terms of trade and saving: the Harberger-Laursen-Metzler effect, through which an improvement in the terms of trade is supposed to lead to an increase in saving and an improvement of the trade balance. The modern literature integrates this effect into intertemporal models and stresses the distinction between transitory and permanent changes in the terms of trade. A transitory improvement, because it causes only a transitory change in income, should lead to higher saving rather than higher consumption, confirming the direction of the Harberger-Laursen-Metzler effect (Obstfeld (1982) and Svensson and Razin (1983)). Permanent shocks to the terms of trade would have ambiguous effects that should be small in magnitude. The empirical literature has tended to confirm a positive correlation between transitory terms of trade shocks and saving (for example, Ostry and Reinhart (1992)).

Empirical Results

In order to examine the outstanding empirical issues discussed above, saving rates for industrial and developing countries were regressed on a number of potential explanatory variables. The set of explanatory variables was limited to those that could be collected on a reasonably comparable basis for all countries. Although, because of differences in data availability, the regressions were initially done separately for the two groups of countries, a combined regression, also reported below, pooled the two groups by using common explanatory variables. The regressions focus on four principal explanatory factors as determinants of private saving: fiscal variables; demographics; GDP per capita and GDP growth; and interest rates, inflation, and changes in the terms of trade.

Industrial Countries

A panel data set comprising 21 industrial countries[13] over the period 1971 to 1993 was used to regress the ratio of private saving to nominal GDP on the following variables: the general government budget surplus, general government current expenditure, general government investment, and private sector

---

[12]A preliminary attempt to assemble such information (though not on a strictly comparable basis) for the seven largest industrial countries is presented in Poterba (1994).

[13]The 23 industrial countries, excluding Iceland and Luxembourg. See appendix for data resources.

Table 1. Decomposition of Overall Variance into Cross-Sectional and Time-Series Variances for 21 Industrial Countries over 1971–93

(In percent of total)

Variable	Across Countries	Over Time
Private saving/GDP	65.6	34.4
General government budget surplus/GDP	60.5	39.5
General government current expenditure/GDP	67.3	32.7
General government investment/GDP	62.1	37.9
GDP growth rate	8.2	91.8
Real interest rate	13.2	86.8
Wealth/GDP	66.7	33.3
Inflation rate	24.5	75.5
Percent change in terms of trade	1.1	98.9
Per capita GDP relative to United States	94.7	5.3
Dependency ratio	62.3	37.7

Source: IMF staff estimates.

wealth[14] (all measured as ratios of nominal GDP); growth rates of real output, consumer prices, and the terms of trade; the real short-term interest rate; GDP per capita relative to that in the United States (measured by using purchasing power parities); and the dependency ratio (the ratio of those under the age of 20 and over the age of 65 and to those aged 20–64).[15]

The advantage of panel data is that they provide variation both across countries and over time. Ideally, one would exploit both dimensions simultaneously, using a single specification across all countries. Unfortunately, the statistical assumptions required to make such an approach valid do not generally hold, a common problem with panel estimation. In what follows, the results from different approaches that give more or less weight to one or another aspect of the data are reported, and the similarities and differences found in the empirical results using alternative methods are discussed.

Table 1 provides information on some of the characteristics of the underlying data. It divides the total variance of each of the series into the part that can be ascribed to changes over time within countries (the time-series variation) and the part that can be ascribed to long-term differences across countries (the cross-

sectional variation).[16] Private saving, the dependent variable, contains significant amounts of variation in both dimensions, with cross-sectional differences explaining about two thirds of the total variance and changes over time the remaining third. The importance of the cross-sectional differences presumably reflects the persistence of differences in saving behavior across countries. For example, Japan and Italy had relatively high saving ratios throughout the sample period, while the United Kingdom and United States had relatively low ratios.

Cross-sectional differences are also more important than changes over time for the fiscal variables, the dependency ratio, the wealth ratio, and per capita GDP relative to the United States. By contrast, most of the variation in real short-term interest rates, output growth, inflation, and the change in the terms of trade is across time, presumably reflecting the greater importance of cyclical variation in these cases. However, all of the variables except the ratio of per capita GDPs and the change in the terms of trade have significant variation across both countries and time, indicating that useful information can be extracted in both dimensions.

In order to focus on the time-series information, a specification was run in which the constant terms were allowed to vary by country while the coefficients on the independent variables were made equal across all countries. Accordingly, these regressions are best seen as a way of using data across a large number of different economies to estimate the response of saving in a typical country with more precision than is possible by using individual country data. Although the constraint that all of the coefficients are equal across countries was rejected by the data, it was considered that the benefits from a greater number of observations outweighed the potential biases in the estimates for individual countries. Moreover, the large number of variables and countries involved in the analysis made it impractical to report the results of individual country regressions.

Table 2 reports the results from both a general specification including all the variables and a more restricted one. Most of the variables in the general specification are correctly signed and significant. Increases in the general government budget surplus (the fiscal position), government current and capital expenditure, per capita output relative to the United States, and the dependency ratio all lower private saving, while increases in the

---

[14]The private wealth variable includes the stock of government debt. To the extent that individuals are Ricardian, however, this debt should not be included in private wealth. Results when the stock of government debt was included in the specification as a separate variable were very similar to the main case and are not reported.

[15]Separating the overall dependency ratio into dependency ratios for the young and the old gave coefficients that were not significantly different.

[16]See Kessler, Perelman, and Pestieau (1993) for a more detailed description of this approach. Briefly, the variation over time is calculated by summing the individual variances across countries, on the assumption that each country has a different mean. The cross-sectional variation is calculated as the variance across these country means multiplied by the number of time periods. The two measures sum to the total variation.

Table 2. Private Saving–GDP Ratio: 1971–93 Panel Estimates for 21 Industrial Countries with Separate Country Constant Terms

(Absolute t-ratios in parentheses)

	General Model	Restricted Model	Instrumental Variables
Explanatory variables			
General government budget surplus/GDP	−0.51	−0.52	−0.53
	(8.5)	(8.8)	(4.8)
General government current expenditure/GDP	−0.42		
	(10.5)	−0.40	−0.42
		(10.3)	(7.2)
General government investment/GDP	−0.52		
	(4.9)		
GDP growth rate	−0.04	—	—
	(0.8)		
Real interest rate	0.22	0.17	0.24
	(4.5)	(3.5)	(2.8)
Wealth/GDP	0.016	—	—
	(3.9)		
Inflation rate	0.18	0.13	0.17
	(4.6)	(3.5)	(3.1)
Percent change in terms of trade	0.05	0.05	0.05
	(3.0)	(3.2)	(3.2)
Per capita GDP relative to United States	−0.07	−0.04	−0.05
	(2.1)	(1.3)	(1.3)
Dependency ratio	−0.13	−0.15	−0.14
	(4.5)	(5.4)	(4.4)
Fit statistics			
Adjusted R^2	0.23	0.25	0.25
S.E.R.	2.36	2.40	2.41
Number of observations	483	483	483

Source: IMF staff estimates.

real interest rate, inflation (included as a proxy for measurement biases in national accounts measures of saving caused by the nominal component in interest payments[17]), and the terms of trade raise it. However, the coefficient on the growth in real GDP was small and insignificant, while that on wealth was significant but incorrectly signed.

The results from excluding the growth in real output and the wealth ratio are shown in Table 2 under the "Restricted Model" column. The implied effects from the remaining variables appear reasonable.[18] About one half of all changes in the fiscal position caused by tax changes are estimated to be offset by changes in private saving; if the fiscal position changes are caused by changes in government expenditure, the offset on private saving is much less (about 10 percent, the difference between the two coefficients). A 6 percentage point increase in the real interest rate raises the private saving ratio by 1 percent of GDP, a result that would also come from a rise in the terms of trade or a fall in per capita income relative to the United States of 20 percent. Finally, a 7 percentage point increase in the dependency ratio lowers private saving by 1 percent of GDP, an effect that, although within the (wide) range of existing estimates, is somewhat lower than the typical value found in cross-country studies.

One potential problem with these results is that saving may be determined simultaneously with some of the other variables, in particular the real interest rate and fiscal variables, causing the estimated coefficients to be biased downward. Accordingly, the restricted regression was re-estimated using instrumental variables to test for biases in the coefficients on the fiscal deficit, government current

---

[17]Similar results were found by using an alternative proxy for the inflation bias in the national accounts measures of saving, namely, the product of the inflation rate and the general government debt ratio. This alternative proxy was used because it is a measure of the increase in private saving required to keep the real value of claims on the government unchanged.

[18]Regressions including time dummies for each year produced broadly similar results.

expenditure, and the real interest rate.[19] As indicated in the third column of Table 2, the coefficient on the real interest rate rises by over one third of its original value, from 0.17 to 0.24, indicating that the original coefficient may indeed have been biased downward. The size and significance of the other estimated coefficients, by contrast, are similar to those found in the regression without instruments.

The R^2 statistics indicate that these regressions explain about one fourth of the variation in the private saving ratio over time.[20] To summarize, the results indicate that the relevant economic variables are generally correctly signed and have significant effects on the level of private saving, but that a reasonably large amount of the variance of saving over time remains unexplained, at least when the coefficients on the explanatory variables are assumed equal across countries.

The same variables were included in a cross-sectional equation in which private saving ratios averaged over time were regressed on average values of the explanatory variables; there are thus 21 observations, one for each country. As can be seen in Table 3, only three variables (the fiscal position, output growth, and the dependency ratio) were found to be significant in the general regression. The small number of significant variables presumably reflects two factors: the much smaller number of observations and, hence, limited degrees of freedom; and the inclusion of variables whose main explanatory power appears likely to be in variation over time, either because there is little variation across countries (the change in the terms of trade) or because of problems of data comparability.

The second column of Table 3 reports the results from a restricted regression using only the fiscal position, growth in output, per capita GDP relative to the United States, and the dependency ratio. A comparison of the results in Tables 2 and 3 indicates that the impact of these variables on saving is estimated to be noticeably greater in the cross-sectional regression than in the time-series results. The most dramatic difference is in the case of real growth, which has a coefficient of over 2 in the cross-sectional regression. If, as seems reasonable, the time-series regressions measure the sensitivity of saving to changes over the economic cycle while the cross-sectional regressions measure the impact of long-

---

[19]The instrumental variables chosen for each country were time dummies, the first lags of the fiscal surplus, the ratio of government current spending to GDP, and the real interest rate, as well as contemporaneous values of the change in the terms of trade, inflation, per capita GDP relative to the United States, and the dependency ratio. Contemporaneous values were used for these latter variables as they were regarded as exogenous to the simultaneity issues being investigated.

[20]When the impact of differing country intercepts is included, over 70 percent of the total variation in saving is explained.

Table 3. Private Saving–GDP Ratio: Average 1971–93 Cross-Sectional Estimates for 21 Industrial Countries

(Absolute t-ratios in parentheses)

	General Model	Restricted Model
Explanatory variables		
General government budget surplus/GDP	−0.80 (3.7)	−0.71 (4.6)
General government current expenditure/GDP	−0.02 (0.2)	—
General government investment/GDP	0.22 (0.4)	—
GDP growth rate	2.29 (2.1)	2.77 (3.87)
Real interest rate	−0.03 (0.1)	—
Wealth/GDP	−0.00 (0.2)	—
Inflation rate	−0.34 (1.07)	—
Percent change in terms of trade	−0.52 (0.5)	—
Per capita GDP relative to United States	−0.08 (1.5)	−0.06 (1.7)
Dependency ratio	−0.25 (2.4)	−0.28 (3.8)
Fit statistics		
Adjusted R^2	0.65	0.74
S.E.R.	2.42	2.06
Number of observations	21	21

Source: IMF staff estimates.

term differences in behavior, saving may be more sensitive to long-term differences in fiscal positions, output growth, and demographic changes than to shorter-term movements in these variables.

Finally, the restricted version of the cross-sectional regressions was re-estimated over three subsample periods, the 1970s, the 1980s, and 1990–93, in order to investigate whether the estimated coefficients were robust to alternative time periods, and whether they showed any pattern over time. These results, reported in Table 4, show that the underlying pattern found over the full sample period also holds over all three subsamples. At the same time, there does appear to be some diminution in the coefficients on the fiscal position and the growth in output over time, possibly owing to rising international capital mobility. As access to international capital markets has expanded over time, the linkages between national saving, investment, and growth, and between government and private saving, may have been reduced. The corollary may be an increase in the sensitivity of domestic saving to international influences, as domestic and world financial markets have become more integrated.

Table 4. Private Saving–GDP Ratio: Cross-Sectional Estimates for 21 Industrial Countries Across Subperiods

(Absolute t-ratios in parentheses)

	1970s	1980s	1990–93
Explanatory variables			
General government	−0.88	−0.61	−0.20
budget surplus/GDP	(3.7)	(4.0)	(0.9)
GDP growth rate	1.91	2.88	1.30
	(2.3)	(3.5)	(3.0)
Per capita GDP relative	−0.05	−0.11	−0.08
to United States	(0.8)	(2.7)	(1.6)
Dependency ratio	−0.31	−0.29	−0.27
	(2.8)	(3.3)	(2.5)
Fit statistics			
Adjusted R^2	0.58	0.65	0.49
S.E.R.	3.28	2.45	2.75
Number of observations	21	21	21

Source: IMF staff estimates.

Developing Countries

In estimating saving functions for developing countries, further considerations should be taken into account. First, because most developing countries face constraints on their external borrowing, foreign saving—to the extent that it is exogenous—is likely to be a determinant of domestic saving. The current account surplus (equal to minus foreign saving) was therefore included as an extra explanatory variable in the regressions.[21] Second, broad money as a ratio to GDP was included in the initial estimation as a proxy for financial development; however, this variable was not significant and hence was omitted from the regressions reported below. Third, for the period 1970–93, data on private saving and the interest rate were not available for a sufficiently large set of countries; therefore, two sets of regressions were run. For the 1970–93 period, national as opposed to private saving was used as the dependent variable, and the interest rate and fiscal variables were excluded from the regression. In this case, the wealth variable was altered to include both private and public wealth. For the 1982–93 period, a specification similar to that for the industrial countries was estimated, with the private saving ratio used as the dependent variable. Thus, the Ricardian equivalence hypothesis was tested only for the shorter sample. Finally, in all regressions a quadratic function of per capita income was included to test the hypothesis that the saving ratio may increase at the initial stages of development but decrease at later stages. This hypothesis would require the coefficients of per capita income and per capita income squared to be positive and negative, respectively.

Some differences relative to the industrial country data should also be noted. Because of the lack of reliable independent data, national saving was calculated as domestic investment plus the current account surplus. This means that foreign transfers are included as part of national saving. Private saving (for the 1982–93 period) was then calculated as national saving minus the central government fiscal surplus and minus central government expenditure on capital goods.[22] Nominal private and public wealth were, respectively, derived as the cumulative sum of nominal private and public savings. Data sources are given in the appendix. The sample includes 64 developing countries for the 1970–93 regressions and 40 countries for the 1982–93 regressions.

Separate estimations were carried out for the entire set of countries, as well as for countries classified as high-income, middle-income, and low-income groups based on 1990 per capita incomes (see the appendix for a list of countries in each group). All panel estimations allowed for the presence of fixed country effects, that is, separate country intercepts. The inclusion of time dummies did not significantly influence the estimated coefficients, and these are excluded in the results reported below. Cross-section regressions were of poor fit and are not reported here.

Table 5 reports the contributions made by the cross-country and over time variances to the total variance of each of the variables, for all the countries together and for the three subgroups. Private and, to a lesser degree, national saving rates show more variability across countries than over time. Apart from the ratios of fiscal position and wealth to GDP, the explanatory power of other variables differs widely in those two dimensions. As is true for industrial countries, most of the variance in GDP growth, the real interest rate, the percent change in the terms of trade, and inflation is over time, while, for per capita income, the dependency ratio, and the ratio of central government expenditure to GDP, the reverse is true. The relative variances are similar across different income groups.

Table 6 presents the results of estimating the model for the four groups for the period 1970–93 by using the national saving ratio as the dependent variable, while Table 7 reports the preferred specifications. For the group of all developing countries (column 1 of Tables 6 and 7), the included variables are all significant at 5 percent with the right sign, except for the inflation rate, which does not have a significant

---

[21]Because the current account includes net private and official transfers, it excludes foreign aid as a measure of foreign saving. In any event, data on foreign aid were not available on a balance of payments basis and the estimations reported below thus do not test for the effect of foreign aid on national saving.

[22]Data on central rather than general government were used as the latter were not available for many countries.

Table 5. Decomposition of Overall Variance into Cross-Sectional and Time-Series Variances for Developing Countries
(In percent of total)

Variable	All Countries		High-Income Countries		Middle-Income Countries		Low-Income Countries	
	Across countries	Over time	Across countries	Over time	Across countries	Over time	Across countries	Over time
National saving rate[1]	58.5	41.5	53.0	47.0	51.6	48.4	56.2	43.8
GDP growth rate[1]	10.5	89.5	13.1	86.9	5.1	94.9	9.3	90.7
Percent change in terms of trade[1]	2.6	97.4	3.9	96.1	2.0	98.0	1.7	98.3
Per capita income[1]	89.8	10.2	74.3	25.7	73.9	26.1	70.9	29.1
Total wealth/GDP[1]	58.3	41.7	56.0	44.0	41.7	58.3	69.3	30.7
Dependency ratio[1]	81.7	18.3	72.9	27.1	59.5	40.5	89.8	10.2
Inflation rate[1]	14.2	85.8	20.9	79.1	10.3	89.7	21.6	78.4
Current account surplus/GDP[1]	26.1	73.9	18.1	81.9	13.9	86.1	38.1	61.9
Private saving rate[2]	77.2	22.8	62.5	37.5	70.1	29.9	84.6	15.4
Central government budget surplus/GDP[2]	53.6	46.4	21.3	78.7	54.4	45.6	56.4	43.6
Central government current expenditure/GDP[2]	90.5	9.5	85.4	14.6	91.0	9.0	82.9	17.1
Central government capital expenditure/GDP[2]	72.5	27.5	67.9	32.1	76.7	23.3	68.2	31.8
Real interest rate[2]	36.7	63.3	20.4	79.6	45.1	54.9	24.9	75.1

Source: IMF staff estimates.
[1]Over the 1970–93 period.
[2]Over the 1982–93 period.

coefficient. The estimated coefficient of the dependency ratio indicates that a 1 percentage point rise in this variable leads to a fall of just over 0.1 percent in the national saving rate.[23] Foreign saving is a significant determinant of domestic saving,[24] and the coefficient of the current account surplus indicates that an increase in foreign saving equal to 1 percent of GDP reduces the national saving rate (and increases the consumption-GDP ratio) by about 0.4 percent. Finally, the results support the hypothesis of a quadratic relationship between the national saving rate and per capita income; however, the estimated coefficients suggest that the turnaround is mild and occurs at relatively high levels of per capita income (84 percent of the U.S. level).

The estimation results vary considerably across country groups (columns 2–4 of Tables 6 and 7), with the fit being the best for the high-income group. GDP growth turns out to be significant in all the subgroups (at the 10 percent level for the low-income countries), while per capita income, the percent change in the terms of trade, and wealth are not significant in the case of the low-income countries. These results may indicate that, for these countries, subsistence considerations do not allow higher incomes to lead to higher saving rates. Demographic factors are significant for all but the middle-income countries.

Tables 8 and 9 report the results for the private saving rate over the period 1982–93, with the fiscal surplus, central government current expenditure, central government capital expenditure, and the real interest rate also included as regressors. The coefficient of the ratio of the fiscal position to GDP indicates a 0.63 percent offset of government dissaving by increased private saving for all developing countries. The Ricardian equivalence hypothesis of a full offset is rejected for all but the high-income countries. The fiscal balance used here includes only the central government, implying that private saving includes the noncentral government fiscal balance. If central and noncentral government saving ratios are negatively correlated, the estimated coefficient of the fiscal position will be biased upward. When the fiscal deficit is reduced by cuts in central government investment, rather than by increases in taxes, there is a smaller offset on private saving (except in the case of the middle-income countries). However, government current expenditure does not have such a differentiated effect.

---

[23]As was done for the industrial countries, youth and elderly dependency ratios were first included separately and then combined into a single variable, as the coefficient on the elderly dependency ratio was not well determined (perhaps reflecting the very small proportion of the population in this age group).

[24]However, this may partly result from data problems, as national saving is calculated as the sum of domestic investment and the current account deficit. Therefore, the estimated coefficient of the current account surplus will be biased if that variable is itself influenced by national saving or if—as is quite likely—it contains measurement errors that also affect the calculation of national saving.

Table 6. National Saving–GDP Ratio: 1970–93 Panel Estimates for 64 Developing Countries with Separate Country Constant Terms

(Absolute t-ratios in parentheses)

	All Countries	High-Income Countries	Middle-Income Countries	Low-Income Countries
Explanatory variables				
GDP growth rate	0.125	0.176	0.103	0.100
	(4.28)	(5.00)	(2.06)	(1.69)
Percent change in terms of trade	0.032	0.045	0.059	0.006
	(3.70)	(3.95)	(4.12)	(0.38)
Per capita income	0.843	0.613	2.776	−0.687
	(9.17)	(7.40)	(6.23)	(0.45)
Per capita income squared	−0.005	−0.003	−0.005	0.078
	(5.88)	(4.43)	(4.08)	(0.62)
Total wealth/GDP	−0.008	−0.019	0.018	−0.009
	(2.56)	(6.01)	(2.73)	(1.28)
Dependency ratio	−0.114	−0.144	−0.022	−0.309
	(6.83)	(8.34)	(0.77)	(4.56)
Inflation rate	−0.000	−0.000	0.000	−0.000
	(0.50)	(0.72)	(0.38)	(0.04)
Current account surplus/GDP	0.414	0.521	0.112	0.562
	(14.18)	(13.81)	(2.18)	(9.44)
Fit statistics				
Adjusted R^2	0.264	0.585	0.203	0.233
S.E.R.	5.93	4.10	5.77	6.82
Number of observations	1,536	504	504	528

Source: IMF staff estimates.

Table 7. National Saving–GDP Ratio: 1970–93 Preferred Panel Estimates for 64 Developing Countries with Separate Country Constant Terms

(Absolute t-ratios in parentheses)

	All Countries	High-Income Countries	Middle-Income Countries	Low-Income Countries
Explanatory variables				
GDP growth rate	0.126	0.180	0.102	0.108
	(4.34)	(5.14)	(2.04)	(1.87)
Percent change in terms of trade	0.032	0.045	0.058	—
	(3.70)	(3.95)	(4.10)	
Per capita income	0.849	0.620	2.824	—
	(9.31)	(7.53)	(6.41)	
Per capita income squared	−0.005	−0.004	−0.056	—
	(5.97)	(4.52)	(4.33)	
Total wealth/GDP	−0.008	−0.019	0.021	—
	(2.53)	(5.97)	(3.44)	
Dependency ratio	−0.114	−0.142	—	−0.316
	(6.82)	(8.32)		(5.88)
Inflation rate	—	—	—	—
Current account surplus/GDP	0.414	0.520	0.119	0.598
	(14.19)	(13.80)	(2.35)	(10.80)
Fit statistics				
Adjusted R^2	0.265	0.585	0.205	0.234
S.E.R.	5.93	4.10	5.77	6.81
Number of observations	1,536	504	504	528

Source: IMF staff estimates.

Table 8. Private Saving–GDP Ratio: 1982–93 Panel Estimates for 40 Developing Countries with Separate Country Constant Terms

(Absolute t-ratios in parentheses)

	All Countries	High-Income Countries	Middle-Income Countries	Low-Income Countries
Explanatory variables				
Central government budget surplus/GDP	−0.626 (9.40)	−0.931 (8.74)	−0.434 (3.38)	−0.629 (5.38)
Central government current expenditure/GDP	0.007 (0.11)	−0.054 (0.57)	0.045 (0.29)	0.097 (0.70)
Central government capital expenditure/GDP	−0.233 (2.69)	−0.392 (2.99)	−0.089 (0.46)	−0.302 (2.14)
GDP growth rate	0.142 (3.59)	0.181 (3.26)	0.090 (1.17)	0.081 (1.18)
Percent change in terms of trade	0.007 (0.63)	−0.026 (1.33)	0.023 (1.11)	0.020 (1.47)
Per capita income	0.823 (3.65)	0.981 (3.32)	3.797 (3.41)	5.343 (2.17)
Per capita income squared	−0.008 (2.67)	−0.010 (2.73)	−0.110 (3.15)	−0.480 (2.24)
Private wealth/GDP	0.007 (1.14)	0.004 (0.38)	−0.003 (0.25)	0.023 (1.78)
Dependency ratio	−0.198 (6.33)	−0.250 (6.03)	−0.097 (1.29)	−0.196 (3.25)
Inflation rate	−0.049 (1.60)	−0.076 (2.81)	−0.009 (0.09)	0.166 (1.22)
Current account surplus/GDP	0.463 (11.19)	0.709 (11.94)	0.253 (3.47)	0.578 (6.58)
Real interest rate	−0.021 (0.63)	−0.032 (1.02)	−0.014 (0.13)	0.233 (1.64)
Fit statistics				
Adjusted R^2	0.306	0.626	0.117	0.455
S.E.R.	3.36	2.52	4.14	2.62
Number of observations	480	168	156	156

Source: IMF staff estimates.

The real interest rate is not significant at the 5 percent level for any of the groups. This result, which is in line with most earlier studies, may reflect the importance of liquidity constraints and subsistence considerations in many developing countries, but the poor quality of the data may also be significant. The results for the 1982–93 period also show the importance of growth (although not for middle- and low-income countries), per capita income, and foreign saving in the determination of private saving. The results also suggest that the effect of the terms of trade is insignificant, probably because of the smaller degree of variation in this variable during the shorter period, which excludes the two major oil price increases.

Results from the Combined Panel

The industrial country and the shorter developing country data sets were combined to produce an unbalanced panel involving a total of 61 countries: 21 industrial countries with 23 years of data (1971–93); and 40 developing countries with 12 years of data (1982–93). The private saving ratio was then regressed upon those series available in both panels.[25] The data were treated identically across all countries, except in the case of the current account, which was set to zero for the industrial countries because the availability of foreign saving was not considered to be an exogenous determinant of saving in these economies. As the constant terms were allowed to vary by country, this effectively eliminated the current account from the estimation for industrial countries.

Table 10 reports the results from a general specification and from a more restricted version, in which a

---

[25]Available series include the government balance, government current and investment expenditures, and wealth (all as a ratio to GDP), the growth in real output, the real short-term interest rate, inflation, the change in the terms of trade, per capita GDP relative to the United States and its square, the current account surplus as a ratio to GDP, and the dependency ratio.

Table 9. Private Saving–GDP Ratio: 1982–93 Preferred Panel Estimates for 40 Developing Countries with Separate Country Constant Terms
(Absolute t-ratios in parentheses)

	All Countries	High-Income Countries	Middle-Income Countries	Low-Income Countries
Explanatory variables				
Central government budget surplus/GDP	−0.659 (11.43)	−0.940 (11.19)	−0.349 (3.90)	−0.673 (6.99)
Central government current expenditure/GDP	—	—	—	—
Central government capital expenditure/GDP	−0.298 (3.91)	−0.408 (4.80)	—	−0.397 (3.11)
GDP growth rate	0.156 (3.97)	0.197 (3.75)	—	—
Percent change in terms of trade	—	—	—	—
Per capita income	0.870 (3.98)	1.086 (4.19)	3.881 (4.28)	5.504 (2.54)
Per capita income squared	−0.009 (2.82)	−0.011 (3.31)	−0.117 (3.93)	−0.520 (2.64)
Private wealth/GDP	—	—	—	—
Dependency ratio	−0.181 (6.04)	−0.241 (6.29)	—	−0.159 (2.79)
Inflation rate	—	−0.056 (3.15)	—	—
Current account surplus/GDP	0.469 (11.39)	0.697 (11.96)	0.268 (3.86)	0.572 (6.49)
Real interest rate	—	—	—	—
Fit statistics				
Adjusted R^2	0.302	0.627	0.136	0.423
S.E.R.	3.37	2.52	4.10	2.69
Number of observations	480	168	156	156

Source: IMF staff estimates.

number of the explanatory variables have been eliminated. All of the coefficients in the restricted model are correctly signed and significant. The fiscal offset is 0.64, indicating that slightly over half of any change in the fiscal balance is offset by changes in private saving. Rises in the ratio of government expenditure to GDP that do not affect the fiscal position (because they also involve higher taxes) are found to lower the corresponding private saving ratio by about one third. Both output growth and per capita income relative to the United States are found to have significant impacts on saving, with the quadratic term implying that rises in relative per capita income boost saving when the ratio is below about 60 percent of the value in the United States, and lower it after this point. The real interest rate has a significant but relatively small impact on saving, while, at −0.16, the coefficient on the dependency ratio is very similar to that found in the earlier time-series regressions. The equation explains 30 percent of the variance of saving in the combined panel.[26]

[26]As noted above, this result understates the explanatory power because it ignores the contribution of separate country intercepts.

Uniting the combined panel results with the results obtained separately for industrial and developing countries permits some conclusions to be drawn. First, the fiscal position induces an offset in private saving, but only a partial one, estimated to be about three fifths. Therefore, fiscal consolidation has an appreciable positive impact on national saving. Moreover, given the typical negative coefficient on government spending, fiscal consolidation that takes the form of spending reduction rather than tax increases induces less of a private saving offset. Second, higher output growth is generally associated with higher saving rates. Third, the real interest rate generally seems to have a positive effect on private saving. Fourth, the dependency ratio is generally significant, with the expected negative sign. Finally, per capita income has an effect on saving that depends on its level: it is initially positive but turns negative at higher levels. These conclusions seem relatively insensitive to changes in specification, time period, and the countries included in the sample.

Other hypotheses discussed in the preceding section fare less well. Wealth effects seem to be either insignificant or perverse. Inflation, which was expected to increase measured saving because of the omission of real capital losses on nominal assets, is generally insignificant. There is strong evidence that the current account matters for developing countries' private saving, although, given the identity linking the two variables, the evidence should be treated with caution. Moreover, the current account variable was not considered a legitimate regressor for industrial countries, which do not typically face exogenous financing constraints. As for the terms of trade, there is generally a positive coefficient on this variable, but it is only significant when a sufficiently long data period is used.

The Implications for Saving of Projections for Selected Variables

The estimated equations can be used to examine the prospects for saving in the future by focusing over the longer term on slow-moving variables that are easier to forecast. In particular, the results for both industrial and developing countries suggest that saving is significantly influenced by demographic factors, economic growth, relative per capita income, and government fiscal positions. Another important factor in evaluating the prospects for world saving is the change in the relative size of the countries concerned; if high-saving countries both continue to grow faster than other countries and maintain their high saving, world saving will rise.

Population projections from the United Nations (UN) were used to investigate the impact of changes in the dependency ratio. The fraction of the elderly in the population is relatively predictable for industrial countries as it is mainly influenced by the behavior of birthrates many years before, rather than by changes in life expectancy. While a gradual increase in life expectancy is normal, large changes are unlikely in the absence of major wars, epidemics, or medical discoveries, as the effect of improved public health in extending life has been largely exploited (although its full effect in increasing the proportion of those over the age of 75 has not yet been observed). Projections for the number of elderly in the population for developing countries are somewhat more uncertain, both because of the heterogeneity of the countries concerned and because life expectancy is considerably lower at present than in industrial countries. Moreover, when the dependency ratio also includes the young, as it does in the regression equations reported above, the projections are much more sensitive to future fertility rates, which are also uncertain.

Charts 4 and 5 give the UN projections for industrial and developing countries, respectively. The extent to which they diverge is striking, with industrial countries showing a marked increase in dependency ratios and developing countries exhibiting a trend decline, at least until 2025. Given the coefficient estimated in the com-

Table 10. Private Saving–GDP Ratio: Results from the Combined Industrial and Developing Country Panel

(Absolute t-ratios in parentheses)

	General Model	Restricted Model
Explanatory variables		
Government budget surplus/GDP	–0.62 (13.7)	–0.64 (14.8)
Government current expenditure/GDP	–0.32 (11.1)	–0.32 (11.5)
Government investment/GDP	–0.26 (4.2)	
GDP growth rate	0.10 (3.4)	0.11 (3.9)
Real interest rate	0.03 (1.2)	0.03 (2.0)
Wealth/GDP	0.01 (2.7)	—
Inflation rate	–0.01 (0.3)	—
Percent change in the terms of trade	0.01 (1.3)	—
Per capita GDP relative to United States	0.55 (5.0)	0.51 (5.0)
Square of per capita GDP relative to United States	–0.005 (5.3)	–0.004 (5.1)
Current account surplus/GDP (developing countries only)	0.44 (12.5)	0.44 (12.7)
Dependency ratio	–0.15 (7.2)	–0.16 (8.0)
Fit statistics		
Adjusted R^2	0.31	0.30
S.E.R.	2.96	2.97
Number of observations	963	963

Source: IMF staff estimates.
Note: Estimated using 1971–93 data for 21 industrial countries and 1982–93 data for 40 developing countries.

bined panel regression and the projected relative sizes of the two country groups, these divergent trends would imply that saving rates could be expected to fall by $1\frac{1}{2}$ percent of GDP in 2025 relative to 1995 in industrial countries but rise by 4 percent of GDP in developing countries and by $\frac{2}{3}$ of 1 percent worldwide (Table 11).[27] It is interesting also to note differences across countries. Japan's population is expected to undergo a larger increase in its dependency ratio than other industrial countries (Chart 4, top panel), which will produce a larger fall in its saving rate.

These projections are subject to a number of uncertainties. It may not be appropriate to measure the de-

---

[27]Individual country effects are aggregated by using GDP weights (because total saving is derived from saving rates in that way); however, the aggregation in Charts 4 and 5 is based on population weights.

Chart 4. Industrial Countries: Dependency Ratios
(In percent)

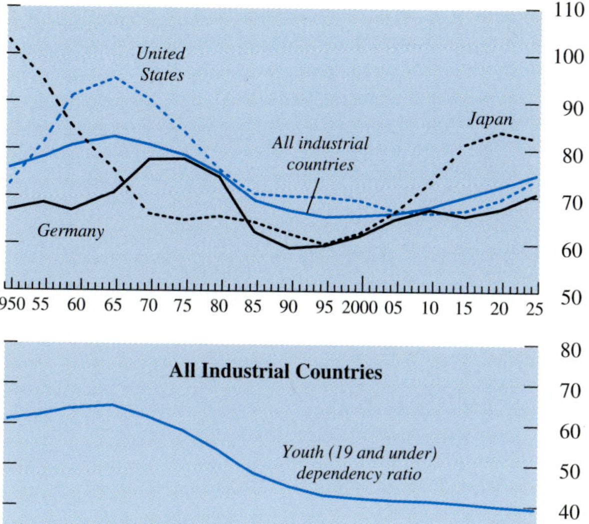

Source: United Nations, *World Population Prospects,* 1992.

Chart 5. Developing Countries:Dependency Ratios
(In percent)

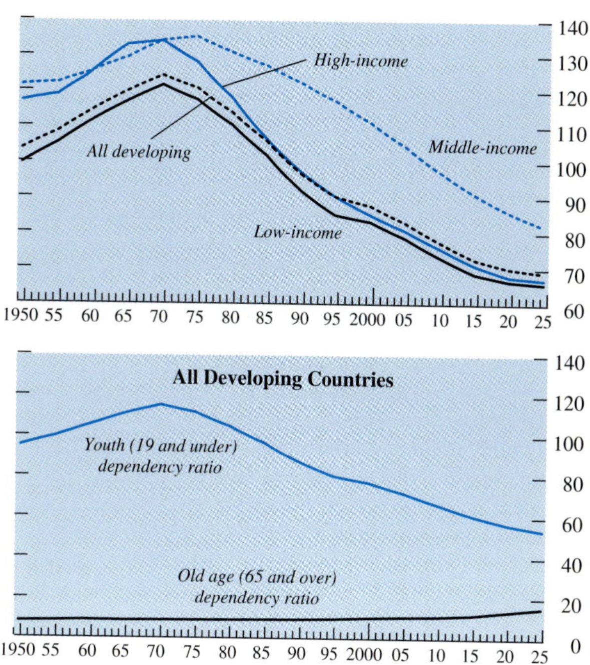

Source: United Nations, *World Population Prospects,* 1992.

pendency ratio in the same way for the two sets of countries. The effective retirement age is probably lower for developing countries, as mortality rates are higher and life expectancy is lower. The proportion of the aged is increasing in developing countries in the projection period, but this trend will be offset by a decline in the number of young (see bottom panel of Chart 5). Using a broader definition of the elderly would produce a smaller decline or an increase in the developing country dependency ratio. Moreover, if the impact of the old on saving is larger than that of the young, as some researchers have found, the net effect of the demographic trends could be a fall of the projected saving rate in developing countries.[28]

Per capita GDP for each country was projected by combining the average growth rate over the period 1997–2000 in the *World Economic Outlook*'s medium-term projections, with the assumption that growth rates will converge as per capita income rises toward U.S. levels. Rather than a forecast, this is intended merely to understand the effects of a continuation of current trends. Chart 6 plots the resulting values for per capita

income by subgroup, relative to the United States. It can be seen that a continuation of faster growth in developing countries permits a catch-up in per capita income, from an average of 12 percent of the U.S. level for developing countries in 1995 to 35 percent in 2025.[29] The panel regressions for private saving attribute an effect to relative per capita income that is nonlinear: for low- and middle-income countries, an increase in relative per capita income tends to raise saving; for those countries closer to the U.S. level (in particular, those that are within about 60 percent of it, including most industrial countries), the effect is negative. Growth also has a small but significant direct effect on the panel regression for saving. The growth coefficient of 0.11 implies that the projected saving rates will be higher, the higher is projected GDP growth. The assumed slowdown in GDP growth relative to 1995 in itself would lower saving rates in the future by a small amount (only about 0.1 percent of GDP). The net effect of projected GDP on world saving, which depends on both the per capita income distribution across countries and the direct growth rate effect, would be to raise saving by half a percentage point

---

[28]See World Bank (1994b) for a discussion of problems arising from aging populations. World Bank projections show an increase in the proportion of those over the age of 60 in the populations in both industrial and developing countries. By 2030, that proportion is expected to be 31 percent for the former and about 15 percent for the latter, excluding Eastern Europe and the former Soviet Union (World Bank (1994b, Table A.2)).

[29]The rankings of what are initially low- and middle-income countries change as a result of faster growth in the former group, in particular, China.

in 2025, with a rise in developing countries more than offsetting a decline in industrial countries (Table 11).

The projections for population (Chart 7) and for per capita income also imply evolving shares of world GDP. These weights are needed to assess the actual flow of saving resulting from the predicted saving ratios. These calculations are done country by country and then aggregated. To indicate the importance of this factor—the *composition effect*—each country's saving ratio was kept at its 1990–93 average, but the GDP weights were modified in the manner described. The results are shown in Table 11. It can be seen that the composition effect tends on balance to raise world saving because the high-saving countries grow faster than the others. The amount of the increase, about 3.6 percent of GDP, is substantial.

These positive developments for world saving come mainly from a rise in saving in the developing countries, as unfavorable demographics and rising per capita income relative to the United States would imply a large decline in saving in industrial countries. It is important to recognize, however, how much the results for developing countries depend on one country, China, which currently has a very high real growth rate (about 10 percent) and a high national saving rate (about 35 percent of GDP). Even though the illustrative calculations assume some decline in China's growth rate, a continuation of relatively rapid growth for several decades could well prove to be optimistic. Moreover, there may be cultural or political factors not captured in the regression coefficients that could lead to a decline in China's saving. If China were excluded from the set of countries for purposes of the calculation, the demographic effects in Table 11 would be little changed; however, the effect on developing country saving of rel-

Chart 7. Population Growth

(Five-year percent changes)

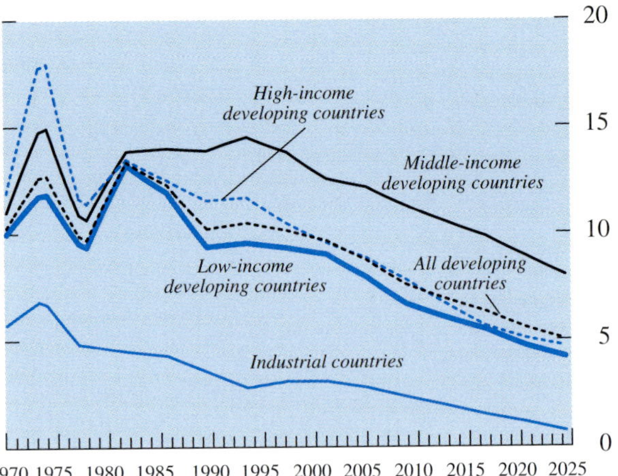

Source: United Nations, *World Population Prospects.*

ative per capita income and growth rate changes would fall to less than 3 percent from the 6.07 percent indicated in the table, while the composition effect would show an increase of only about half a percentage point, not 2.64 percent.

A final factor that is relevant for both private and national saving is the evolution of taxes and government spending. As there is only a partial offset on private saving of government dissaving, a reduction in the fiscal deficit through tax increases would raise national saving by an amount equal to 40 percent of that reduction.[30] A reduction in the deficit owing to spending cuts would induce a private saving offset of only 0.3 and, hence, increase national saving by more, namely, 70 percent of the deficit reduction. Table 12 gives the implied effects on national saving of eliminating government deficits by either tax increases or spending cuts. If deficits were to be reduced to zero by tax increases, national saving rates relative to 1990–93 would increase by about 1.2 percent of GDP in both industrial countries and developing countries, while a similar reduction through spending cuts would increase national saving by about 2.2 percent of GDP.

It should be emphasized that these calculations are not intended as a forecast of what will happen but are rather a way to examine the sensitivity of projections to various factors. Demographic factors and growth are both projected to depress saving in the industrial countries. However, the positive effects on developing countries offset this downward tendency. Finally, government deficits will be important determinants of saving.

Chart 6. Per Capita Income Relative to the United States

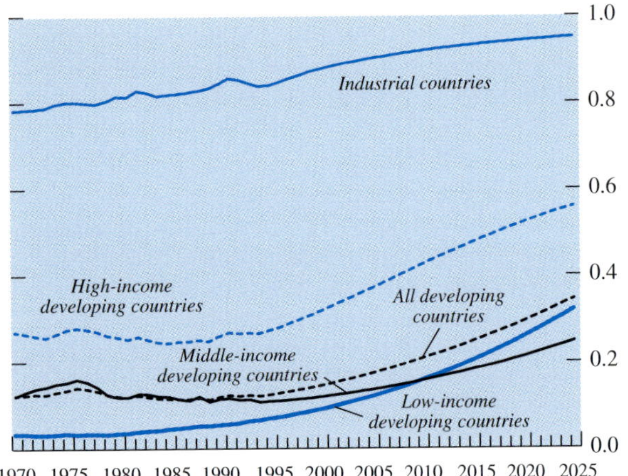

Source: IMF staff estimates.

---

[30]Using the combined panel's coefficient estimate on the fiscal position of –0.6.

Table 11. Sensitivity of Projections to Selected Factors

(Changes in percentage points of GDP)

	Changes in Saving Rate Relative to 1995					
	2000	2005	2010	2015	2020	2025
Effect of projected changes in dependency ratio on private saving						
Industrial countries	−0.01	−0.05	−0.26	−0.64	−0.98	−1.37
Developing countries	0.84	1.87	2.96	3.84	4.17	4.16
World	0.12	0.34	0.58	0.76	0.80	0.68
Effect of projected relative per capita income and growth rate changes on private saving						
Industrial countries	−0.50	−0.95	−1.27	−1.53	−1.76	−1.96
Developing countries	0.76	1.64	2.66	3.78	4.96	6.07
World	−0.38	−0.62	−0.62	−0.41	−0.01	0.51
Composition effect of changing GDP shares on aggregate private saving						
Industrial countries	0.10	0.14	0.14	0.12	0.09	0.05
Developing countries	0.54	1.04	1.51	1.94	2.27	2.64
World	0.54	1.12	1.73	2.37	3.02	3.63

Source: IMF staff estimates.

Table 12. National Saving Rates Implied by Assumption of Different Fiscal Policies

(In percent of GDP)

	Memorandum Item	Deficit-Reduction Scenarios	
	1990–93 actual	By tax increases	By spending reduction
Industrial countries			
Fiscal deficit	3.2	0.0	0.0
National saving	19.7	20.8	21.9
Developing countries			
Fiscal deficit	3.3	0.0	0.0
National saving	26.8	28.0	29.0
World			
Fiscal deficit	3.3	0.0	0.0
National saving	21.5	22.7	23.7

Source: IMF staff estimates.

Concluding Remarks

Several conclusions emerge clearly from the regressions, despite some heterogeneity in the results between industrial and developing countries, and, within the latter, among different income groups. First, there seems to be a substantial offset of changes in the government fiscal position from private saving—of the order of 30–60 percent—depending on whether those changes are due to government spending or tax changes, respectively. While this offset is large, it is considerably below

unity, implying that changes in the government's fiscal position can have a significant impact on national saving. Thus, prospects for world saving depend importantly on decisions with respect to fiscal policies.

Another conclusion that can be drawn from both country groups' estimates is that demographic effects are an important determinant of private saving rates. The size of the effect of the dependency ratio on private saving is somewhat lower than in most previous studies that found a significant saving impact from demographic variables. Nevertheless, the results suggest that the projected aging of the population in most industrial countries will generate significant downward pressure on private saving rates over the next three decades. Developing countries show an opposite trend in the overall dependency ratio, despite an increase in those over the age of 65, owing to a decline in the proportion of those under the age of 20. Provided that these two age groups have the same effect on aggregate saving, the net effect on world saving would be a small positive figure.

The results identify a number of channels through which growth influences saving. A direct positive association between GDP growth and private saving emerges from most of the specifications, although it is unclear whether there is a causal effect in either direction or a joint response to a third factor. There is also a suggestive result concerning the level of per capita income (relative to the United States) and saving. For developing countries, the level of this variable has a generally significant positive effect, but the square of the level has a negative effect, implying that beyond a certain point higher income has a negative effect on the private saving rate. The industrial country panel estimates, which suggest a negative level effect (the squared term was not significant), are consistent with this finding, as are the results of the combined panel. Given the distribution of per capita incomes, a continuation of growth trends has positive and negative effects through this channel, but the positive effects on world saving dominate. Finally, a composition effect of the changes in the relative sizes of the countries concerned can also affect the aggregate rate of saving. If countries with high saving rates continued to grow faster, their increasing share of world output could induce an upward trend to world saving of several percentage points. However, such a favorable outcome is very sensitive to assumptions concerning one country, China.

The real interest rate seems to have a positive, and significant, coefficient for industrial countries and for the combined panel. Though there clearly are measurement problems related to the choice of the appropriate interest rate and measure of inflation—and this may in particular affect the results for developing countries, which did not show a significant coefficient—it appears that a shift to increased investment, to the extent that it raised interest rates, could induce higher global saving through this channel.

Changes in the terms of trade were also found to have a significantly positive effect on saving, both for industrial and developing countries. Clearly, the deterioration in many countries' terms of trade owing to the oil price shocks of 1973 and 1979 had large effects in reducing their saving rates, and, conversely, the improvement in oil exporters' terms of trade increased their saving, at least for a time. However, the effect is transitory, and, because terms of trade changes balance out at the world level, there is no presumption that this variable will durably affect world saving. An additional external factor that negatively affects private saving in developing countries is the level of foreign saving. As in the case of the government fiscal position, however, the offset is only partial. Thus, greater availability of foreign saving should help contribute to higher investment in these countries.

Clearly, many interrelated factors combine to generate observed saving behavior. With respect to the future, two factors stand out as being of particular importance. First, aging populations in the industrial countries appear likely to put downward pressure on their saving rates over the next few decades. Even if this decline in industrial country saving is offset by increases in saving in the developing world, which is by no means certain, this trend in industrial countries implies significant changes in the location and structure of world saving. Second, the simplest and most direct way in which governments can boost national and worldwide saving is by reducing their fiscal deficits.

Appendix

Measurement Issues

The main reason for using private, not household, saving is related to the adequacy of the data. As the government sector is usually fairly clearly delineated, private spending and saving can be calculated residually. Measuring the household sector is more difficult because it requires a further split, whose dividing line is less clear. In particular, this measurement requires a judgment about whether to include unincorporated businesses in the household or the business sector. Especially in countries at early stages of economic development and where agriculture is important, it may be impossible to separate such unincorporated businesses from the household sector. Their treatment differs across countries, with the result that household sector data are not comparable. Another reason for using private saving is that, even for incorporated businesses, decisions to make transfers in the form of dividends or to acquire assets or debt will reflect the interests of shareholders. Conversely, households may adjust their saving behavior in response to changes in corporate saving behavior. Such offsetting changes are likely to make household and business saving more difficult to explain than total private saving, although cyclical variations in corporate profits may make private income more variable than household income.

No attempt is made to adjust private saving as measured by the national accounts to approximate better the change in private net worth. Various adjustments have been made by others, but the conclusion of that work has generally been that the evolution of saving is not affected in a major way (for example, Bosworth (1993) and Dean and others (1990)),[31] and that the ranking of countries as low or high savers is generally independent of these adjustments (for example, Horioka (1993)).[32] However, it must be recognized that national accounts measures of saving are subject to substantial error, even relative to what they purport to measure (Elmeskov, Shafer, and Tease (1991)).

A number of other adjustments have been made by various authors. Net saving, instead of gross saving, has been calculated by subtraction of the depreciation of the capital stock; however, capital consumption is poorly measured and not comparable across countries (Blades and Sturm (1982)). The two saving series in any case show similar trends. Purchases of consumer durables have for some countries been included in saving, and their services in consumption, but this is difficult to do across a range of countries because of lack of data. In order to adjust properly for capital gains and losses on assets, including the capital loss on unindexed government debt owing to inflation, detailed information is needed about asset holdings; furthermore, saving that includes such adjustment is much more variable than the unadjusted data, suggesting that it would also be more difficult to explain.[33] Other possible adjustments would be to include education and research and development expenditure in investment (and saving) rather than in current spending.

Industrial Country Data

Most of the data come from the World Economic Outlook database, supplemented in some cases by OECD sources.

Private saving: World Economic Outlook database except for Portugal, which was derived from the OECD Analytical Database.

General government fiscal surplus: either the World Economic Outlook database or OECD Analytical Database, depending on the availability of historical numbers. In some cases, central government numbers were used to infer historical general government values.

General government current expenditures: calculated as total general government expenditures (World Economic Outlook database) less general government investment.

---

[31]However, the inflation adjustment to saving changes a decline in U.S. saving into an increase when comparing the 1980s with the 1970s.

[32]However, Lipsey and Kravis (1987) find that adjustment for consumer durables eliminates a good part of the measured saving rate difference between the United States and an average of 11 other industrial countries.

[33]For instance, measured saving rates in most countries showed little movement after the substantial loss of wealth caused by the 1987 stock market crash, and, in Japan, private saving was little affected by the tremendous rise in wealth (and subsequent fall) resulting from the property price bubble in the late 1980s.

General government investment: most series from the World Economic Outlook database. However, in some cases, the OECD Analytical Database was used. This is most important in the case of the United States, whose national accounts define all government spending as consumption. The OECD source was used in this case as it measures government investment in the United States in a manner compatible with the conventions used in other countries.

Real GDP: World Economic Outlook database.

Inflation (rate of change of consumer price index): World Economic Outlook database.

Real interest rate: short-term rate minus current inflation (from the World Economic Outlook database).

Private wealth: calculated as the sum of the beginning-of-period capital stock (from the OECD Analytical Database where available), otherwise cumulated investment, government debt, and net foreign assets. Some of the historical values for net foreign assets were calculated by cumulating current account values backward from the earliest available net foreign asset figures.

The terms of trade: calculated as the ratio of unit values from total exports and total imports, using series from the World Economic Outlook database.

Per capita income: calculated by using purchasing power parity exchange rates from the World Economic Outlook database.

Dependency ratio: calculated from data in the United Nations' *World Population Prospects*, 1992.

Developing Country Data

The data source for the developing countries is the World Economic Outlook database except for the interest rate, where the IMF's *International Financial Statistics* has been used in the case of some countries to extend the data. These include China, Myanmar, Israel, Paraguay, Bhutan, Oman, and Liberia. For Uruguay, the data are entirely from *International Financial Statistics*.

The regressions on national saving include 64 developing countries. The countries in each group (ranked by per capita income) are as follows:

High-income countries: Singapore, Hong Kong, Cyprus, Israel, Oman, Malta, Korea, Venezuela, Malaysia, Gabon, Mauritius, Uruguay, Mexico, Chile, Algeria, Brazil, Argentina, Costa Rica, Turkey, Colombia, and Thailand.

Middle-income countries: Fiji, Tunisia, Panama, Jamaica, Ecuador, Islamic Republic of Iran, Paraguay, Peru, Morocco, Egypt, Guatemala, Sri Lanka, Indonesia, Philippines, Lesotho, Ghana, El Salvador, Cameroon, Pakistan, Nigeria, and Zimbabwe.

Low-income countries: Honduras, Bhutan, China, Mauritania, Benin, Nepal, Kenya, Central African Republic, India, Bangladesh, The Gambia, Liberia, Lao People's Democratic Republic, Mozambique, Rwanda, Burundi, Niger, Mali, Burkina Faso, Malawi, Myanmar, and Chad.

The regression results reported for private saving include the following 40 countries: Cyprus, Oman, Malta, Korea, Venezuela, Malaysia, Gabon, Mauritius, Uruguay, Chile, Algeria, Costa Rica, Turkey, Colombia, Panama, Jamaica, Ecuador, Islamic Republic of Iran, Paraguay, Morocco, Egypt, Indonesia, Lesotho, El Salvador, Cameroon, Nigeria, Zimbabwe, Honduras, China, Benin, Nepal, Kenya, Central African Republic, India, Bangladesh, The Gambia, Rwanda, Burundi, Mali, and Burkina Faso.

Bibliography

Aghevli, Bijan, and others, *The Role of National Saving in the World Economy: Recent Trends and Prospects*, IMF Occasional Paper No. 67 (Washington: International Monetary Fund, March 1990).

Auerbach, Alan J., and Kevin Hassett, "Corporate Savings and Shareholder Consumption," in *National Saving and Economic Performance*, ed. by B. Douglas Bernheim and John B. Shoven (Chicago and London: University of Chicago Press, 1991).

Barro, Robert J., "Are Government Bonds Net Wealth?" *Journal of Political Economy*, Vol. 82 (No. 6, 1974), pp. 1095–117.

Bayoumi, Tamim, "Financial Deregulation and Household Saving," *Economic Journal*, Vol. 103 (November 1993), pp. 1432–43.

Bernheim, B. Douglas, "Ricardian Equivalence: An Evaluation of Theory and Evidence," in *NBER Macroeconomics Annual 1987*, ed. by Stanley Fischer (MIT Press, Cambridge, Massachusetts: MIT Press, 1987).

———, Andrei Shleifer, and Lawrence H. Summers, "The Strategic Bequest Motive," *Journal of Political Economy*, Vol. 93 (December 1985), pp. 1045–76.

Bernheim, B. Douglas, and John B. Shoven, "Pension Funding and Saving," in *Pensions in the U.S. Economy*, ed. by Zvi Z. Bodie, John B. Shoven, and David A. Wise (Chicago: University of Chicago Press, 1988).

Blades, Derek W., and Peter H. Sturm, "The Concept and Measurement of Savings: The United States and Other Industrialized Countries," paper presented at conference on Saving and Government Policy, sponsored by the Federal Reserve Bank of Boston, Melvin Village, New Hampshire, October 1982.

Blanchard, Olivier Jean, "Debt, Deficits, and Finite Horizons," *Journal of Political Economy*, Vol. 93 (April 1985), pp. 223–47.

Bosworth, Barry P., *Saving and Investment in a Global Economy* (Washington, Brookings Institution, 1993).

Buiter, Willem H., "Death, Birth, Productivity Growth and Debt Neutrality," *Economic Journal*, Vol. 98 (June 1988), pp. 279–93.

Campbell, John Y., and N. Gregory Mankiw, "Consumption, Income, and Interest Rates: Reinterpreting the Time Series Evidence," NBER Working Paper No. 2924 (Cambridge, Massachusetts: National Bureau of Economic Research, April 1989).

Carroll, Christopher D., and Lawrence Summers, "Consumption Growth Parallels Income Growth: Some New Evidence," in *National Saving and Economic Performance*, ed. by B. Douglas Bernheim and John B. Shoven (Chicago and London: University of Chicago Press, 1991).

Carroll, Christopher D., and David N. Weil, "Saving and Growth: A Reinterpretation," *Carnegie-Rochester Conference Series on Public Policy*, Vol. 40 (June 1994), pp. 133–92.

Corbo, Vittorio, and Klaus Schmidt-Hebbel, "Public Policies and Saving in Developing Countries," *Journal of Development Economics*, Vol. 36 (July 1991), pp. 89–115.

De Gregorio, José, and Pablo Guidotti, "Financial Development and Economic Growth," (unpublished, Research Department, International Monetary Fund, 1994).

Dean, Andrew, and others, "Saving Trends and Behaviour in OECD Countries," *OECD Economic Studies*, No. 14 (Spring 1990), pp. 7–58.

Deaton, Angus S., "Saving and Liquidity Constraints," *Econometrica*, Vol. 59 (September 1991), pp. 1221–48.

———, *Understanding Consumption* (Oxford: Clarendon Press, 1992).

Elmeskov, Jorgen, Jeffrey Shafer, and Warren Tease, "Saving Trends and Measurement Issues," OECD Economics and Statistics Department Working Papers, No. 105 (Paris: Organization for Economic Cooperation and Development, 1991).

Evans, Paul, "Are Consumers Ricardian? Evidence for the United States," *Journal of Political Economy*, Vol. 96 (October 1988), pp. 983–1004.

Feldstein, Martin, "Social Security, Induced Retirement and Aggregate Capital Accumulation," *Journal of Political Economy*, Vol. 82 (September/October 1974), pp. 905–26.

Fisher, Irving, *The Theory of Interest* (New York: Macmillan, 1930).

Flavin, Marjorie A., "The Adjustment of Consumption to Changing Expectations About Future Income," *Journal of Political Economy*, Vol. 89 (October 1981), pp. 974–1009.

Friedman, Milton, *A Theory of the Consumption Function* (Princeton, New Jersey: Princeton University Press, 1957).

Fry, Maxwell J., "Money and Capital or Financial Deepening in Economic Development?" *Journal of Money, Credit, and Banking*, Vol. 10 (November 1978), pp. 464–75.

_____, "Saving, Investment, Growth and the Cost of Financial Repression," *World Development*, Vol. 8 (April 1980), pp. 317–27.

Giovannini, Alberto, "Saving and the Real Interest Rate in LDCs," *Journal of Development Economics*, Vol. 18 (August 1985), pp. 197–217.

Graham, John W., "International Differences in Saving Rates and the Life Cycle Hypothesis," *European Economic Review*, Vol. 31 (December 1987), pp. 1509–29.

Hadjimichael, M.T., and others, *Sub-Saharan Africa: Growth, Savings, and Investment, 1986–93*, IMF Occasional Paper No. 118 (Washington: International Monetary Fund, January 1995).

Hall, Robert E., "Stochastic Implications of the Life Cycle-Permanent Income Hypothesis: Theory and Evidence," *Journal of Political Economy*, Vol. 86 (December 1978), pp. 971–87.

Haque, Nadeem U., and Peter Montiel, "Consumption in Developing Countries: Tests for Liquidity Constraints and Finite Horizons," *Review of Economics and Statistics*, Vol. 71 (August 1989), pp. 408–15.

Hayashi, Fumio, "The Permanent Income Hypothesis and Consumption Durability: Analysis Based on Japanese Panel Data," *Quarterly Journal of Economics*, Vol. 100 (November 1985), pp. 1083–113.

_____, "Explaining Japan's Saving: A Review of Recent Literature," *Monetary and Economic Studies*, Bank of Japan, Vol. 10 (November 1992), pp. 63–78.

Horioka, Charles Y., "Saving in Japan," in *World Savings: An International Survey*, ed. by Arnold Heertje (Cambridge, Massachusetts: Blackwell, 1993).

Hurd, Michael D., "Research on the Elderly: Economic Status, Retirement, and Consumption and Saving," *Journal of Economic Literature*, Vol. 28 (June 1990), pp. 565–637.

Jappelli, Tullio, and Marco Pagano, "Consumption and Capital Market Imperfections: An International Comparison," *American Economic Review*, Vol. 79 (December 1989), pp. 1088–105.

Kennickell, Arthur B., "Demographics and Household Savings," Finance and Economics Discussion Series No. 123 (Washington: Board of Governors of the Federal Reserve System, May 1990).

Kessler, Denis, Sergio Perelman, and Pierre Pestieau, "Savings Behavior in 17 OECD Countries," *Review of Income and Wealth*, Vol. 39 (March 1993), pp. 37–49.

Koskela, Erkki, and Matti Viren, "International Differences in Saving Rates and the Life Cycle Hypothesis: A Comment," *European Economic Review*, Vol. 33 (September 1989), pp. 1489–98.

Kotlikoff, Laurence J., "Intergenerational Transfers and Savings," *Journal of Economic Perspectives*, Vol. 2 (Spring 1988), pp. 41–58.

Leff, Nathaniel H., "Dependency Rates and Savings Rates," *American Economic Review*, Vol. 59 (December 1969), pp. 886–96.

Lehmussaari, Olli-Pekka, "Deregulation and Consumption: Saving Dynamics in the Nordic Countries," *IMF Staff Papers*, Vol. 37 (March 1990), pp. 71–93.

Levy, Victor, "Aid and Growth in Sub-Saharan Africa: The Recent Experience," *European Economic Review*, Vol. 32 (November 1988), pp. 1777–95.

Lipsey, Robert E., and Irving B. Kravis, *Saving and Economic Growth: Is the United States Really Falling Behind?*, American Council of Life Insurance and Conference Board Report No. 901 (New York: Conference Board, 1987).

Maddison, Angus, "A Long-Run Perspective on Saving," *Scandinavian Journal of Economics*, Vol. 94 (No. 2, 1992), pp. 181–96.

Masson, Paul R., and Ralph W. Tryon, "Macroeconomic Effects of Projected Population Aging in Industrial Countries," *IMF Staff Papers*, Vol. 37 (September 1990), pp. 453–85.

McKinnon, Ronald I., *Money and Capital in Eco-nomic Development* (Washington: Brookings Institution, 1973).

Modigliani, Franco, "The Life Cycle Hypothesis of Saving, the Demand for Wealth and the Supply of Capital," *Social Research*, Vol. 33 (Summer 1966), pp. 160–217.

_____, "The Life Cycle Hypothesis of Saving and Intercountry Differences in the Saving Ratio," in *Induction, Growth and Trade: Essays in Honour of Sir Roy Harrod*, ed. by Walter A. Eltis, Maurice F. Scott, and James N. Wolfe (London: Clarendon Press, 1970).

_____, "The Role of Intergenerational Transfers and Life Cycle Saving in the Accumulation of Wealth," *Journal of Economic Perspectives*, Vol. 2 (Spring 1988), pp. 15–40.

_____, and Richard Brumberg, "Utility Analysis and the Consumption Function: An Interpretation of Cross-Section Data," in *Post-Keynesian Economics*, ed. by Kenneth K. Kurihara (New Brunswick, New Jersey: Rutgers University Press, 1954).

Modigliani, Franco, and Albert Ando, "Tests of the Life Cycle Hypothesis of Savings: Comments and Suggestions," *Oxford Institute of Statistics Bulletin*, Vol. 19 (May 1957), pp. 99–124.

Modigliani, Franco, and Arlie Sterling, "Determinants of Private Saving with Special Reference to the Role of Social Security—Cross-country Tests," in *The Determinants of National Saving and Wealth*, ed. by Franco Modigliani and Richard Hemming (New York: St. Martin's Press, 1983).

Munnell, Alicia H., "The Impact of Social Security on Personal Savings," *National Tax Journal*, Vol. 27 (December 1974), pp. 553–67.

Nagatani, Keizo, "Life Cycle Saving: Theory and Fact," *American Economic Review*, Vol. 62 (June 1972), pp. 344–53.

Obstfeld, Maurice, "Aggregate Spending and the Terms of Trade: Is There a Laursen-Metzler Effect?" *Quarterly Journal of Economics*, Vol. 97 (May 1982), pp. 251–70.

Ogaki, Masaoi, Jonathan D. Ostry, and Carmen M. Reinhart, "Saving Behavior in Low- and Middle-Income Developing Countries: A Comparison," IMF Working Paper, WP/95/3 (Washington: International Monetary Fund, January 1995).

Ostry, Jonathan D., and Carmen M. Reinhart, "Private Saving and Terms of Trade Shocks," *IMF Staff Papers*, Vol. 39 (September 1992), pp. 495–517.

Ostry, Jonathan D., and Joaquim Levy, "Household Saving in France: Stochastic Income and Financial Deregulation," IMF Working Paper, WP/94/136 (Washington: International Monetary Fund, November 1994).

Poterba, James M., *Public Policies and Household Saving* (Chicago and London: University of Chicago Press, 1994).

Ramsey, F.P., "A Mathematical Theory of Saving," *Economic Journal*, Vol. 38 (December 1928), pp. 543–59.

Rebelo, Sergio, "Long-Run Policy Analysis and Long-Run Growth," *Journal of Political Economy*, Vol. 99 (June 1991), pp. 500–21.

Schmidt-Hebbel, Klaus, Steven B. Webb, and Giancarlo Corsetti, "Household Saving in Developing Countries: First Cross-Country Evidence," *World Bank Economic Review*, Vol. 6 (September 1992), pp. 529–47.

Seater, John, "Ricardian Equivalence," *Journal of Economic Literature*, Vol. 31 (March 1993), pp. 142-90.

Shaw, Edward S., *Financial Deepening in Economic Development* (New York: Oxford University Press, 1973).

Smith, Roger S., "Factors Affecting Saving, Policy Tools, and Tax Reform: A Review," *IMF Staff Papers*, Vol. 37 (March 1990), pp. 1–70.

Svensson, Lars E.O., and Assaf Razin, "The Terms of Trade and the Current Account: The Harberger-Laursen-Metzler Effect," *Journal of Political Economy*, Vol. 91 (February 1983), pp. 97–125.

Tobin, James, "Life Cycle Saving and Balanced Growth," in *Ten Economic Studies in the Tradition of Irving Fisher*, ed. by William J. Fellner (New York: John Wiley and Sons, 1967).

Weil, David N., "The Saving of the Elderly in Micro and Macro Data," *Quarterly Journal of Economics*, Vol. 109 (February 1994), pp. 55–81.

World Bank (1994a), *Adjustment in Africa: Reform, Results, and the Road Ahead*, World Bank Policy Research Report (New York: Oxford University Press for the World Bank, 1994).

______ (1994b), *Averting the Old Age Crisis: Policies to Protect the Old and Promote Growth*, World Bank Policy Research Report (New York and Oxford: Oxford University Press for the World Bank, 1994).

Yaari, Menahem E., "Uncertain Lifetime, Life Insurance, and the Theory of the Consumer," *Review of Economic Studies*, Vol. 32 (April 1965), pp. 137–50.

II

The Global Real Interest Rate

Thomas Helbling and Robert Wescott

The global real interest rate is arguably the most important price in world financial markets. It determines the rate at which agents in the world economy are willing to substitute today's consumption for consumption in the future, and, at the same time, it signals the pressures that investment demands impose on the supply of world saving. By some accounts, the global real interest rate in the mid-1990s is high by historical standards. Is it? Do world economic policies influence the real interest rate over the medium to long term, or do other factors, such as technological change, matter more? And has government dissaving really been a driving force behind the rise of the global real interest rate since the early 1980s, as claimed by some? This paper analyzes these issues. It has two main objectives. First, it develops measures of the global real interest rate and provides historical evidence to help judge whether the rate today is high or low. Second, it examines the factors that influence the global real interest rate over time and quantifies the extent to which shifts in government policies and other factors have caused it to move.

A key challenge in economic research has been to estimate the impact of government dissaving on real interest rates. Many economists believe that there must be some linkage because of crowding-out effects, but most studies over the past decade have found little empirical support for this hypothesis. Blanchard and Summers (1984) provide one of the first examinations of the increase in global real interest rates in the 1980s. They conclude that most of the increase was due to higher stock market returns, not bigger budget deficits. Barro and Sala-i-Martin (1990) and Barro (1992) use an analytical framework in which saving equals investment to study the determinants of short-term real interest rates, and they also find little effect of fiscal policy. More recently, Gagnon (1995) claims that, if ten-year historical inflation is a good proxy for inflation expectations, real U.S. interest rates did not really increase much in the 1980s and 1990s, and so there is nothing for the larger budget deficits or higher ratios of government debt to GDP to explain.

This paper presents evidence that both short- and long-term global real interest rates have been higher since 1981 than they were in earlier periods. This finding is shown to be robust with respect to the inflation model and also with respect to different real interest rate concepts. The paper also finds that higher government debt in the world economy is associated with higher global real interest rates. In this sense, this study is more in agreement with the work of Howe and Pigott (1991) and Ford and Laxton (1995), who also find significant fiscal effects, than with the economists mentioned above.

A particular feature of this paper is that its analytical framework views the global real interest rate as determined through the equilibration of the supply and demand for world assets. It examines the relationship between a comprehensive global real interest rate and measures of the world rate of return on productive capacity, world government debt, and similar factors—not just national measures, as used in most studies—because, as world capital mobility steadily increases, these issues must be analyzed globally.

This paper has two main parts. The first part looks at the concept of the global interest rate, describes the construction of various global interest rate measures, and tests for the existence of different interest rate regimes. The second part develops a framework for modeling the global interest rate and provides empirical evidence about the factors that seem to explain its movements.

Measurement of the Global Real Interest Rate

In a world with integrated capital markets, arbitrage ensures that (risk-adjusted) returns on similar assets are equalized across countries.[1] Real interest rates are among the most important rates of return, for they determine the rate at which economic agents are willing to substitute present for future consumption.[2] Saving is the reflection of this decision to forgo consumption today; at the same time, it is also related to the rate of capital accumulation and growth in the world econ-

---

[1]This statement ignores the differential effects of taxation, transaction costs, and other measures, which are responsible for incomplete equalization in practice.

[2]Theoretically, of course, all rates of return, not just real interest rates, are determined simultaneously in general equilibrium.

omy. It seems natural, therefore, to include real interest rates in the set of indicators used to evaluate the current state of the world economy. Using a single real interest rate as a sufficient statistic—in the sense that it contains (almost) all the relevant information contained in national real interest rates—could greatly simplify the task. A single real interest rate, which is an average rate at which agents in the world economy are willing to substitute consumption today for consumption in the future, is, therefore, what is meant by the term "global real interest rate."

Barro and Sala-i-Martin (1990) construct a global real interest rate that equilibrates saving and investment in the world economy. Their theoretical basis is the proposition that there must be a common component in real interest rates in all countries that are integrated in the world capital market. If, as is claimed in their paper, this common component is one of the most important sources of variation in real interest rate movements over time, the global real interest rate is a useful concept.

The common component in national real interest rates is the result of transactions in asset and goods markets, both of which are channels of transmission of shocks between countries. In Appendix I, it is shown that in a very stylized model the common component can be thought of as the interest rate for a synthetic asset, a real bond denominated in terms of world output. It is, therefore, an average price for a fictitious world consumer.

The global real interest rate is essentially an empirical concept, although it can be derived rigorously as an implied rate of return in the context of standard asset-pricing relations (as in Appendix I, for example). The reason is that the common component concept puts fewer restrictions on the arbitrage process and expectation formation than most standard asset-pricing models. If assets are priced according to some model, the global real interest rate follows as an implied price. It can still be calculated, however, even if most asset prices cannot be explained by standard models, as long as national real interest rates are correlated.[3] The strong empirical bias is both an advantage and a disadvantage. The concept benefits because it does not require strong assumptions that do not hold on empirical grounds, but it suffers from the lack of theoretical implications that could be tested.

Review of the Measurement of the Global Real Interest Rate

Various methods to extract common factors from a set of national consumption-based real interest rates have been suggested in the literature. Conceptually, it is possible to distinguish between methods that derive the global real interest rate directly and methods that derive a rate by restricting the deviations of national real interest rates from the global real interest rate. The first class of methods assume a common component, whereas, in the second method, the common component is estimated.

Barro and Sala-i-Martin (1990) define the short-term world real interest rate as a weighted average of k national short-term real interest rates:

$$r_t^W = \sum_{k=1}^{K} w_t^k r_t^k, \tag{1}$$

where r denotes an expected real interest rate and w_t^k stands for the GDP weights based on purchasing power parity exchange rates ($\sum w_t^k = 1.0$). Their approach can be rationalized from two different angles. Given the definition of the global real interest rate under equation (1), the first way of rationalizing the weighting procedure would be to look at the implications of constructing an ex post measure in light of actual asset holdings. The average is taken over a set of k countries, assuming that there is one representative investor per country. These investors care about the return in terms of their consumption basket. It is also assumed that there is one bond for each possible maturity and currency. In a setup with K countries, this average is given at any time t by

$$r_t^W = \sum_{k}^{K} c_t^k \sum_{j}^{K} a_{jt}^k (R_t^k + X_t^k - [X_t^j + \pi_t^j]). \tag{2}$$

The first summation averages all the outstanding bonds of the same maturity in the world. The second summation measures the real return on the bond in currency k over all investors j. R_t^k denotes the nominal rate of return in currency k at time t, X_t^k is the nominal one-period-ahead exchange rate change between currency k and the reference currency K at time t ($X^K = 0$), and ($X_t^j + \pi_t^j$) measures the real value in terms of the reference currency of the return for investor j (X_t^j is the nominal exchange rate change between the investors' currency j and the reference currency, and π_t^j is the inflation rate between t and $t+1$ in country j). a_{jt}^k stands for the relative holdings of all the outstanding bonds in currency k by investors in country j, and c_t^k for the relative supply of bonds in currency k.

The implications in terms of restrictions are easier to understand if equation (2) is rewritten for the case of two countries, two currencies, and two noncontingent assets that are free of default risk:

$$r_t^W = c_t^1(R_t^1 - \pi_{1T}) + c_t^2(R_t^2 - \pi_{2t}) + (c_t^1 a_{2t}^1 - c_t^2 a_{1t}^2)$$

$$(X_t^1 + \pi_{1t} - \pi_{2t}) + c_t^1(a_{1t}^1 - a_{2t}^2)\pi_{1t}. \tag{2a}$$

---

[3] This seems to be the case according to the most recent empirical evidence. See the reviews by Goldstein and Mussa (1993) and Obstfeld (1993).

Barro and Sala-i-Martin's weighted average is a good approximation if (a) GDP weights approximate the relative asset supply well, (b) cross-border holdings are close to zero, or (c) all terms except the first two are independently and identically distributed random variables at any point in time (except, possibly, for a constant mean deviation related to the country size).

The weighted-average method can also be considered to be a generalization of the standard consumption formula for pricing capital assets for the risk-free real interest rate, which states that the real interest rate is simply the sum of the rate-of-time preference and the average growth rate of consumption times the intertemporal elasticity of substitution (and a risk term).[4] Any national real interest rate is then determined by the growth rate of national consumption (and the other terms), so that a weighted average of national interest rates is an implicit real interest rate consisting of an average rate-of-time preference and the growth rate of world GDP (weighted by the intertemporal elasticity of substitution). Deviations from the world real interest rate should also be independently and identically distributed over time for the weighted-average method to be appropriate.

Gagnon and Unferth (1993) use a panel data model to estimate global real interest rates. Each national real interest rate is explained by a common world component, which is modeled by a constant and a time factor, as well as by a country-specific factor, which is modeled by a time-invariant dummy. Using annual data, they conclude that interest differentials disappear within a year, that capital markets are integrated, and that a global real interest rate, defined as a common factor, does exist. Their approach imposes more structure on the global real interest rate than the weighted-average method. The world real interest rate is estimated by imposing a model for its mean and the residuals, which have to be independently and identically distributed over time. Thus, Gagnon and Unferth's model implies that, at any point in time, the world real interest rate is a simple average of national real interest rates; however, Gagnon and Unferth provide little economic reasoning for this model of the world real interest rate.

Ford and Laxton (1995) use the first principal component of a set of national real interest rates to construct a proxy for the global real interest rate. The principal component approach is appealing because it can be regarded as a kind of a factor asset pricing model. Excess returns on noncontingent assets that are free of default risk, defined as deviations of national interest rates from the global real interest rate, can be modeled as a function of one or more factors. The problem with this approach is that the risk-free rate of return or, in this case, the world real interest rate, is not defined. Ford and Laxton standardize their raw input series, a set of national real interest rates, to obtain a unique factor representation. The global real interest rate is constructed by renormalizing the squared load factors implied by the first principal component, such that they sum to unity, and then using them as weights for the nonstandardized national real interest rates. However, this approach might bias the level of the global real interest rate because it is constructed with weights derived from deviations.

Brunner and Kaminsky (1994) consider the global real interest rate to be the common trend driving cointegrated national real interest rates. If deviations from bilateral real interest parity are stationary for all possible combinations of a set of national real interest rates, there can be only one common trend, that is, a common nonstationary component. The common trend approach shares the idea underlying the principal component methodology. It has the advantage, however, that it can allow for shifts in the mean. The common trend, a random walk, represents simply a mean shift in every period. This concept is too extreme to be literally true, but it might be a good statistical representation of real interest rates that display unit root properties over fairly long samples. The common trend also can be expressed as a weighted average of national real interest rates in the form

$$r_t^W = \sum_{k=1}^{K} w^k r_t^k, \qquad (3)$$

where the weights are constant over time and, in general, are not equal to GDP weights. (See Appendix III for a more detailed discussion of how the weights can be determined.)

None of these methods is unambiguously superior. The weighted-average approach is pragmatic and offers intuitive appeal, including the feature that the size of a country's economy and its asset markets matter. It also produces a global real interest rate whose mean value is financially meaningful, which allows for an analytical connection to rates of return on stock markets and other real world measures. The assumption that deviations owing to expected real exchange rate changes are independently distributed over time is rather strong, however. Similar arguments apply to the simple averages implied by the panel data approach. The principal component method is appealing because it uses information contained in the data, but it suffers from using standard-

---

[4]The standard consumption formula for pricing capital assets for the risk-free real interest rate is given by

$$r = \rho + \gamma g_c - \tfrac{1}{2}\gamma^2 \sigma^2,$$

where γ denotes the coefficient of relative risk aversion (the inverse of the intertemporal elasticity of substitution), g_c the unconditional mean of the growth rate of consumption (spending), ρ the rate-of-time preference, and σ the unconditional variance of the consumption growth rate. This formula is strictly valid only for the unconditional mean of r; an inflation risk is not taken into account.

ized measures, which leave mean values unexplained. Because no single approach is clearly best, three methods are tested in this paper.

Constructing the Global Real Interest Rate

Data for Belgium, Canada, Germany, Japan, the Netherlands, Switzerland, the United Kingdom, and the United States were used to construct global real interest rates according to three of these methods—the weighted average, principal component, and common trend methodology.[5] The eight countries were selected because they had relatively open capital markets for the period from 1960 to 1994, and because they offer historical data back to the 1960s. The national short-term real interest rates are ex post real interest rates on a quarterly basis, constructed by subtracting the one-period-ahead annualized three-month inflation rate, as measured by the consumer price index, from a representative three-month interest rate.[6] (Summary statistics can be found in Appendix III, Table A1.) Long-term ex ante national real interest rates require an inflation forecast, and an exponential-smoothing formula was used to update the expected annual inflation rate based on consumer prices (see Appendix II).[7] The smoothed value was then subtracted from a representative quarterly long-term government bond yield. Other standard univariate methods of modeling inflation expectations were also developed, but the resulting real long-term interest rates did not differ significantly.

Two sets of global real interest rates were generated for both short- and long-term real interest rates with all three methods (Table 1). The first set includes all eight countries in the sample, while the second set includes just the United States, Japan, and Germany—the so-called G-3 countries. For the rates computed with the weighted-average method, the weights in any time period are given by the share of each country's nominal GDP (in U.S. dollars at current market exchange rates) in the total GDP of all countries included in the calculations in the same period. GDP in current market prices, as well as market exchange rates, is likely to reflect the supply of assets more accurately than GDP weights based on purchasing power parity exchange rates because market clearing in financial markets occurs in nominal terms.[8]

The first principal component of standardized short- and long-term real interest rates was calculated for the period from 1960:QI to 1994:QIII. Global real interest rates were then generated with weights based on the load factors of the first principal component. The estimation results are documented in Appendix III, Tables A2 and A3. The results of the common trend approach for eight countries have to be interpreted with caution because the estimation results suggest that the common trend representation might be inappropriate (see Appendix III, Tables A4 and A5).

Establishing Upper and Lower Bounds for the Global Real Interest Rate

While no single optimal method exists for constructing a global real interest rate, a comparison among the rates generated by the various approaches allows for the establishment of upper and lower bounds for the global real interest rate. As seen in Table 1, the maximum difference in the mean of the global short-term real interest rates for the period from 1960:QI to 1994:QIII is 32 basis points. The largest difference between various mean estimates is for the period from 1973:QI to 1980:QIV. For the years since 1981, the maximum difference in the mean global short-term real interest is about 85 basis points. These differences can be largely attributed to the differences in the weights of Japanese and U.K. short-term real interest rates, as both countries exhibited large negative real interest rates in the 1970s. In the past 13 years, the variation can be attributed to differences in the U.S. weight. Both the principal component approach and the common trend approach generate much smaller weights for the United States and Japan than the weighted-average method. Nevertheless, the qualitative properties of the various estimates are not very different, as shown in Chart 1, and the long-term movements coincide to a large degree.

The differences in means and variances are even smaller for long-term real interest rates. The estimates differ at most by 42 basis points between 1960:QI and 1994:QIII. For the period from 1981:QI to 1994:QIII, this divergence declines to just 32 basis points. The similarity of the various long-term global real interest rates can also be seen in Chart 2. These results suggest that the analysis can safely be continued with only one

---

[5]Barro and Sala-i-Martin (1990) also included France and Sweden in their analysis, and Barro (1992) included Italy. In terms of country coverage, the sample used in this paper is close to Gagnon and Unferth (1993) and Ford and Laxton (1995), except that Denmark is excluded.

[6]The ex ante real short-term interest rate is the more relevant variable from a theoretical perspective, but several studies have shown that short-term ex ante real interest rates are effectively bounded by the short-term horizon and thus cannot deviate from the observed ex post rate by much or for long. See, for example, Barro and Sala-i-Martin (1990) and Laxton, Ricketts, and Rose (1993).

[7]This method was chosen in part to avoid the excessive updating generated by estimated recursive univariate models of inflation; the updated coefficient for all countries is 0.3.

[8]World real interest rates based on OECD estimates of purchasing power parity exchange rates have also been constructed. The impact on the mean, variance, and unit root properties of the corresponding world real interest rates is so small that it can safely be concluded that the exchange rate choice does not matter for the conclusions drawn in the paper. All calculations are available from the authors upon request.

Table 1. Summary Statistics for Global Short- and Long-Term Real Interest Rates

	Mean[1]				ADF t-statistics[2]	ADF t-statistics[3]	Break Date[4]
	60:QI–94:QIII	60:QI–72:QIV	73:QI–80:QIV	81:QI–94:QIII			
Short-term real interest rates							
Weighted average							
Eight countries[5]	1.631	1.169	–1.230	3.733	–2.026 (6)	–4.015 (6)	79:QIV
	(2.568)	(1.140)	(2.309)	(1.734)			
Three countries[6]	1.636	1.229	–1.081	3.603	–2.210 (2)	–4.069 (6)	79:QIV
	(2.556)	(1.100)	(2.417)	(1.929)			
Principal component[7]							
Eight countries[5]	1.939	0.945	–0.773	4.457	–1.526 (4)	–3.498 (6)	79:QII
	(2.846)	(1.917)	(2.499)	(1.372)			
Three countries[6]	1.734	1.167	–0.730	3.703	–2.230 (3)	–4.407 (6)	80:QI
	(2.812)	(1.945)	(3.187)	(1.716)			
Common trend[7]							
Eight countries[5]	1.769	0.718	–0.847	4.286	–1.557 (4)	–3.588 (6)	79:QII
	(2.948)	(2.135)	(2.719)	(1.446)			
Three countries[6]	1.952	1.311	–0.212	3.818	–2.241 (3)	–4.578 (6)	80:QI
	(2.625)	(2.008)	(2.522)	(1.585)			
Long-term real interest rates							
Weighted average							
Eight countries[5]	3.084	2.978	0.451	4.716	–2.137 (3)	–4.054 (3)	80:QII
	(1.944)	(0.441)	(1.457)	(1.193)			
Three countries[6]	3.235	3.058	0.586	4.945	–1.927 (4)	–4.331 (3)	80:QII
	(2.003)	(0.421)	(1.475)	(1.306)			
Principal component[7]							
Eight countries[5]	3.037	2.927	0.433	4.655	–1.443 (6)	–3.019 (3)	83:QI
	(1.956)	(0.816)	(1.902)	(0.821)			
Three countries[6]	3.247	3.557	0.377	4.624	–1.808 (4)	–3.375 (4)	80:QIII
	(2.117)	(1.150)	(1.971)	(0.990)			
Common trend[7]							
Eight countries[5]	3.250	3.079	0.757	4.864	–1.216 (5)	–3.217 (3)	80:QIII
	(1.903)	(0.704)	(1.747)	(0.817)			
Three countries[6]	3.439	3.584	0.978	4.734	–1.749 (4)	–3.650(3)	80:QIII
	(1.775)	(0.819)	(1.415)	(0.976)			

Source: IMF staff estimates.

[1]In percent; standard deviation in parentheses.

[2]t-statistics of the coefficient on the lagged level of series in an augmented Dickey-Fuller unit root regression. Lag length (in parentheses) selected according to significance of coefficients of lagged first difference of series (Campbell and Perron (1991)).

[3]Minimum t-statistics of the coefficient on the lagged level of a series of augmented Dickey-Fuller unit root regressions with a 1–0 dummy variable for every period in the sample (excluding end points). Lag length in parentheses. Critical values for test statistics taken from Perron and Vogelsang (1992).

[4]Period in which minimum t-statistic occurs.

[5]Belgium, Canada, Germany, Japan, Netherlands, Switzerland, United Kingdom, and United States.

[6]Germany, Japan, and the United States.

[7]See Appendix III for details.

Chart 1.   Annual Short-Term World Real Interest Rates
(In percent)

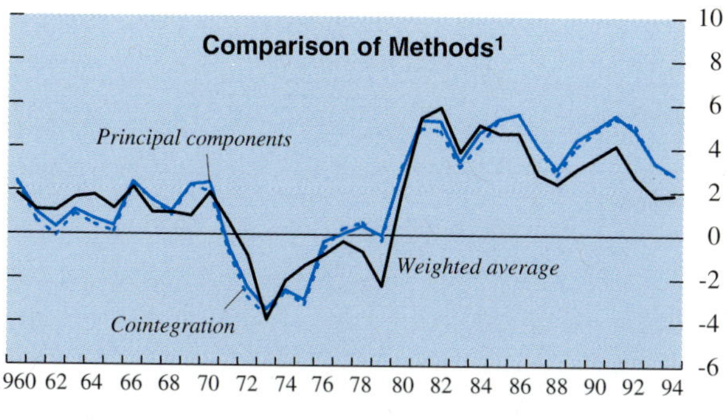

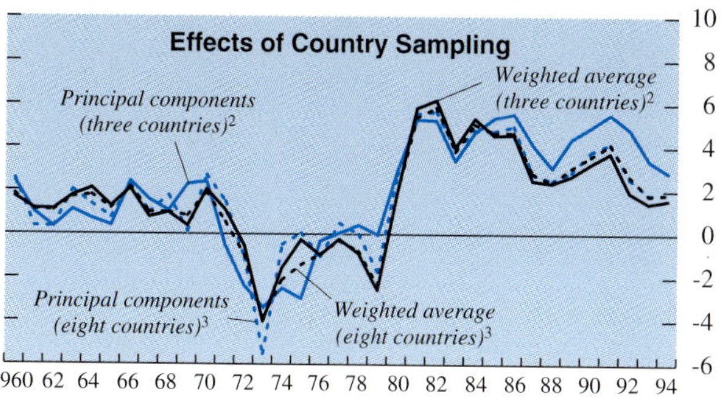

Source: IMF staff estimates.
¹Results for each method based on full sample of eight countries.
²Germany, Japan, and United States.
³Belgium, Canada, Germany, Japan, Netherlands, Switzerland, United Kingdom, and United States.

Chart 2.   Annual Long-Term World Real Interest Rates
(In percent)

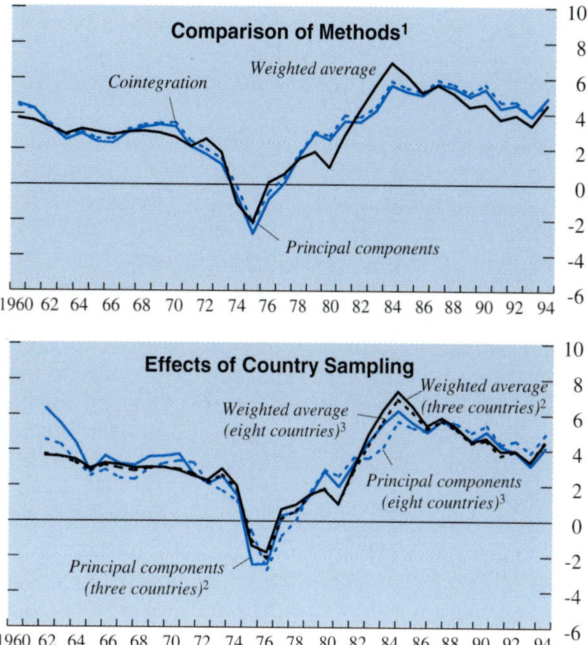

Source: IMF staff estimates.
¹Results for each method based on full sample of eight countries.
²Germany, Japan, and United States.
³Belgium, Canada, Germany, Japan, Netherlands, Switzerland, United Kingdom, and United States.

short-term and one long-term global real interest rate.[9] The choice was made to work with global real interest rates constructed according to the weighted-average method because it generates mean estimates that can be rationalized most easily on the grounds of economic theory.

Have There Been Different Global Real Interest Rates Regimes over the Past Third of a Century?

A main reason for attempting to define and construct a global real interest rate is to answer the question of whether it is high or low today, relative to earlier periods. The arbitrarily selected subperiods in Table 1 suggest that there have been three distinct global interest rate regimes over the past third of a century—the first between 1960 and 1972, the second between 1973 and 1980 (the period of adjustment to the oil price shocks), and a third since 1981. In this subsection, the selection of dates for the different

regimes is tested by means of a nonlinear time-series model, proposed by Hamilton (1989) and (1990), that incorporates regime changes. In this class of model, a random variable—the global real interest rate, in this case—is assumed to be normally distributed. The parameters of the distribution are not time invariant, however. They depend, at any point in time t, on the unobserved state of the world at time t, denoted with s_t, which is itself a random variable and which in this model can take values from $i = 1, \ldots, 3$. This implies the following model for the global real interest rate:[10]

$$r_t^W(s_t = i) \sim N(\mu_i, \sigma_i), \quad i = 1, \ldots, 3. \tag{4}$$

---

[9]The further results of this analysis confirm that the conclusions do not depend on the interest measure used.

[10]The model could be more general; the interest rate could follow an autoregressive process of order p, for example. In the case of an AR(1) process, the model would have to rewritten as

$$r_t^W(s_t = i) \sim N(\mu_i + \rho(r_{t-1}^W - \mu_i), \sigma_i).$$

The simple model is used because only the unconditional mean and variance in each regime is of interest in this study. (Hamilton (1994) used the same model for U.S. real interest rates.) AR(1) and AR(2) specifications were also estimated; these models led to the same conclusions with respect to the timing and the means of the different regimes, however.

The probability of switching between states in the subsequent period, that is, $Pr\{s_t = j \mid s_{t-1} = i\} = p_{ij}$, is given by the matrix

$$P = [p_{ji}] = \begin{bmatrix} p_1 & 0 & 1-p_3 \\ 1-p_1 & p_2 & 0 \\ 0 & 1-p_2 & p_3 \end{bmatrix}. \tag{5}$$

The unconditional probability density function for the global real interest rate is a probability-weighted mixture of the densities for each regime. The probability weights are determined by the probability that the world is in state i at time t, given information up to time t. These probabilities can be evaluated using an adapted Kalman filter algorithm. The unconditional probability density function can then be used to construct the log likelihood function and to estimate the parameters in the usual way. The model was estimated using quarterly data for the period from 1960:QI to 1994:QIII for both short- and long-term global interest rates.

Results can be found in Table 2 and Chart 3. The estimates for the mean global real interest rate for each regime differ less than the estimates reported in Table 1. These parameters also allow one to estimate the probability that a global real interest rate was in regime i in period t. Two different probability concepts must be distinguished. One is the conditional probability of $s_t = i$, given information up to time t. These probabilities are plotted as black lines in Chart 3. The other concept is that of the smoothed probability that $s_t = i$, given the information in the whole sample, that is from $t = 1,\dots,T$. These smoothed probabilities, which are shown as blue lines in Chart 3, are interesting because they add information to the estimates of the unobserved regimes.

This three-regime characterization, based upon sample statistics for subsample periods, seems to be appropriate. The degree of uncertainty about the current regime, as measured by the difference between the conditional and the smoothed probabilities, is surprisingly small, particularly in the case of the long-term global real interest rate. The estimated unconditional probabilities for the short- and long-term global real interest rates overlap almost perfectly.

Determinants of the Global Real Interest Rate

Previous Attempts to Explain the Global Real Interest Rate

As the above analysis finds that the global real interest rate has moved over time and currently *does* appear to be high by historical standards, the question

Table 2. Time-Series Model with Regime Changes for Global Real Interest Rates, 1960:QI–1994:QIII

(Standard errors of parameter estimates in parentheses)

	Short-Term Global Real Interest Rate[1]	Long-Term Global Real Interest Rate[1]
Mean		
μ_1 (regime 1)	1.432	2.822
	(0.133)	(0.062)
μ_2 (regime 2)	−1.525	0.437
	(0.332)	(0.257)
μ_3 (regime 3)	3.986	4.653
	(0.235)	(0.143)
Standard deviation		
σ_1 (regime 1)	0.892	0.139
	(0.179)	(0.033)
σ_2 (regime 2)	3.298	2.002
	(0.817)	(0.507)
σ_3 (regime 3)	2.687	1.193
	(0.540)	(0.215)
Probability of switching		
$p1$ (between regime 1 and 2)	0.989	0.973
	(0.012)	(0.023)
$p2$ (between regime 2 and 3)	0.965	0.964
	(0.030)	(0.031)
$p3$ (between regime 3 and 1)	0.975	0.990
	(0.021)	(0.010)

Source: IMF staff estimates.
[1]Weighted average.

arises of why this might be so. Empirical research on the determinants of the global real interest rate has split into structural and reduced-form modeling approaches. Barro and Sala-i-Martin (1990) and Barro (1992) follow the first route and model the short-term global real interest rate as the price that equilibrates worldwide investment and saving.[11] Their specification of the investment and saving ratios is such that both ratios depend on a large, unexplained, persistent part and a short-term, business cycle part driven by stock prices, the relative price of oil, and changes in money supply growth and in fiscal policy. They conclude that stock markets and oil prices play a major role in explaining real interest rates, and that world monetary growth and public debt exert only a secondary influence.[12] Barro's (1992) results indicate that a 1 percentage point increase in the ratio of world

---

[11]The main difference between Barro and Sala-i-Martin (1990) and Barro (1992) lies in their aggregation and estimation procedures: in the first article, the world interest rate is modeled and estimated directly, whereas in the second article, only country-specific interest rates are modeled and estimated.

[12]This result is from Barro (1992), who derives results very similar to those in Barro and Sala-i-Martin (1990), except that fiscal variables are not significant in the latter.

Chart 3.   Probabilities of Regime Changes for Global Real Interest Rates
(Based on GDP weightst)

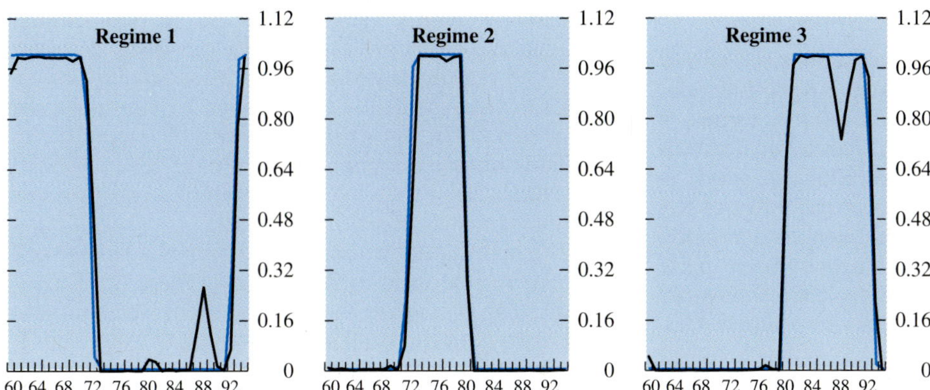

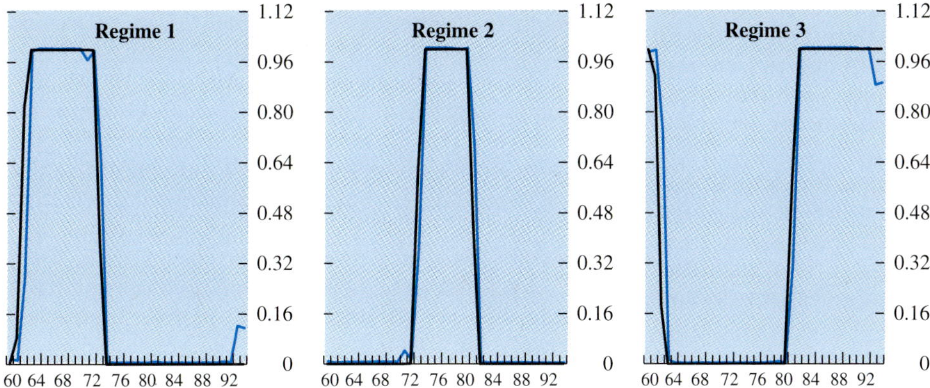

Source: IMF staff estimates.

public debt to GDP raises the world real short-term interest rate by 12 basis points.

Most other empirical studies use reduced-form equations of the form

$$r_t^W = \alpha_0 + \alpha_1 d_t + \alpha_2 g_t + \varepsilon_t, \qquad (6)$$

where d_t and g_t denote government debt and government consumption, both normalized by GDP. The studies differ as to whether national real interest rates or global real interest rates were taken as the dependent variables (Evans (1987), Ford and Laxton (1995), and Howe and Pigott (1991)), whether other arguments were included in the reduced form (see, for ex-

ample, Howe and Pigott (1991) and Coorey (1991)), and whether ε_t is assumed to be an independently and identically distributed residual (Ford and Laxton (1995)) or a stationary variable with zero mean only (Coorey (1991), Evans (1987), and Howe and Pigott (1991)).

Ford and Laxton (1995) estimate a system of equations of the form

$$r_t^i = \alpha_i + \alpha_1 d_t + \alpha_2 g_t + \varepsilon_{it}, \qquad (7)$$

where d_t and g_t denote the normalized net debt and normalized government purchases for all Organization for Economic Cooperation and Development

(OECD) countries. Their specification is similar to that of Gagnon and Unferth (1993), except that the global real interest rate is replaced by that part of the rate explained by world fiscal aggregates. They find that a 1 percentage point increase of the ratio of net public debt to GDP in the OECD area raises interest rates by about 30 basis points. Ford and Laxton's work is unique in that they assume ε_{it} to be a white-noise process.

In most of the other empirical studies, equations analogous to equation (7) represent a long-run relationship only. Evans (1987), for example, estimates cointegration equations for nominal three-month U.S. treasury bill rates using both the inflation rate and U.S. fiscal variables as regressors; he does not find any stationary residual for this kind of equation. Furthermore, his coefficients on d_t are always negative and quite large for the period from 1948 to 1986.[13] Coorey (1991) estimated long-run equations for various U.S. real interest rates using a larger set of variables, including fiscal and monetary policy, demographic, wealth, and productivity variables. She also obtained sizable fiscal policy effects, although the strength of the effect depends upon the exact specification.

Howe and Pigott (1991) use a two-step process to estimate the determinants of real interest rates for five industrial countries. They use cointegration equations to define what they call the "equilibrium real interest rate" for each country as a function of the rate of return on business capital, total nonfinancial debt relative to GDP, and the relative riskiness of bonds. They then use an error-correction model to estimate the actual changes in real interest rates as a function of the deviations between the calculated real interest rates and the equilibrium rates, as well as of fiscal and monetary policy factors and business cycle factors. They find small but significant effects of government debt on real interest rates: a 1 percentage point increase in the total debt (government debt and total nonfinancial debt) raises real interest rates between 3 basis points (in the United States) and 30 basis points (in France). A limitation of their work is that they do not take into account linkages among countries.

Brunner and Kaminsky (1994) estimate a structural vector autoregression (VAR) model for their (derived) global real interest rate using fiscal deficits as a fraction of GDP and the world money supply growth in Germany, Japan, and the United States as explanatory variables. They find that U.S. fiscal shocks and an unexplained residual, which they call a "worldwide real shock," account for most of the variation in global real interest rates over the past 15 years.

A Modeling Framework for the Global Real Interest Rate

The global real interest rate is best seen as determined through a framework of demand and supply for assets. If all countries that are part of the integrated world goods and capital markets are viewed as a single entity, the global real interest rate should be determined by world aggregates. One of the critical conceptual problems in isolating the main determinants of real interest rates is the simultaneity among asset markets, whereby equilibrium is determined for all assets at the same time. However, it is possible to isolate dominant common factors in all asset demand functions, such as wealth, for example, and to focus on their impact on real interest rates.

The starting point for the modeling is a framework similar to that used in Appendix I. There are households that maximize their utility from consumption over two periods. Unlike in the model of Appendix I, however, it is now assumed that there are overlapping generations—that is, households exist for two periods and work only in the first period. Each household receives some wage income, which, after taxes, is either consumed or invested in risky stocks and risk-free government bonds. The gross return on this investment is the source for this second-period consumption. Firms invest so as to maximize the value of firms or, in other words, to maximize the value of the outstanding shares that represent claims on the return on the capital stock. Uncertainty is resolved in the beginning of each period, so that new households know about their labor income and the marginal productivity of capital. Future marginal products of capital are uncertain because of productivity shocks.

In this framework, new households consume a fraction of their net wealth in the first period. Their asset demands are also a function of net wealth, which is equal to the value of the initial labor income (net of taxes) and other initial wealth. The level of their asset demand, as well as the fraction of their assets held in risk-free bonds, depends on the real interest rate, as well as on the real return on the world stock portfolio (r^s). Therefore, the bond demand function of new households in country i can be written as

$$b^i = \alpha^i(\overset{+}{r^i},\overset{-}{r^s})a^i, \tag{8}$$

where the signs on top of a variable indicate the sign of the partial derivative with respect to that variable, and where a^i denotes the net wealth of an investor in country i in terms of world output. (All variables are in a common currency.) An increase in national real interest rates raises asset demand in general if it is assumed that the substitution effect dominates the income effects (including discounting of future income), so that present consumption becomes expensive relative to future consumption. A real interest rate

---

[13]A negative coefficient on debt has also been found in previous studies.

increase also raises the demand for bonds relative to that for stocks.[14] An increase in world stock returns relative to the real interest rate decreases the demand for bonds. An increase in net wealth increases asset demand because investors will consume only part of that increase in the current period.

For the discussion of the effects of fiscal policy, it is important to know whether so-called Ricardian equivalence holds. If the equivalence holds, investors do not include outstanding government debt in their net wealth as they anticipate future tax increases. If Ricardian equivalence does not hold, a fraction of the outstanding debt, ø, is part of investors' net wealth.[15] It is most likely that Ricardian equivalence holds to some degree, that is $-1 < ø < 1$, because investors anticipate that they will suffer from some of the future tax increases.[16] Net wealth can therefore be decomposed into a private component, h, and the government component, $øb^i$, where b^i denotes government debt as a fraction of GDP in country i. The bond demand function of an investor in country i can therefore be rewritten as

$$b^i = \alpha^i(r^i, r^s)[h^i + øb^i]. \tag{9}$$

In equilibrium, only government bonds can be in positive net supply. The supply of government bonds, for simplicity, is assumed to be strictly exogenous.[17] If it is also assumed that all government bonds issued by each national government, denoted by b_s^i, are perfect substitutes for each other, and that national real interest rates deviate from the world real interest rate by an independently and identically distributed error term, equilibrium in the world bond market can be defined by

$$\sum_{i=1}^{I} \alpha^i(r,r^s)[h^i + øb^i] = \sum b_s^i = b. \tag{10}$$

The assumptions that technology shocks are the sole determinant of the return on capital (given the level of technology) and that there are integrated capital markets allow the model to be solved recursively. Given the world real interest rate, stock returns are

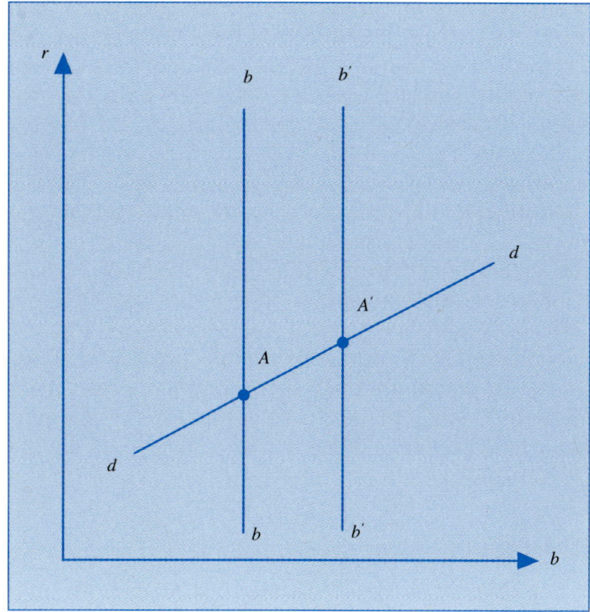

Chart 4. The Global Real Interest Rate (r) and an Increase in Government Debt (b)

determined by net investment, which, in turn, is a function of the level of technology and the expected technology shock, summarized in the variable θ. It can be shown that stock returns also depend positively on real interest rates. Therefore, the equilibrium condition (10) can be written as[18]

$$\sum_{i=1}^{I} \alpha^i(r,r^s(r,\theta))[h^i + øb^i] = b. \tag{11}$$

Equilibrium is represented in Chart 4. The bb schedule represents the exogenous supply of government bonds, whereas the upward sloping locus dd portrays demand. The slope of this locus depends on the Ricardian parameter ø. If it is equal to one, that is, if households fully take into account the future tax implications of the current government debt, the locus is horizontal for all values of b, so that an increase in government debt has no effect on interest rates. If the parameter θ is smaller than one, an increase in government debt leads to a rise in the real interest rate, as the shift in the bb schedule to $b'b'$ demonstrates.

This model is an oversimplification in two dimensions. First, by assuming the existence of a world stock market, and by assuming that various countries' government bonds are perfect substitutes, a degree of capital mobility is assumed that is not yet realized in

---

[14]For the partial derivative to be positive, only an overall positive net effect is needed.

[15]This very simple device introduces the real interest effects of government debt; see Masson and Knight (1986).

[16]In general, ø can be expected to be positive (as in Masson and Knight (1986)). This outcome leaves the exact tax structure in the model unspecified, that is, h^i would be income net of taxes. One could also have a ø that is negative and equal to r, as in Diamond (1965). The result in this case would be a fully specified steady state in which the government just rolls over the constant government debt (as a fraction of labor income). It can be shown that the conclusions of this section do not depend on whether ø is positive or negative as long as it lies within the specified range.

[17]The asset supply of an old household is completely inelastic.

[18]This representation of the equilibrium is possible if the technology shock in each period is assumed to be distributed log normally (with time-invariant parameters).

today's world economy. Second, the model focuses only on long-run equilibria, abstracting from short-term influences, such as monetary policy and the business cycle. It is clear that, in the short term, real interest rates are determined by other factors besides the level of outstanding government debt (and private net wealth) and stock returns. Monetary policy instruments, for example, have an impact on real interest rates in the short run because of various frictions that prevent prices from adjusting immediately or within a short time span. But it is also well established that the effects of monetary tightening or easing are only transitory, and that, in the long run, monetary policy mainly determines only the price level (see Friedman (1968)). Real movements of interest rates are affected only through risk premiums (the covariation of inflation with consumption). These premiums are most likely to be small in the countries included in this sample, and their sign is by no means certain (see Labadie (1989)).

Model Specification

Because asset demands are interrelated through considerations of risk and return, a proper structural model would require the estimation of a whole system of asset demand and supply functions, as well as the evolution of aggregate wealth. As such an estimation is beyond the scope of this study, a reduced-form modeling strategy has been chosen instead. The general two-step modeling procedure described by Howe and Pigott (1991) has been followed; however, this procedure has been applied to the concept of a global real interest rate rather than a set of national rates. This choice is based on the results of the unit root tests in Table 1, which show no mean reversion in global real interest rates in the sample period. This study does not assume that the global real interest rate literally follows a random walk process that is without bounds, but rather that there are mean shifts—owing to preference shifts, shifts in demographics, and so forth—that occur too frequently to be handled with dummy variables.

The first step is to estimate the equilibrium global real interest rate as a function of the variables described above. Because the equilibrium global interest rate is a long-run concept, it can be thought of as the natural real interest rate that would occur if there were no transitory determinants of the real interest rate, such as monetary policy and the business cycle. It is important that the equilibrium function generate stationary residuals. The second step is to account for transitory movements in the global real interest rate owing to factors such as monetary policy shifts or business cycle factors.

In the approach followed in this study, the equilibrium global real interest rate is determined by the return on capital in the real economy and the outstanding public debt. It is assumed that other factors are captured by a constant and a stationary error process. This approach raises the question of how to measure the return on capital in the real sector, and of which public debt variable to use. Two natural candidates for the variable for return on capital in the real sector are the return on the capital stock derived from national accounts statistics and the real aggregate stock market returns. Both variables measure average returns. From a theoretical perspective, the marginal rate of returns would be preferable; however, from a long-run perspective, this should be only a minor problem because the two measures should coincide. Stock market returns are appealing because they represent a financial market return and reflect the market valuation of physical and human capital.

From an asset demand and supply perspective, gross public debt seems to be the relevant variable because it represents the outstanding stock of bonds. One might argue, however, that only the net outstanding public debt matters for the non-Ricardian effects of debt on interest rates. The answer to the question of whether gross or net debt should be used depends on the definition of these aggregates. It is clearly preferable to use a debt aggregate that includes only the consolidated liabilities of the general government sector (that is, liabilities of both central and local governments). It is less certain whether one should use debt measures that include the consolidated liabilities of the general government and the social security sectors. As, most likely, future taxes will also have to cover liabilities of the social security sector, a gross measure that does *not* include consolidated liabilities of the general government and the social security sector seems preferable. For this reason, gross public debt figures compiled by the OECD have been used.

Although stock returns and gross public debt are preferable as long-run determinants of real interest rates, equation (12) uses other arguments as explanatory variables to facilitate comparison with other studies, as follows:

$$R_{i\,t}^{W} = \alpha_0 + \alpha_1 R_t^K \ + \alpha_2 \left(\frac{B_t}{NGDP_t} \right)_t^{W} + \varepsilon_t, \qquad (12)$$

where B denotes government debt (in current prices), $NGDP_t$ the GDP in current prices, and R_t^K the world real return on the productive capital in the economy. All aggregates are GDP-weighted world aggregates based on the same eight countries used in the previous section. Both the rate of return on capital and stock return are used as measures of the return on capital in the real economy, and both gross and net periodic debt are used for outstanding public debt.

These equations are only semireduced forms. The return on capital depends partly, as shown above, on the real interest rate because of the relationship between risk and return in asset markets. This might

Table 3. Cointegration Regressions for Global Real Interest Rates, 1960–93[1]

(Coefficients and asymptotic errors based on Stock and Watson's (1993) dynamic ordinary least squares estimator)

	Short-Term Global Real Interest Rate[2]				Long-Term Global Real Interest Rate[2]			
Return on capital[3]	0.663 (0.196)		−0.427 (0.208)		0.534 (0.197)		−0.396 (0.233)	
Capital gains on stock index[4]		0.162 (0.047)		0.071 (0.077)		0.210 (0.034)		0.196 (0.053)
Gross government debt (in percent of GDP)	0.195 (0.038)	0.1574 (0.032)			0.129 (0.065)	0.102 (0.029)		
Net government debt (in percent of GDP)			0.550 (0.083)	0.372 (0.117)			0.421 (0.090)	0.161 (0.089)
ADF *t*-statistics[5]	−2.437	−2.759	−2.967	−2.284	−1.798	−2.522	−3.588	2.968
PP *t*-statistics[6]	−3.301**	−3.778*	−3.528*	−3.889**	−4.724***	−3.920**	−3.467	3.792*

Source: IMF staff estimates.

[1]Annual data.

[2]Weighted average.

[3]Capital income in the business sector as percentage of capital stock.

[4]Percentage changes in stock prices.

[5]Augmented Dickey-Fuller unit root test.

[6]Philips-Perron unit root test. Three asterisks denote rejection of the null hypothesis of a unit root in the residuals at the 1 percent level, two asterisks at the 5 percent level, and one asterisk at the 10 percent level.

cause some simultaneity problems. If equation (12) is thought of as a cointegration relationship, the simultaneity question might be less acute. The asymptotic bias is known to be zero, although the finite sample bias can be considerable. This is taken into account by using Stock and Watson's (1993) dynamic least squares estimator. Also, an advantage of the cointegration approach is that actual debt figures can be used because targeted and actual debt should coincide in the long run.

The second step of the modeling process, the modeling of the transitory movements, must deal with both a short- and a long-term equilibrium global interest rate. From a theoretical perspective, the long-term equilibrium value for both should be equal because of term structure linkages.[19] Therefore, the long-term equilibrium values for long-term global interest rates are used to explain both the short- and the long-term deviations from equilibrium. The transitory dynamics are modeled using the following error-correction models:

$$\Delta R_{st}^{W} = X_{t}\beta + \gamma_{s}\,\varepsilon_{t-1}^{s} + \eta_{st}, \text{ and}$$
$$\Delta R_{1t}^{W} = X_{t} + \gamma_{1}\,\varepsilon_{t-1}^{l} + \eta_{1t}, \tag{13}$$

where variables in the vector X_t capture business cycle factors as well as monetary and fiscal policy variables that have a transitory impact on real interest rates, and

where ε_i^l is the deviation of the interest rate from its long-run equilibrium value.

Empirical Results

Only annual data were available for the return on capital and the outstanding public debt variables, so all the regression results are based on annual data. The stationarity of the residuals was tested using both augmented Dickey-Fuller and Philips-Perron tests. The coefficients were estimated using Stock and Watson's lead-lag estimator to correct for finite sample biases owing to the simultaneity problem. The asymptotic standard errors were calculated using an autocorrelation-consistent variance-covariance matrix for the coefficients. Given the relatively short sample (1960–93), the number of leads and lags was restricted to one on a priori grounds.

The results for both short- and long-term global real interest rates are presented in Table 3.[20] The short-term global real interest rate based on GDP weights was used as the dependent variable. The Philips-Perron unit root tests allow for the rejection of the null hypothesis of no cointegration. The coefficients for the public debt variables have the right sign and are always significant. The long-term effects on global real interest rates of an increase in the ratio of gross public debt to GDP of 1 percentage point vary between 16 and 20 basis points. For each percentage point rise in the ratio, net public debt generates larger interest rate

---

[19]That is, long-term interest rates are weighted averages of future short-term interest rates.

[20]Results for the constants are not reported.

effects—between 37 basis points and 55 basis points—than gross public debt. With the ratio of gross public debt to GDP as the fiscal variable, the coefficients on the rate of return on capital, as well as on stock market returns (the index of capital gains on stock), are both significant and of the right sign. The coefficient on the return on capital has the wrong sign if the ratio of net public debt to GDP is used as a regressor, whereas the coefficient on stock market returns has the right sign but is insignificant. Only the cointegration estimations using gross public debt as a ratio to GDP seem to be robust, with a significant coefficient with the right sign.

The results for the long-term real interest rate are very similar to those for the short-term rate. The coefficients on the rate of return on business capital are of similar magnitude and significant as well. As with the short-term rate, these coefficients also have the wrong sign if the ratio of net public debt to GDP is used as a regressor. The coefficients on the stock market returns have the right sign, are roughly similar, and are significant independent of the debt measure used. These coefficients are also larger in size than with the short-term rate, indicating that the link between stock and bond markets is more important in the market for bonds with longer maturities. The results also indicate that the effects of government debt on real interest rates are smaller if long-term yields are used. These estimates on the long-term effects of government debt are close to those of Barro (1992) in the case of gross government debt, and close to those of Ford and Laxton (1995) in the case of net public debt (with stock market returns used as regressors).

Some versions of equation (12) have also been estimated with national real interest rates as left-hand variables to show that the global real interest rate is a significant factor in their determination. The long-run level of national real interest rates is explained by a world return variable, a world government debt measure, and a country-specific constant. The results confirm that world aggregates can explain national real interest rates reasonably well, based on the Philips-Perron unit root test on the residuals. All equations display cointegration at the 10 percent confidence level. The coefficients have the right sign, with the return on capital and gross government debt as explanatory variables for all countries except the Netherlands. The rate of return on stocks is more problematic. The effects expected for long-term interest rates hold in seven out of the eight countries; however, they hold for short-term real interest rates in only four out of the eight countries.

Cointegration results have to be interpreted with some caution in small samples.[21] Given the considerable degree of uncertainty concerning the size of the

long-run coefficients, the study also used Johansen's maximum likelihood estimator to test for cointegration and to estimate the long-run coefficients. All results strongly support the existence of a single unique cointegration vector. The most noteworthy aspect of the estimated cointegration vectors is how close the coefficients for stock returns and gross government debt (as a fraction of GDP) are both for short-term and long-term global real interest rates. The estimates for the long-run coefficients on stock return lie in the interval [.2, .3] and the estimates for the coefficient on gross government debt in the interval [.08, .11]. Also the coefficients on debt depend less on which debt measure is used, as both gross and net world public debt produce similar long-run effects. A final consideration is the possibility that each variable is weakly exogenous when it comes to the estimation of the cointegration vectors. Gross public debt is weakly exogenous in almost all cases. The results are much more ambiguous when it comes to real interest rates and real stock returns. The real stock return is almost never weakly exogenous, whereas there is some indication that global real interest rates are. However, these results are quite sensitive to specification issues, such as the lag length and the inclusion of a constant in the cointegration vector, and strong conclusions cannot be drawn.

These results show that much of the long-term variation in real interest rates can be explained by rates of return in the real economy and by the ratio of gross government debt to GDP. The link between rates of return and long-term variation in real interest rates is less solid, although the relation is stronger for long-term bond yields. The results also suggest that the estimates for the long-term real interest rates come closer to the underlying equilibrium relationship than do those for the short-term real interest rates, as the coefficients in the former regressions are more in line with theory.

The final regression results concern the transitory deviations of the short- and long-term global real interest rates from the long-term equilibrium real interest rate. Table 4 reports the regression results for the weighted-average global real interest rates.[22] Only the reduced equations, that is, equations that underwent the reduction from the general to the specific, are shown. (The first and second lags of all variables, as well as the current values for the change in the real discount rate and the GDP growth rate, are included in the general specifications.) For the short-term rate, monetary and fiscal policies, measured by changes in the world real discount rate and the ratio of world budget deficits, are significant determinants, as well

---

[21]Stock and Watson (1993) emphasize this point.

[22]Given the analogy among world real interest rates, the results for other interest rates are also analogous. Results with other world real interest rates as left-hand variables are available from the authors upon request.

Table 4. Error-Correction Models for Global Real Interest Rates

(Standard errors in parentheses)

	Changes in Global Real Interest Rate[1]	
	Short term	Long term
Independent variables		
Lagged changes in short-term real interest rate		0.377 (0.077)
Lagged changes in long-term global real interest rate	0.210 (0.071)	0.275 (0.084)
Current changes in real world discount rate	0.945 (0.049)	
Lagged changes in debt-to-GDP ratio	−5.124 (2.515)	
Current growth rate of world GDP		0.246 (0.037)
Lagged growth rate of world GDP		−0.270 (0.037)
Lagged change in stock returns	0.001 (0.003)	
Lagged deviation from equilibrium value	−0.153 (0.041)	−0.119 (0.032)
Fit statistics		
$\bar{R}^2$	0.937	0.775
$\hat{\sigma}$	0.382	0.477
AR(1)[2]	0.25	1.64

Source: IMF staff estimates.

[1]Weighted average.

[2]Lagrange multiplier test of residual first order serial correlation.

as the error-correction adjustment, the lagged long-term changes, and the changes in the return on stocks. The world GDP growth rate and changes in the long-term global real interest rate were insignificant.[23] The results for the long-term global real interest rate were remarkably different. Monetary and fiscal policies have no significant direct impact. But the business cycle, as measured by the growth in

world GDP, is a primary determinant of the short-term dynamics. Fiscal and monetary policies still influence the long-term global real interest rate, however, through the lagged change in short-term real interest rates and the error-correction term.

Conclusions

Until recently, it was probably sufficient to look at trends in national interest rates to get a sense of the pressures that ex ante investment demands place on the world supply of saving. With the increasing integration of world capital markets, however, it now makes more sense to think about the concept of a global real interest rate that reflects global financial forces. Although several methodologies can be employed to measure such a global real interest rate—a weighted-average approach, a principal components approach, and a common trend approach—the analysis in this paper suggests that they all indicate the same basic trend over the past third of a century. Global real interest rates averaged 1–2 percent in the 1960s and early 1970s, roughly zero in the oil shock period of 1973–1980, and a much higher 3–4½ percent in the 1981–94 period. This paper's model of shifts in global interest rate regimes finds strong empirical support for such a breakdown.

These findings raise the obvious question of why real interest rates have been so much higher over the past decade and a half than they were from 1960 to 1972, which can be considered to be a useful reference period. The paper's modeling structure suggests that increased levels of world government debt relative to GDP since the early 1980s are the most important factor in the increase in the global real interest rate. This increase in debt explains a larger share of the increase in real rates than other commonly posited factors, including the general worldwide increase in the rate of return on productive capacity. Because the real interest rate is such an important determinant of economic growth, and because higher interest rates are associated with lower levels of capital formation, productivity, and income growth, governments worldwide need to be concerned about the repercussions of increases in not only their own ratios of debt to GDP, but also their neighbors'.

---

[23]The residuals in the error-correction equations seem to be plagued by heteroscedasticity. For this reason, all standard errors reported are calculated using a heteroscedasticity-consistent variance-covariance matrix of coefficients. The same variance-covariance matrix was used in the process of reducing the general error-correction model to the specific model reported in Table 4.

Appendix I

Common Components in Global Real Interest Rates

In this appendix, a two-period, two-country asset-pricing model is used to provide a theoretical basis for the discussion of global real interest rates in the first section of the paper. Assuming that each of the two countries is populated with identical consumers whose preferences might be country specific, consumers in both countries face two decisions. The first concerns the intertemporal allocation of spending over the two periods; the second concerns the temporal allocation between traded and nontraded goods. The real spending of a consumer in country i ($i = 1,2$) in period t ($t = 0,1$) is denoted as C_t^i, and the consumer's expected lifetime utility is given by

$$U^i = \ln(C_o^i) + \beta^i E[\ln(C_1^i)], \tag{A1}$$

where β^i denotes the inverse of one plus the rate-of-time preference. The consumer's spending is allocated between traded goods C_{Tt}^i and nontraded goods C_{Nt}^i, according to the function

$$C_t^i = C_{Tt}^{i\gamma^i} C_{Nt}^{i(1-\gamma^i)}, \tag{A2}$$

with spending restricted by the requirement that the present value of consumption expenditures equal the present value of the consumer's endowment over the two periods

$$X_o^i + p_o^i Y_o^i - P_o^i C_o^i - B_o^i = 0, \text{ and}$$
$$x_1^i + p_1^i Y_1^i - P_1^i C_1^i + (1+r)B_o^i = 0, \tag{A3}$$

where X_t^i stands for the endowment of traded goods, Y_t^i for the endowment of nontraded goods that consumer i receives in period t, p_t^i for the relative price of nontraded goods in terms of traded goods in period t, and P_t^i the consumption price index in period t. B_o^i, finally, denotes the number of bonds that consumer i buys in period 0. One bond can be acquired with one unit of the tradable good and yields a net return of r units of the tradable good in period 1.

In equilibrium, the consumption of nontraded goods must be equal to the endowment of nontradables in each period and in each country. That is,

$$C_{Nt}^i = Y_t^i. \tag{A4}$$

Also, the total consumption of tradables must be equal to the total endowment of tradables in each period, that is,

$$C_{Tt}^1 + C_{Tt}^2 = X_t^1 + X_t^2. \tag{A5}$$

Finally, the net supply of bonds has to be equal to zero:

$$B_o^1 + B_o^2 = 0. \tag{A6}$$

The endowments X_t^i and Y_t^i are random variables that are distributed log normally with mean ω_{ij} and variance σ_{ij}, where $j = X,Y$. Given the notation above, it also follows that consumers in both countries are assumed to know the state of the world in period 0 when they form their decisions or, in other words, to have learned about the realizations of the endowment shocks in that period.

The intertemporal spending decision is governed by the following familiar first-order condition:

$$\beta^i(1 + r) \, E\left[\frac{C_o^i}{C_1^i} \cdot \frac{P_o^i}{P_1^i} \right] = 1, \tag{A7}$$

which requires the marginal rate of substitution of spending to be equal to the marginal rate of transformation, that is, the return on savings. Using the goods market equilibrium conditions in this first-order condition leads to the equation[24]

$$e\left[\begin{array}{c} \beta^i(1 + r)[X_0^i(1 + \tilde{\gamma}) + (\tilde{\gamma} - 1)b_0^i] \\ -\ln(1+ \tilde{\gamma}) - \omega_i^X + \dfrac{\sigma_{ix}}{2} - \dfrac{X_0^i(\tilde{\gamma} - 1)(1 + r)b_0^i)}{X_1^i(1 + \tilde{\gamma})} \\ \tilde{\gamma} = \dfrac{1-\gamma^i}{\gamma^i}, \end{array} \right] = 1, \tag{A8}$$

---

[24]This equation is based on a first-order Taylor expansion around $X_1^i = e^{-\omega}$ and $b_0^i = 0$ and is therefore only an approximation for small trade flows between the two countries. Otherwise, no closed-form solution could be obtained, even in this simple setup.

which defines the demand for bonds for consumers who are price takers in world capital markets (b_0^i denotes B_0^i as a fraction of world output in tradables X_0^i). The bond demand functions B_o^1 and B_o^2, where the signs over the variables denote the sign of the partial derivative of the function with respect to that variable, can therefore be written as

$$B_0^i = b(X_0^i, E[X_1^i], \overset{+}{r}, \overset{+}{\sigma}_{ix}, \overset{+}{\beta}^i, \overset{+}{\gamma}^i. \tag{A9}$$

The bond market equilibrium condition (equation (A6)), finally, leads to the following function for the equilibrium global real interest rate:

$$r = R(\bar{X}_0^1, E[\overset{+}{X}_1^1], \bar{X}_0^2, E[\overset{+}{X}_1^2], \bar{\sigma}_{X1}, \bar{\sigma}_{X2}, \bar{\beta}^1, \bar{\beta}^2, \bar{\gamma}^1, \bar{\gamma}^2). \tag{A10}$$

The determination of real interest rates in this setup is standard and will not be discussed in more detail; instead, the focus will be on only the aspects relevant for the measurement of the global real interest rate. X_0^1 and X_0^2 are realizations of the endowment shocks, which, although uncorrelated, still affect consumption allocation decisions in both countries because of capital mobility.

There is a well-defined world real interest rate in this setup because there is an asset denominated in tradable goods that allows consumers to smooth their consumption of tradable goods. In empirical work, only so-called consumption-based real interest rates, that is, nominal interest rates deflated by some consumer price index, are available for most countries. This model, however, can be used to analyze the determination of the consumption-based real interest rate and to discuss the implications for empirical work. The gross consumption-based real interest rate for country i is defined (according to Frenkel and Razin (1992, p. 140)) as

$$1 + r_c^i = (1 + r)\frac{P_o^i}{P_1^i}. \tag{A11}$$

Taking natural logarithms, the net real interest rate can be approximated by

$$r_c^i = r - q^i, \tag{A12}$$

where q^i denotes the percentage change in the consumption price index P_t^i between period 0 and period 1 in country i. To illustrate the role of this new real interest rate concept, it is useful to rewrite the first-order conditions (equation (A7)) as

$$\beta^i E\left[\frac{C_o^i}{C_1^i}(1 + r_c^i)\right] = 1. \tag{A13}$$

This equation clearly illustrates the role of the consumption-based real interest rate: it determines the intertemporal allocation of spending. Households take the expected price change in the consumption price index into account when they decide on their intertemporal allocation.

It can be shown that the consumption price index P_t^i in this model is given by

$$P_t^i = k\, p_t^i{}^{\gamma^i}, \tag{A14}$$

and that in equilibrium the relative price of nontraded goods is

$$P_t^i = \left(\frac{1 - \gamma^i}{\gamma^i}\right)\frac{C_{Tt}^i}{Y_t^i}. \tag{A15}$$

Using the fact that the consumption of traded goods is a function of the same factors as the bond demand function (equation (A9)) because of the trade balance constraints, that is,

$$C_{T0}^i = X_0^i - B_0^i, \tag{A16}$$

$$C_{T1}^i = X_1^i + (1+r)B_0^i$$

allows one to write the change in the consumption price index q as

$$q^i = q(\bar{X}_0^1, E[\overset{+}{X}_1^1], \bar{X}_0^2, E[\overset{+}{X}_1^2], \bar{\sigma}_{1X},$$
$$\bar{\sigma}_{2X}, \bar{\beta}^1, \bar{\beta}^2, \bar{\gamma}^1, \bar{\gamma}^2; \bar{Y}_0^i, E[\overset{+}{Y}_1^i]\sigma_{i\gamma}). \tag{A17}$$

Consequently, the consumption-based real interest rate of country i is a function such that

$$r_c^i = q(\bar{X}_0^1, E[\overset{+}{X}_1^1], \bar{X}_0^2, E[\overset{+}{X}_1^2], \bar{\sigma}_{1X}, \bar{\sigma}_{2X},$$
$$\bar{\beta}^1, \bar{\beta}^2, \bar{\gamma}^1, \bar{\gamma}^2; \bar{Y}_0^i, E[\overset{+}{Y}_1^i], \sigma_{i\gamma}). \tag{A18}$$

Equation (A18) is the foundation of the claim that there are common factors in national consumption-based real interest rates that can be extracted to construct a global real interest rate. The country-specific shocks, that is, shocks to the endowments of nontradable goods Y_0^i and Y_1^i, have no impact on the world real interest rate r, but they do have an impact on the consumption-based real interest rates r_c^i.[25] It is clear from equations (A17) and (A18) that both the interest

---

[25]It is, of course, assumed that the endowment shocks for nontradable goods are less than perfectly correlated across countries.

rate r and the expected real exchange rate changes q move with common components, that is X_0^1 and X_0^2.

What are the consequences of using consumption-based real interest rates in empirical work? The common component picks up the impact of shocks that are transmitted to both countries, in particular, the impact of the realized shocks X_0^1 and X_0^2 and of the expected shocks $E[X_1^1]$ and $E[X_1^2]$. The level of the world real interest rate provided by the common component, however, is "wrong" because it does not reflect only r, the rate of interest on the global asset B, but also expected changes in real exchange rates. If there were no shocks to the endowments of nontraded goods, this fact would not constitute any problem because the common movements in the expected ratios of tradable consumption in period 0 and period 1, that is, C_0/C_1, are exactly offset across the two countries (note that these ratios are perfectly negatively correlated in this model). Shocks to the endowments of nontradables also induce real exchange rate changes, however; these effects are not necessarily related to other shocks nor can they be expected to be offset. It follows, therefore, that the global real interest rate, defined as the common component in consumption-based real interest rates, should be seen as an average real interest rate on world spending growth rather than on the growth of spending in tradable goods alone.[26] However, this average interest rate is not a real price

in the sense of a decision variable because no underlying asset exists.[27]

It is argued in the text that a global real interest rate is an interest rate on world spending or, in equilibrium, on world output. This claim can be illustrated by rewriting the first-order conditions in terms of world spending:

$$\beta^i \, E\left[\frac{(1 - Z_o^i)S_o^i}{\Omega(1 - Z_1^i)S_1^i} \cdot (1 + r_c^i) \right] = 1, \qquad (A19)$$

where Ω denotes the growth rate of world GDP, that is the sum of all traded and nontraded goods, Z_t^i stands for the share of country i's real spending in world output, and S_t denotes the consumption price index of country i in terms of the country in which world output/spending is measured, that is, the ratio P_t^2/P_t^1, at time t. Equation (A19) is yet another indication that it is possible to construct an average consumption-based real interest rate that is a synthetic asset return in terms of world GDP.

---

[26]See Stulz (1994) for a discussion of asset pricing in terms of world consumption growth.

[27]The global real interest rate as defined in this section is therefore an implication of asset-pricing relations; it does not define an asset-pricing relation. This is a drawback in the sense that restrictions on global real interest rates are always also restrictions on the asset-pricing model that "prices" the national real interest rates. There is also an advantage to it, however. Assuming that national real interest rates are correctly priced, a global real interest rate can be constructed without specifying the exact underlying asset-pricing model.

Appendix II

Modeling Inflation Expectations

Measuring real average bond yields to maturity requires an inflation forecast for the same period as the bond. Blanchard and Summers (1984) propose a duration-weighted average of expected future inflation rates. Given that average yields to maturity are used for long-term government bond rates, the question arises of which forecast horizon to choose. The answer depends on the time-series properties of inflation. If inflation is nonstationary and can be modeled as a random walk, the problem of the forecast horizon is irrelevant. If inflation can be approximated by an autoregressive moving average (ARMA(p,q)) model, choosing the forecast horizon depends on the parameters of the model.

The three-month inflation rates in all countries included in the sample display unit root or near unit root properties over the sample period.[28] Any recursive univariate model, therefore, will lead to forecasts in which innovations in the current inflation rate are incorporated as (almost) permanent shifts.[29] This feature turns out to have rather problematic implications for the real long-term interest rates in the years 1973–74 and 1979. It seems rather unlikely, however, that market participants expected oil-shock-induced innovations in the inflation rates to be permanent. Surveys of inflation expectations show that, although there is a certain degree of inertia in these expectations, they are updated with respect to events in the recent past. It is also likely that agents learn and react differently in different monetary policy regimes. For that reason, nonlinear univariate time-series models might capture the process of inflation expectation formation more accurately than linear time-series models. However, an adaptive expectations formula comes close to observed expectation formation patterns. Given the near-random-walk properties of inflation, this procedure also generates optimal linear forecasts (see Muth (1961)). Adaptive expectations were generated by using the exponential-smoothing formula

$$\hat{\pi}_t = 0.7\hat{\pi}_{t-1} + 0.3\pi_t,$$

where π_t denotes the annual inflation rate and $\hat{\pi}_t$ the forecast value.

---

[28]Results are available from the authors upon request.

[29]Univariate fixed and time-varying ARMA(p,q) models—with and without an autoregressive conditional heteroscedasticity (ARCH) specification—were experimented with for the error processes (See Evans (1991) for an AR(1) model with time-varying parameters and an ARCH specification for the forecast errors). In all cases, the estimated models implied a considerable degree of updating to current innovations in forecasts.

Appendix III

Constructing Global Real Interest Rates

In this appendix, the construction of a global real interest rate using the principal component and the common trend estimation approaches are documented.

Principal Components Approach

The first principal components of standardized short- and long-term real interest rates were calculated for the period from 1960:QI to 1994:QIII. Global real interest rates were then generated as a weighted average of national real interest rates, with weights based on the load factors of the first principal component of standardized national real interest rates.[30] Global real interest rates based on both eight and three countries were calculated. The results of the principal component analysis can be found in Tables A2 and A3. The first principal component explains roughly half of the variation in short-term real interest rates and about 65 percent in long-term real interest rates. The additional explanation by other principal components declines rapidly, although the importance of country-specific factors is remarkable.[31] It is interesting that the weights implied by the load factors are much more equal than the GDP weights.

Common Trend Approach

For the extraction of the common trend in national real interest rates, the cointegration vectors describing the long-run relations between national real interest rates are needed. These were estimated for the period from 1960:QI to 1994:QIII using Johansen's (1991) maximum likelihood estimator. The lag length of the underlying vector autoregression was determined using likelihood ratio tests based initially on eight lags. Two different systems were estimated for both the short- and the long-term real interest rate, including one for the so-called G-3 countries and one for eight countries (see Tables A4 and A5). The outcome was quite sensitive to the number of countries included. The results for the G-3 countries are sensible: two cointegration vectors seem to be significant, so that only one common trend determines the nonstationary part of national real interest rates.

In the case of the eight countries, the evidence of one common trend is weaker. Although real interest rates seem to be cointegrated bilaterally (except possibly between Germany and Belgium), the number of significant cointegration vectors in the eight-country estimation system was always less than seven, suggesting more than one common trend. This outcome might be the result of a rapid loss in the power of the multivariate unit root tests caused by the introduction of more countries into the system.[32] The whole concept of the global real interest rate being associated with a single common trend would therefore be misleading. For this reason, seven cointegration vectors were imposed on a priori reasoning rather than on statistical grounds. This procedure can be justified on the grounds that bilateral real interest rate differentials seem to be stationary in all cases. Nevertheless, given these shortcomings, the conclusions from the common trend calculations should be interpreted with caution.

The estimated cointegration vectors were then used to construct the orthogonal complement $\beta_\perp$ of the matrix of cointegration vectors β, in order to implement Kasa's (1992) version of the common trend representation for the vector of national real interest rates X_t:[33]

$$X_t = \beta(\beta'\beta)^{-1}\beta'X_t + \beta_\perp(\beta_\perp'\beta_\perp)^{-1}\beta_\perp'X_t. \qquad (A20)$$

---

[30]The $(T \times k)$ matrix of k standardized national real interest rates is denoted by X (T is the number of observations), and the first eigenvalue and the first eigenvector of $X'X$ with λ and v. The vector of load factors is then given by

$$\Xi = (T\sqrt{\lambda})^{-1}X'Xv.$$

The weights are computed by normalizing the squared elements of Ξ with λ.

[31] This result seems not to be specific to the sample period in the calculations. If the principal component analysis is undertaken for the period 1981:QI–1993:QIV, the contribution of the first principal component is remarkably similar to the one for the whole sample period 1960:QI–1993:QIV. It is striking, however, that the weight for the U.S. real interest rate increases somewhat for both long- and short-term real interest rates.

[32]The results were even more problematic when cointegration vectors were estimated for all eight countries.

[33]Kasa proposes to decompose the space spanned by the vector X_t, that is, the vector of national real interest rates, into two orthogonal subspaces. One of these subspaces is given by the cointegration vectors, so that the orthogonal subspace follows quite naturally.

Table A1. Summary Statistics for National Real Interest Rates

| | Mean[1] | | | | | Break |
	60:QI–94:QIII	60:QI–72:QIV	73:QI–80:QIV	81:QI–94:QIII	ADF t-statistics I[2,5]	ADF t-statistics II[3,5]	Date[4]
Short-term interest rates							
Belgium	3.019	1.322	0.950	5.829	−1.627 (6)	−3.472 (6)	76:QI
	(3.751)	(2.612)	(4.643)	(1.943)			
Canada	3.073	2.235	−0.059	5.686	−2.278 (3)	−7.047 (0)***	80:QIII
	(3.281)	(2.243)	(8.173)	(4.622)			
Germany	2.893	1.995	1.988	4.268	−3.715 (4)***	−5.657 (5)***	79:QII
	(2.688)	(2.698)	(2.946)	(1.850)			
Japan	1.396	0.556	−1.365	3.796	−3.476 (4)**	−5.986 (3)***	73:QIV
	(5.037)	(3.231)	(7.352)	(2.688)			
Netherlands	1.814	−0.311	0.469	4.807	−2.606 (4)	−4.981 (4)**	78:QII
	(4.186)	(5.727)	(4.001)	(2.126)			
Switzerland	0.084	−0.807	−1.520	1.860	−2.326 (3)	−4.313 (3)	73:QI
	(3.166)	(2.586)	(3.777)	(2.367)			
United Kingdom	1.050	0.746	−4.832	4.760	−2.420 (3)	−4.206 (4)	80:QI
	(6.188)	(3.290)	(7.915)	(4.132)			
United States	1.281	1.202	−1.942	3.225	−2.093 (2)	−3.761 (1)	79:QIV
	(2.849)	(1.113)	(4.585)	(6.421)			
Long-term interest rates							
Belgium	3.834	3.521	1.176	5.676	−1.778 (4)	−3.261 (4)	77:QIII
	(2.492)	(0.896)	(3.373)	(0.922)			
Canada	3.559	3.411	0.701	5.362	−1.379 (5)	−3.765 (1)	82:QIV
	(2.135)	(0.574)	(1.373)	(1.442)			
Germany	4.026	4.174	2.932	4.524	−2.177 (1)	−3.131 (3)	82:QIV
	(1.154)	(0.841)	(0.842)	(1.183)			
Japan	2.490	3.720	−1.937	3.903	−2.032 (4)	−3.474 (3)	77:QII
	(3.812)	(3.034)	(4.628)	(1.002)			
Netherlands	2.947	1.597	1.399	5.124	−1.553 (4)	−3.891 (3)	77:QII
	(2.285)	(1.079)	(2.163)	(1.248)			
Switzerland	0.889	0.779	0.149	1.418	−2.866 (6)*	−3.964 (6)	82:QIV
	(2.658)	(1.242)	(1.768)	(1.184)			
United Kingdom	2.303	2.746	−1.732	4.233	−2.178 (6)	−3.577 (4)	77:QI
	(3.265)	(1.489)	(3.916)	(1.650)			
United States	3.410	2.863	0.728	5.487	−2.307 (3)	−5.372 (3)***	80:QII
	(2.237)	(0.386)	(1.327)	(1.640)			

Source: IMF staff estimates.

[1]In percent; standard deviation in parentheses.

[2]Augmented Dickey-Fuller unit root test. Automatic lag length selection according to significance level of last lag of lagged first difference of series. Initial lag length is six lags (lag length in parentheses).

[3]Minimum t-statistics from a series of augmented Dickey-Fuller regressions with a 1–0 dummy variable in every period (excluding observations near end points). Lag lengths in parentheses. Critical values of test statistics taken from Perron and Vogelsang (1992).

[4]Period in which minimum t-statistics occurs.

[5]Three asterisks denote rejection of the null hypothesis of a unit root in the residuals at the 1 percent level, two asterisks at the 5 percent level, and one asterisk at the 10 percent level.

Because common trend representations are not unique, some identification scheme needs to be imposed. Kasa's proposition of normalizing $\beta_\perp$ such that the elements $(\beta_\perp' \beta_\perp)^{-1} \beta_\perp'$ sum to one is a natural normalization in this case. It also allows a direct comparison between the different methods of constructing global real interest rates. The global real interest rate follows then as

$$R_t^W = (\beta_\perp' \beta_\perp)^{-1} \beta_\perp' X_t. \qquad (A21)$$

The results of the cointegration analysis and the weights in the common trend representation are shown in Tables A4 and A5. In the system for the short-term real interest rates of the G-3 countries, the trace statistics suggest two cointegration vectors, whereas the lambda-max statistics suggest one cointegration vector. In the case of long-term real interest rates, both the trace and the lambda-max statistics suggest two cointegration vectors. In the systems for eight countries, there seem to be at most five stationary linear combinations of both short- and long-term real interest rates. It is noteworthy that the weights attached to the countries outside the G-3 group are larger than those inside the group for short-term real interest rates.

Table A2. Principal Component Analysis of National Short-Term Real Interest Rates, 1960:QI–1994:QIII[1]

	United States	United Kingdom	Belgium	Netherlands	Canada	Germany	Switzerland	Japan
Eight countries								
Eigenvalues	3.8953	0.9867	0.7750	0.7132	0.6300	0.4535	0.3043	0.2418
Eigenvectors	−0.3561	−0.5841	0.0479	0.0893	0.2498	−0.1640	0.3072	0.5815
	−0.3675	0.0492	0.1015	0.5092	0.3640	0.6103	−0.2798	−0.0987
	−0.4071	0.0425	0.2238	−0.2008	−0.4421	−0.1065	−0.6605	0.3146
	−0.3549	0.4812	0.2297	0.0934	−0.4055	0.1733	0.6069	0.1351
	−0.3821	−0.4008	0.3589	−0.2672	−0.0545	−0.0529	0.1310	−0.6858
	−0.3198	0.5024	0.0675	−0.0810	0.5720	−0.5488	−0.0462	−0.0604
	−0.3097	0.0626	−0.5904	−0.6210	0.1277	0.3807	0.0559	0.0402
	−0.3197	−0.0785	−0.6346	0.4691	−0.3143	−0.3322	−0.0177	−0.2437
Percentage of variance	0.4869	0.1233	0.0969	0.0892	0.0788	0.0567	0.0380	0.0302
Weight	0.1268	0.1351	0.1657	0.1260	0.1460	0.1023	0.0959	0.1022
Three countries								
Eigenvalues	1.6575	. . .	. . .	. . .	. . .	0.7769	. . .	0.5657
Eigenvectors	−0.6103	. . .	. . .	. . .	. . .	0.3616	. . .	0.7048
	−0.5034	. . .	. . .	. . .	. . .	−0.8640	. . .	0.0074
	−0.6116	. . .	. . .	. . .	. . .	0.3503	. . .	−0.7094
Percentage of variance	0.5525	. . .	. . .	. . .	. . .	0.2590	. . .	0.1886
Weight	0.3725	. . .	. . .	. . .	. . .	0.2534	. . .	0.3741

Source: IMF staff estimates.

[1]See Appendix III for details.

Table A3. Principal Component Analysis of National Long-Term Real Interest Rates, 1960:QI–1994:QIII[1]

	United States	United Kingdom	Belgium	Netherlands	Canada	Germany	Switzerland	Japan
Eight countries								
Eigenvalues	5.1578	0.8688	0.5982	0.4888	0.4513	0.2321	0.1587	0.0443
Eigenvectors	−0.3395	−0.5375	0.0387	0.3936	−0.1376	−0.4105	−0.4082	0.2921
	−0.3591	−0.3327	0.2017	−0.2730	−0.3810	0.6842	−0.1430	−0.1066
	−0.4025	0.1180	−0.0070	−0.1903	0.4718	−0.1801	0.1639	0.7113
	−0.3650	0.2597	0.3488	0.2349	0.5227	0.0694	−0.3576	−0.4653
	−0.3944	−0.2371	−0.0455	0.3098	0.0225	−0.0538	0.7792	−0.2823
	−0.3199	0.4249	0.4859	−0.2794	−0.4471	−0.4326	0.1112	0.0590
	−0.2929	0.5211	−0.5319	0.4114	−0.3541	0.2055	−0.1357	0.0668
	−0.3418	−0.1035	−0.5613	−0.5795	0.1192	−0.3064	−0.1421	−0.3055
Percentage of variance	0.6447	0.1086	0.0748	0.0611	0.0564	0.0290	0.0198	0.0055
Weight	0.1153	0.1290	0.1620	0.1333	0.1555	0.1024	0.0858	0.1168
Three countries								
Eigenvalues	1.9212	. . .	. . .	. . .	. . .	0.6363	. . .	0.4425
Eigenvectors	−0.5851	. . .	. . .	. . .	. . .	0.5146	. . .	0.6268
	−0.5365	. . .	. . .	. . .	. . .	−0.8252	. . .	0.1767
	−0.6082	. . .	. . .	. . .	. . .	0.2329	. . .	−0.7589
Percentage of variance	0.6404	. . .	. . .	. . .	. . .	0.2121	. . .	0.1475
Weight	0.3423	. . .	. . .	. . .	. . .	0.2878	. . .	0.3699

Source: IMF staff estimates.

[1]See Appendix III for details.

Table A4. Cointegration Analysis of Short-Term Real Interest Rates, 1960:QI–1994:QIII

r^1	$\hat{\lambda}_r$	$-T\ln(1-\hat{\lambda}_r)$	$\hat{\lambda}_{max}(0.9)$	$-T\sum\ln(1-\hat{\lambda}_r)$	$\hat{\lambda}_{Tr}(0.9)$	Cointegration Vectors (Row Vectors)							
						United States	Germany	Japan	Belgium	Canada	Switzerland	United Kingdom	Netherlands
1	0.1710	55.13	15.59	36.06	21.63	0.215	0.168	−0.398					
2	0.0636	8.80	9.52	10.93	10.47	−0.537	0.275	0.142					
3	0.0158	2.13	2.86	2.13	2.86	0.101	0.199	0.056					
$\beta\perp^2$						0.8428	1.1587	0.9457					
$(\beta\perp\beta\perp)^{-1}\beta\perp$						0.2860	0.3931	0.3209					
1	0.4711	81.52	44.99	274.50	135.24	0.243	−0.161	−0.394	0.540	0.169	−0.280	−0.090	−0.034
2	0.3875	62.74	38.98	192.98	104.77	0.154	−0.243	−0.218	−0.208	−0.094	0.464	0.159	−0.051
3	0.3405	53.29	33.62	130.24	78.36	−0.261	0.090	−0.015	−0.077	−0.236	−0.130	0.095	0.300
4	0.2234	32.36	27.62	76.95	55.44	0.347	0.252	−0.078	0.206	0.046	0.120	−0.666	−0.008
5	0.1931	27.46	21.58	44.59	36.58	0.141	−0.270	0.106	0.205	−0.455	0.095	−0.107	−0.011
6	0.0730	9.70	15.59	17.14	21.63	0.377	−0.199	−0.006	−0.143	0.117	0.075	−0.029	0.024
7	0.0466	6.10	9.52	7.44	10.47	−0.354	−0.221	0.036	0.151	0.150	0.009	0.018	0.094
8	0.0104	1.34	2.86	1.34	2.86	0.014	−0.057	−0.041	−0.085	−0.025	−0.003	−0.057	−0.028
$\beta\perp^2$						0.6481	0.8583	0.8934	1.2912	0.3979	1.0385	1.1586	1.0785
$(\beta\perp\beta\perp)^{-1}\beta\perp$						0.0880	0.1165	0.1213	0.1753	0.0540	0.1410	0.1573	0.1464

Source: IMF staff estimates.

[1]Number of cointegration vectors under the null hypothesis (trace statistics).

[2]Normalized (see Appendix III for details).

Table A5. Cointegration Analysis of Long-Term Real Interest Rates, 1960:Q1–1994:QIII

r^1	$\hat{\lambda}_r$	$-T\ln(1-\hat{\lambda}_r)$	$\hat{\lambda}_{max}(0.9)$	$-T\sum\ln(1-\hat{\lambda}_r)$	$\hat{\lambda}_{Tr}(0.9)$	United States	Germany	Japan	Belgium	Canada	Switzerland	United Kingdom	Netherlands
1	0.1710	55.13	15.59	36.06	21.63	0.215	0.168	−0.398					
0	0.1106	15.82	15.59	30.27	21.63	−0.561	0.450	0.121					
1	0.1000	14.23	9.52	14.45	10.47	0.040	0.152	−0.320					
2	0.0016	0.22	2.86	0.22	2.86	−0.135	−0.159	0.059					
$\beta\perp^2$						1.0582	1.1392	0.6727					
$(\beta\perp\beta\perp)^{-1}\beta\perp$						0.3687	0.3969	0.2344					
0	0.3408	53.33	44.99	185.11	135.24	1.106	0.151	0.239	0.719	−2.023	−0.204	−0.050	−0.108
1	0.2766	41.44	38.98	131.78	104.77	0.248	−0.283	0.111	0.893	−0.286	1.081	−0.667	−0.600
2	0.2377	34.75	33.62	90.33	78.36	0.292	0.884	0.452	−1.550	−0.752	0.725	−0.057	0.809
3	0.1677	23.50	27.62	55.59	55.44	0.084	−0.082	0.529	−0.632	0.818	−0.448	−0.495	−0.017
4	0.1432	19.78	21.58	32.08	36.58	1.123	−0.513	−0.574	1.255	−0.741	0.886	0.012	−1.158
5	0.0551	7.25	15.59	12.30	21.63	0.468	−0.184	−0.130	0.426	−0.224	−0.352	−0.545	0.002
$\beta\perp^2$						0.1512	0.1653	0.0921	0.1653	0.1500	0.0394	0.0945	0.1415
$(\beta\perp\beta\perp)^{-1}\beta\perp$						1.0860	1.1873	0.6617	1.1873	1.0830	0.2829	0.6787	1.0165

Source: IMF staff estimates.

[1]Number of cointegration vectors under the null hypothesis (trace statistics).

[2]Normalized (see Appendix III for details).

Bibliography

Barro, Robert J., "World Interest Rates and Investment," *Scandinavian Journal of Economics*, Vol. 94 (No. 2, 1992), pp. 323–42.

______, and Xavier Sala-i-Martin, "World Real Interest Rates," in *NBER Macroeconomics Annual 1990*, ed. by Olivier J. Blanchard and Stanley Fischer (Cambridge, Massachusetts: MIT Press, 1990).

Blanchard, Olivier, and Lawrence H. Summers, "Perspectives on High World Real Interest Rates," *Brookings Papers on Economic Activity*, No. 2 (1984), pp. 273–324.

Brunner, Allan D., and Graciela L. Kaminsky, "World Interest Rates: Do Fiscal and Monetary Policies Matter After All?" (unpublished; Washington: U.S. Board of Governors of the Federal Reserve System, 1994).

Campbell, John Y., and Pierre Perron, "Pitfalls and Opportunities: What Macroeconomists should know about Unit Roots," in *NBER Macroeconomics Annual 1991*, ed. by Stanley Fischer (Cambridge, Massachusetts: MIT Press, 1991).

Coorey, Sharmini, "The Determinants of U.S. Real Interest Rates in the Long Run," IMF Working Paper, WP/91/118 (Washington: International Monetary Fund, December 1991).

Diamond, Peter A., "National Debt in a Neoclassical Growth Model," *American Economic Review*, Vol. 55 (December 1965), pp. 1126–50.

Evans, Martin, "Discovering the Link Between Inflation Rates and Inflation Uncertainty," *Journal of Money, Credit, and Banking*, Vol. 23 (May 1991), pp. 169–84.

Evans, Paul, "Do Budget Deficits Raise Nominal Interest Rates? Evidence from Six Industrial Countries," *Journal of Monetary Economics*, Vol. 20 (September 1987), pp. 281–300.

Ford, Robert, and Douglas Laxton, "World Public Debt and Real Interest Rates," IMF Working Paper, WP/95/30 (Washington: International Monetary Fund, March 1995).

Frenkel, Jacob A., and Assaf Razin, *Fiscal Policies and the World Economy* (Cambridge, Massachusetts: MIT Press, 1992).

Friedman, Milton, "The Role of Monetary Policy," *American Economic Review*, Vol. 58 (March 1968), pp. 1–17.

Gagnon, Joseph E., "The Slow Adjustment of Nominal Interest Rates: A Study of the Fisher Effect" (unpublished; Washington: U.S. Department of the Treasury, February 1995).

______, and Mark D. Unferth, "Is There a World Interest Rate?" U.S. Board of Governors of the Federal Reserve System, International Finance Discussion Papers, No. 454 (Washington: U.S. Board of Governors of the Federal Reserve System, September 1993).

Goldstein, Morris, and Michael Mussa, "The Integration of World Capital Markets," IMF Working Paper, WP/93/95 (Washington: International Monetary Fund, December 1993).

Hamilton, James D., "A New Approach to the Economic Analysis of Nonstationary Time Series and the Business Cycle," *Econometrica*, Vol. 57 (March 1989), pp. 357–84.

______, "Analysis of Time Series Subject to Changes in Regime," *Journal of Econometrics*, Vol. 45 (July/August 1990), pp. 39–70.

______, "State-Space Models," in *Handbook of Econometrics*, Vol. IV, ed. by Robert F. Engle and Daniel L. McFadden (Amsterdam and New York: North-Holland, 1994).

Howe, Howard, and Charles Pigott, "Determinants of Long-Term Interest Rates: An Empirical Study of Several Industrial Countries," *Federal Reserve Bank of New York Quarterly Review*, Vol. 16 (Winter 1991/92), pp. 12–28.

Johansen, Soren, "Estimation and Hypothesis Testing of Cointegration Vectors in Gaussian Vector Autoregressive Models," *Econometrica*, Vol. 59 (November 1991), pp. 1551–80.

Kasa, Kenneth, "Common Stochastic Trends in International Stock Markets," *Journal of Monetary Economics*, Vol. 29 (February 1992), pp. 95–124.

Labadie, Pamela, "Stochastic Inflation and the Equity Premium," *Journal of Monetary Economics*, Vol. 24 (September 1989), pp. 277–98.

Laxton, D., N. Ricketts, and D. Rose, "Uncertainty, Learning and Policy Credibility," in *Economic Behavior and Policy Choice Under Price Stability* (Ottawa: Bank of Canada, 1993).

Masson, Paul R., and Malcolm Knight, "International Transmission of Fiscal Policies in Major Industrial Countries," *IMF Staff Papers*, Vol. 33 (September 1986), pp. 387–438.

Muth, John F., "Optimal Properties of Exponentially Weighted Forecasts," *Journal of American Statistical Association*, Vol. 55 (1961), pp. 299–306.

Obstfeld, Maurice, "International Capital Mobility in the 1990s," NBER Working Paper No. 4534 (Cambridge, Massachusetts: National Bureau of Economic Research, November 1993).

Perron, Pierre, and Timothy J. Vogelsang, "Nonstationarity and Level Shifts With an Application to Purchasing Power Parity," *Journal of Business and Economic Statistics*, Vol. 10 (July 1992), pp. 301–20.

Stock, James H., and Mark W. Watson, "A Simple Estimator of Cointegrating Vectors in Higher Order Integrated Systems," *Econometrica*, Vol. 61 (July 1993), pp. 783-820.

Stulz, Rene M., "International Portfolio Choice and Asset Pricing: An Integrative Survey," NBER Working Paper No. 4645 (Cambridge, Massachusetts: National Bureau of Economic Research, February 1994).

III

A Monetary Impulse Measure for Medium-Term Policy Analysis

Bennett T. McCallum and Monica Hargraves[1]

For a number of years, the biannual issues of the *World Economic Outlook* have regularly featured a measure of "fiscal impulse" for each of the seven major industrial economies in the discussion of conditions and prospects of the industrial countries. Although it has recently been given less emphasis, as attention has shifted to the concepts of structural and cyclical fiscal balances, the fiscal impulse measure continues to be reported. In contrast, there has been no presentation of a comparable common or standardized measure of monetary impulse for the major industrial countries. As monetary policy is unquestionably crucial for the success or failure of macroeconomic policies, it would seem that some additional attempt at systematization could be useful; in particular, it could provide a complement to the ranges of monetary indicators relied upon by individual monetary authorities and to the analysis of the world economic outlook itself. Consequently, the present paper is devoted to the development and investigation of one potential measure of monetary policy stance.

Organizationally, the paper proceeds as follows. The design and rationale of the proposed monetary impulse measure are discussed in the first section, followed by a presentation of the values of the proposed measure for the past 25 years. These annual values illustrate the construction of the measure and provide the basis for an evaluation, presented in the succeeding section, of its historical reliability. Next, values of the measure based on quarterly observations are reported, and some brief comparisons with other potential impulse measures are provided. Concluding remarks are then presented. Information concerning monetary base data is included as an appendix.

Design and Rationale

Two main criteria have guided the design of the proposed measure of monetary impulse. First, the measure should clearly reflect the medium-term inflationary implications of the current stance of monetary policy. Second, the measure should pertain to actions taken by the central bank itself—indeed, should pertain primarily to a variable over which the central bank could exert accurate control if it chose to do so. The first of these criteria suggests the use of some aggregate spending variable, such as the growth rate of nominal GDP, with other possibilities provided by the growth rate of nominal domestic demand, final sales, or personal income, for example.[2] The second criterion, by contrast, points toward use of a measure such as the growth rate of the (adjusted) monetary base. Other controllable reserve aggregates could be considered instead, but the monetary base has the desirable property of reflecting the effect of open market purchases on both reserves and currency. Thus, if adjusted for changes in reserve requirements, the base provides a reasonably comprehensive summary measure of the actions of the central bank.[3] Short-term nominal interest rates are also controllable, of course, and are emphasized by central banks, but these rates are less satisfactory indicators of monetary policy actions for reasons that will be discussed below.

Together, the two main criteria can be reasonably well satisfied by the proposed measure of monetary impulse, which is defined as the growth rate of the (adjusted) monetary base plus the expected medium-term growth rate of base velocity. This expected rate will be represented provisionally in this study by the actual change in base velocity over the most recent four years.[4] To be specific, if DLX and DLB denote growth rates (that is, changes in the logs) of nominal GDP and the monetary base, respectively, the growth rate of velocity over a single period—either a quarter or a year—will be $DLV = DLX - DLB$. Its average over the

---

[1]Bennett T. McCallum is the H.J. Heinz Professor of Economics at Carnegie-Mellon University. Work on this paper was begun when Professor McCallum was a visiting scholar in the Research Department. The authors are indebted to Peter B. Clark and David T. Coe for advice and encouragement, to Robert P. Flood for comments on an earlier draft, and to Toh Kuan, Sheila Bassett, and Sungcha Cha for expert assistance.

[2]Whether the aggregate spending measure should pertain to asset exchanges as well as production (or consumption) flows is an issue, raised by Hargraves and Schinasi (1993), that will be reserved for a future study.

[3]That actual central banks, at least in the major industrial countries, do not use the base as a control instrument is well known and will be discussed below.

[4]Other approaches could be explored, such as extracting the "permanent" component of the velocity series by means of time-series decomposition methods.

past four years will then be $DLVBAR = (1/N)(DLV + DLV(-1) + \ldots + DLV(-N + 1))$, where N equals 16 or 4, depending on the time interval adopted.

With quarterly data, then, the impulse measure to be studied below is

$$IM1 = DLB + DLVBAR(-1), \qquad (1)$$

where $DLVBAR$ is lagged one quarter so as to reflect data available to the central bank when setting DLB. When using annual data, however, the choice has been made to represent the impulse measure as

$$IM = DLB + DLVBAR, \qquad (2)$$

with no time lag for the average velocity term. This choice represents a compromise in terms of the controllability criterion, but to impose a full-year lag would seem to be excessively conservative.

In the sections that follow, values of the impulse measures in equations (1) and (2) will be reported for each of the major industrial economies. As the measures are rates of base growth adjusted by GDP velocity, they represent nominal growth rates of GDP that are implied—on average, from a medium-term perspective—by current monetary policy actions. Consequently, they are appropriately compared with "target" paths of nominal GDP growth that would be consistent with low inflation rates (that is, approximate price stability) in terms of GDP deflators. For presentational purposes, 2 percent has been adopted as the common annual inflation target, and 1 percent to 3 percent will be treated as the range of low inflation.[5] Average growth rates of real output must be accounted for, of course. Accordingly, the charts that present the impulse measures include low-inflation bands that represent the relevant economy's estimated long-run growth rate of real GDP plus 1–3 percent. For several economies, the estimate of long-run real growth is 3 percent, so in those cases the low-inflation bands extend from 4 percent to 6 percent.[6]

It is important to recognize that the impulse measure presented in this paper builds upon growth rates of the monetary base for the reasons mentioned above, not because of a belief that the base (or any other monetary aggregate) has any mystical properties. It should also be

noted that the case for using this measure does not rely on a presumption that technological and regulatory change in the payments and financial industries will be insignificant. Indeed, the purpose of the $DLVBAR$ term is in large part to account for precisely such changes, which have been important over recent decades in several countries and which may be important in the future.

As was mentioned above, the monetary base is not currently used as an instrument or intermediate target variable in any of the countries under study—although a variant (termed "central bank money") served as a target in Germany prior to 1987. That fact does not negate the reasons for focusing upon the base, however: that it could be accurately controlled[7] and that it represents a reasonably comprehensive measure of the impact of central bank actions (however governed) on aggregate demand. It can therefore be argued that the precision that is lost by not using a measure that reflects more specifically individual countries' policy mechanisms is outweighed by the advantages of using one that can be calculated in the same way for different countries and that can be used to study long periods of monetary history.

It is also well known that the base in many countries is largely composed of currency, and that currency is demand determined, in the sense that demand deposits can be redeemed for currency at the wish of the deposit holder. However, that fact does not imply that the base could not be controlled by the central bank or that manipulation of the base (rather than of reserves alone) would not be more effective for influencing total spending. Somewhat more troublesome is the likelihood that a large fraction of recent currency issues in the United States and Germany have gone abroad. In that regard, it should be kept in mind that such movements will eventually be reflected in the velocity growth term $DLVBAR$. For the first year or two after a major change, however, the impulse measures in equations (1) and (2) will reflect their effects only partially and will accordingly yield signals that are somewhat distorted.

The more traditional monetary growth rate measures—of M1 or M2, for example—and interest rates fare poorly in comparison with both of the adopted criteria. Aggregates of the M1 and M2 variety cannot be controlled with a high degree of accuracy, compared with the monetary base, and the growth rate of M1 or M2 that is necessary to yield a target inflation rate (over a decade or two, on average) is much more uncertain than the necessary growth rate for nominal

---

[5]Actual inflation targets and monetary policy objectives vary among the major industrial countries, but annual inflation of 2 percent may be considered roughly consistent with price stability. See International Monetary Fund (1993).

[6]The estimates of long-run real growth rates are not intended to be refined measures. They are simply averages of realized rates over 1961–92, rounded to the nearest ½ of 1 percent (annual basis). The values obtained in this manner are 3 percent, except for Japan (4 percent for 1972–92), Canada (4 percent), and the United Kingdom (2 percent). It would be straightforward to adopt more sophisticated estimates of potential output growth.

[7]As a sum of liability items on the central bank's own balance sheet, the base could be monitored daily—or even more frequently—and adjusted by open market operations whenever observations depart from desired values.

GDP.[8] Even if one added predicted velocity growth to an M1 or M2 measure, as equations (1) and (2) do for the base, this would still fail to produce a variable that is accurately controllable by the central bank.

With regard to interest rates, the most basic point is that the level of any short-term nominal interest rate is an ambiguous indicator of monetary policy stance. Specifically, high interest rates are associated with tight monetary policy from a short-term perspective but with easy monetary policy from a longer-term point of view. Accordingly, the interest rate effects of a monetary tightening—for example, an open market sale of securities—are in opposite directions from the short-term and long-term perspectives. Moreover, whether a particular interest rate level corresponds to a tight or easy monetary stance depends on economic conditions at the time, which would seem to be an extremely undesirable feature for a monetary indicator.

Conceivably, other variables involving interest rates—changes or spreads, for example—could be found that would perform more satisfactorily.[9] A preliminary examination of the performance of one interest spread measure is reported below in the discussion on alternative monetary indicators. A more extensive consideration of other measures is a possible topic for future research.

Annual Measures

The purpose of this section is to calculate and present annual values of the impulse measure *IM*, defined in equation (2), for the major industrial economies.[10] In a fundamental sense, only two basic variables are utilized—nominal GDP and the adjusted monetary base—which is one attractive feature of the proposed measure. The basic source of data for the nominal GDP series is quarterly (seasonally adjusted) observations; for annual series, the quarterly observations are averaged. Natural logarithms of these averages are calculated and first differenced to yield growth rates (denoted *DLX*).

One economy for which more needs to be said is Germany, with the difficulty arising from the east-west reunification of 1990. The procedure adopted in this paper for handling that event is determined in large measure by data availability. Specifically, the monetary statistics are those of the Bundesbank and pertain to west Germany before July 1, 1990, and to unified Germany thereafter. Official quarterly GDP figures since 1990 are available, unfortunately, only for west Germany. (Annual GDP figures are available, however, for west and east Germany separately.) An IMF staff estimate of quarterly GDP for unified Germany has been used for 1990–93.

More discussion is also needed on the monetary base series. As mentioned above, it is important to have a measure of the base—currency held by banks and the private nonbank sector plus banks' reserves at the central bank—that is adjusted for reserve requirement changes.[11] For four of the seven countries, such series have been obtained from national statistics.[12] For Japan, Germany, and France, however, adjustments have been made owing to the unavailability of these series. The basic idea of the procedure is as follows. If only one type of bank deposit were subject to reserve requirements—and if the requirement ratio were a single flat rate of, for example, 10 percent of deposits—the magnitude of deposits would be approximately equal to the ratio of the volume of reserves (R) to the reserve requirement ratio (rr). Consequently, an appropriate measure of adjusted reserves would be R multiplied by the factor rr^o/rr, where rr^o is the value of rr at some reference date. In practice, more than one type of deposit is subject to requirements in these countries, and, in Japan and Germany, the rr values depend on bank size.[13] However, the calculations have been performed as if these complications do not exist by using the rr values pertaining to demand deposits at

---

[8]Much has been made recently of the "stability" of M2 velocity in the United States over the past 30 years. But this phenomenon—more accurately described as the absence of an upward or downward drift—most emphatically did not prevail prior to 1960; see Friedman and Schwartz (1963, p. 640). As reasons for the change in behavior are not known, explicit or implicit predictions of future drift-free behavior should be regarded with some skepticism.

[9]Recent papers on the information content of the term structure spread and the spread between short-term rates on private and government securities have explored their predictive value for aggregate variables. One of the explanations offered for the information content of these spreads is that they reflect the current stance of monetary policy. Some of these studies stress, however, that it is the *real* effects of monetary policy, not the effects on prices, that are relevant. See, for example, Estrella and Hardouvelis (1991). To the extent that the information content does derive from monetary policy, however, the choice between using such interest rate spreads or the monetary impulse measure is in part an empirical one, and some assessments are made in the discussion on alternative monetary indicators.

[10]Data underlying the measures are available from the authors.

[11]The importance of adjusting for reserve requirements can be illustrated by the case of France in 1975. The *International Financial Statistics'* "reserve money" series fell from FF 152.3 billion at the end of 1974 to FF 119.4 billion at the end of 1975, which might appear to be a contraction of epic proportions. Over the same time, however, the ratio of required reserves on sight deposits fell from 17 percent to 2 percent. With initial required reserves in excess of FF 50 billion, roughly FF 44 billion were freed by the reduction in the required ratio, and the overall effect was not strongly contractionary.

[12]In the case of the United Kingdom, the series is not adjusted, but reserve requirements are low enough to be nonbinding.

[13]In Germany, reserve requirements on demand deposits varied according to bank size until March 1977, after which they varied on a "progressive scale" based on the first DM 10 million of a bank's deposits, the next DM 10–100 million, and so forth.

the largest banks.[14] In the case of France, the calculation is nevertheless more complicated than just described because of the zero or very low rr values occurring in parts of the sample. For details, the reader is referred to the appendix.

Once adjusted reserve series have been obtained, they are added to currency magnitudes to yield an adjusted base series. These (quarterly) series are then seasonally adjusted.[15] Finally, averages of the quarterly values—which are used below in the section on quarterly measures—are calculated to yield the annual data used in the present section. Logarithmic differences, denoted DLB, are used as growth rates.

It is a straightforward step to calculate series for $DLV = DLX - DLB$, the rate of change of base velocity, and $DLVBAR = (1/4) (DLV + DLV(-1) + DLV(-2) + DLV(-3))$. The annual impulse measure $IM = DLB + DLVBAR$ is then readily obtained. With observations for GDP and the monetary base beginning in 1960 in the data set, the earliest year for which $DLVBAR$ and IM values are available is 1964. For some countries, one or both of the basic series begins after 1960, so the starting date for the IM values is correspondingly delayed. The charts in the next section present values of the IM measure for each economy, together with a pair of dashed horizontal lines marking the upper and lower limits of the low-inflation band described above. For reference, the charts also present data on the growth of the adjusted monetary base alone (DLB), corresponding to the impulse measure without the velocity adjustment component.

The interpretation of the IM values and low-inflation bands in the charts is as follows. When the IM magnitude is above (or below) the band, current monetary policy as reflected in base growth rates is too rapid (or slow) to be consistent *on a sustained basis* with low inflation. In that sense, the impulse measure suggests that monetary policy is overly expansionary (or restrictive) in the case at hand. The emphasized qualification is important, however, because real-time decision making must recognize the existence of substantial time lags in the inflationary process. In addition, there may be other policy goals besides the attainment of low inflation. Consequently, a value of IM above (or below) the low inflation band does not necessarily imply that policy should be tighter (or easier) from the perspective of that moment.

Evaluation of Annual Measures

This section discusses the interpretations of monetary policy over the years 1965–93 that are suggested by the annual impulse measure plots appearing in Charts 1–8. A leading purpose of the discussion is to consider whether the measure has accurately signaled episodes now generally regarded to have featured monetary policy stances that were inappropriate—either excessively lenient or stringent—from a medium-term perspective.

Before focusing on IM plots for individual economies, accordingly, it should be emphasized that the impulse measures indicate that monetary policy was extremely lenient for a period of several years in the early 1970s in *all seven* major industrial countries. In each of Charts 1–8, that is, the IM measure remained substantially above the low-inflation band for three or more years during the interval 1970–75. In most of the plots, furthermore, this period of leniency extended until 1979 or beyond. However, the plots for two countries, Japan and Germany, stand out by indicating a distinctly earlier movement—about 1974 or 1975—toward the low-inflation range. Thus, taken as a group, the charts very clearly suggest that a widespread inflationary stance in the early 1970s was eliminated during the 1980s by most countries but much earlier in Japan and Germany. That general feature of the charts corresponds quite accurately with views concerning the 1970s and 1980s that are widely accepted today. Although, to some readers, this feature might not seem to represent a major achievement, most alternative measures of monetary policy stance would probably fail to satisfy this basic criterion. For instance, as is demonstrated in the following section, plots of long- and short-term interest rate spreads do not show a contrast between the 1970s and 1980s and do not indicate markedly different policy patterns for Japan and Germany in comparison with the other major industrial economies.

The IM plot for the United States (Chart 1) shows a gradually increasing movement in the inflationary direction before 1980, a tendency that shows up even more strongly in Chart 2 (which begins in 1954 rather than 1964). A sharp drop in the IM measure occurs between 1979 and 1982 and another one between 1987 and 1989. The first of these drops represents the major deflationary episode that began with the Federal Reserve's famous actions of October 6, 1979 and ended in the third quarter of 1982. The second drop pertains to a period of tightening that has not been so widely publicized, but which was arguably quite significant: an attempt by the Federal Reserve to reduce the "trend" rate of inflation from about 4.5 percent to something closer to 2 percent. Whether that attempt was partially responsible for the recession of 1990–91 is debatable, but Chart 1 would certainly provide support to anyone inclined to make such an argument.[16] The sharp upward movement of IM over 1990 and 1991 is probably overstated to some extent

---

[14]For Japan, the reference value of $rr°$ chosen is the 2.5 percent rate that prevailed without change from April 1981 until October 1991. For Germany, the reference value is the 12.1 percent rate that prevailed from February 1987 to February 1992.

[15]Seasonal adjustment has also been required for the Italian series.

[16]Inflation did indeed fall beginning in 1990, but not all the way to 2 percent.

Chart 1. United States: Monetary Impulse Measure, Monetary Base Growth, and Low-Inflation Band

(In percent)

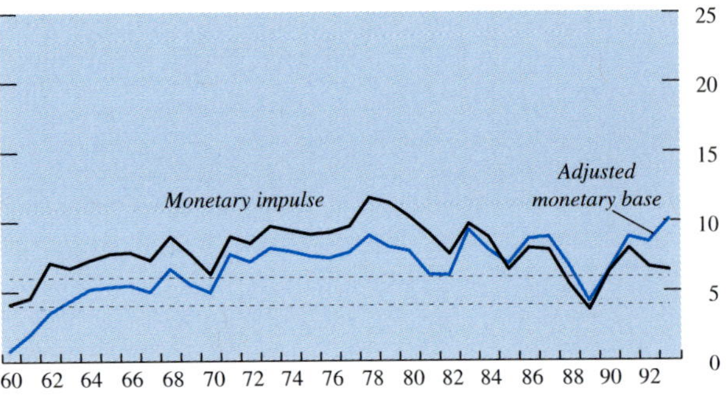

Sources: See appendix.

Chart 2. United States: Monetary Impulse Measure, 1954–93

(In percent)

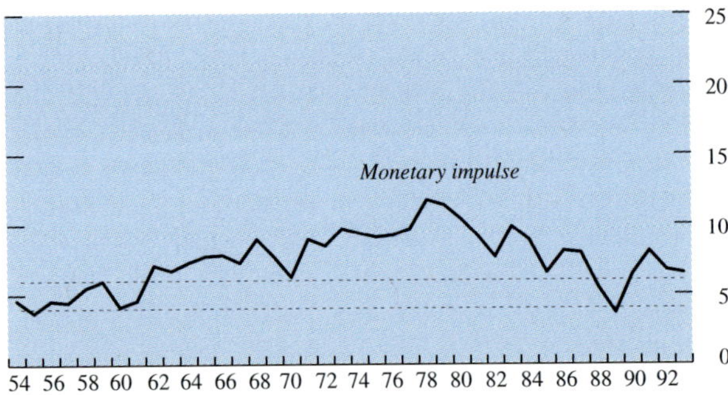

Sources: See appendix.

Chart 3. Japan: Monetary Impulse Measure, Monetary Base Growth, and Low-Inflation Band

(In percent)

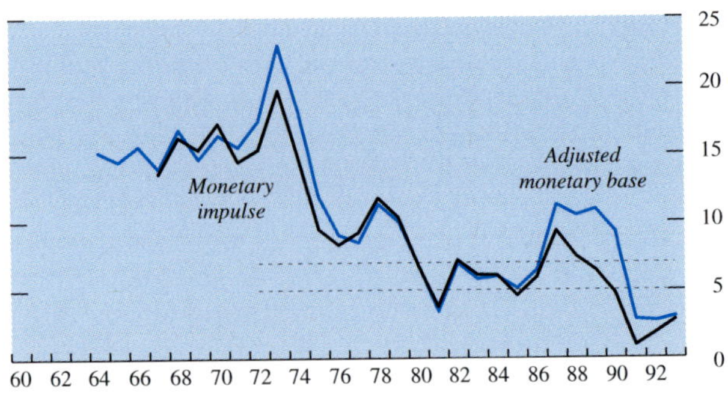

Sources: See appendix.
Note: The low-inflation band for Japan is presented only from 1972 onward because average real growth in Japan was significantly higher during the 1960s than in the following decades.

because of an increase in the fraction of currency outstanding that is held abroad.[17] Changes such as these will eventually be reflected in the *IM* measure, as is pointed out above, but not promptly.

To clarify the contribution of the *DLVBAR* term to the impulse measure, Chart 1 and Charts 3–8 include plots of the growth of the adjusted base alone, that is, just the first component of the impulse measure. In Chart 1, the importance of the velocity adjustment is apparent in the sustained difference between the two series from 1971 through 1981 and in the trend movement of *DLB* from below to above the impulse measure. Base growth during this ten-year period is not much different from its average in the following six years; yet, as the discussion below will make clear, U.S. inflation performance did differ during these

two periods, and the impulse measure captures the change in inflationary pressures much more closely.

Chart 3 plots the monetary impulse measure for Japan, with the first value pertaining to 1967 because of the absence of monetary base data for 1960–62. The low-inflation band limits are not shown before 1972 because average real growth was considerably higher than 4 percent during the 1960s. The Japanese record is dominated by a major tightening of monetary policy over the years 1973–81, with a relatively brief interruption during 1977–79. Since 1975, the *IM* measure has stayed fairly close to the low-inflation band, a pattern that is entirely consistent with the excellent record actually compiled in terms of realized inflation. However, the *IM* measure moves from below the band in 1985 to above it in 1987, thereby representing a tendency toward more lenient monetary conditions. This shift probably reflects actions, prompted by the Louvre Accord and the U.S.-Japan bilateral agreement of October 1986, to prevent major changes in the yen-dollar exchange rate.[18] The ensuing period of easier monetary conditions may have contributed to the asset price "bubble" of the late 1980s.[19] Quite notable in the chart is the degree of monetary stringency indicated for 1991 and 1992. The slight easing of monetary conditions evident in 1993—to a point still well below the

---

[17]In addition, during much of 1992 and 1993, mortgage refinancing activity contributed greatly to faster M1 and reserve growth in the United States because some mortgage funds were mandated to hold demand deposits for a period following the prepayment of mortgages.

[18]The 1986 episode is mentioned by Fischer (1988, p. 33).

[19]Between 1986 and their peak in 1989, stock prices in Japan more than quadrupled, while goods price inflation as reflected in the consumer price index or GDP deflator remained below 2 percent annually. It is noteworthy in Chart 2 that the velocity adjustment term in 1987–90 is relatively large and negative, possibly reflecting in part the shift in the pattern of transactions during this period away from the flow of goods and services and toward assets whose sales are not included in GDP. For a discussion of the role of monetary policy in the asset price inflation in Japan—and, to a lesser extent, in the United States and United Kingdom—see Hargraves and Schinasi (1993).

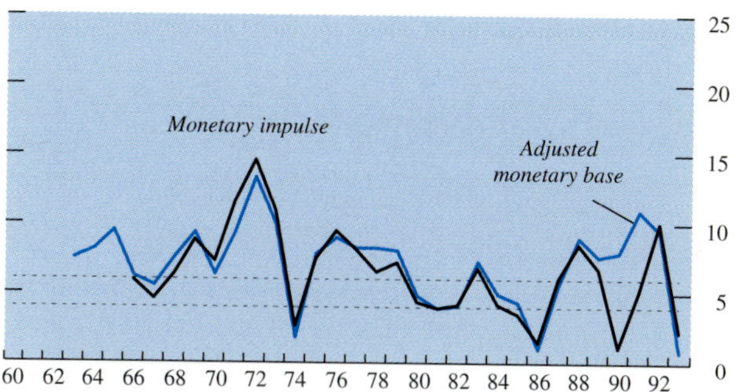

Chart 4. Germany: Monetary Impulse Measure, Monetary Base Growth, and Low-Inflation Band
(In percent)

Sources: See appendix.

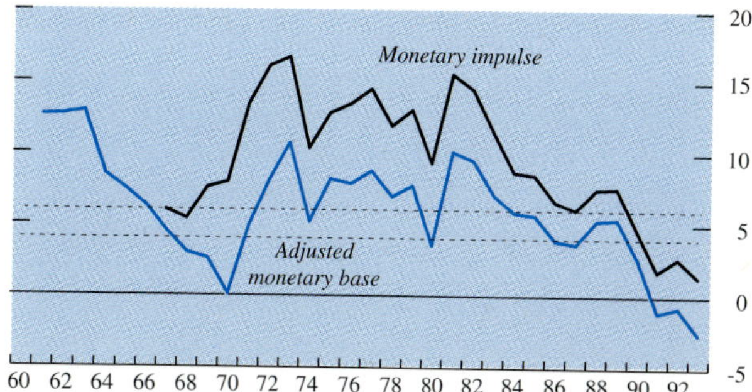

Chart 5. France: Monetary Impulse Measure, Monetary Base Growth, and Low-Inflation Band
(In percent)

Sources: See appendix.

low-inflation range—captures the Bank of Japan's response to the prolonged recession.

Chart 4 pertains to Germany. The proximity of *IM* to the low-inflation band over 1974–89 has already been mentioned. The Bundesbank's sharp tightening during 1973 and 1974 occurred after a five-year buildup of inflationary tendencies had threatened to get out of hand during the final years of the Bretton Woods regime. The other prominent feature of Chart 4 is its suggestion of unusually tight monetary policy in 1990 and distinctly loose policy in 1992–93.[20] With regard to these plotted values, it is important to understand an adjustment that was made to the impulse measure in light of the major event of recent German experience, the unification of mid-1990. In principle, unification might be expected to have had some impact on one component of the impulse measure—velocity—both because of possible differences in money demand relationships in the former east and west Germany, and possibly in reaction to unification itself or to the associated uncertainty. As such, *DLVBAR* would have been affected, and adjustments would be needed. Estimates of such effects are, however, very difficult to make. In this paper, adjustments have been made only for the effects of unification on the other component of the impulse measure, the base growth term. The monetary base expanded very rapidly during 1990 and 1991 to accommodate the jump in the size of the German economy represented by unification. The appropriate adjustment would be to subtract from the unadjusted impulse measure a magnitude equal to the fractional increase in the size of the economy brought about by

unification. But the appropriate distribution over time of this adjustment is not obvious, and the exact magnitude is itself open to question. The adjustment that was implemented, which is reflected in Chart 4, involves a subtraction of terms summing to 0.12 from the raw *IM* measure,[21] with half of the magnitude of this adjustment assigned to 1990 and half to 1991.[22]

From the foregoing discussion it should be apparent that one cannot be confident about the accuracy of the adjustments made in the case of Germany or, therefore, about Chart 4's suggestion that monetary policy was quite tight in 1990, about right in 1991, and rather loose in 1992. Those indications could be altered significantly by a different adjustment magnitude pertaining to unification or a different distribution over time. An additional problem, as mentioned previously, is the increased use of deutsche mark currency outside Germany.

The French *IM* values in Chart 5 show over 1974–80 a beginning of the usual movement away from the inflationary stance of the early 1970s and then a sharp jump upward in 1981 and 1982, clearly representing the so-called Mitterrand Experiment. Since that time, however, the impulse measure has moved toward and finally through the low-inflation zone, with values for 1991–93 that represent a tight policy stance. The contribution of the velocity adjustment term is apparent for much of the period of study, particularly in the early 1970s and again in the early 1990s. Here again, the impulse measure corresponds more closely to subsequent inflation than does base growth by itself.

---

[20]The sharp decline in the *IM* measure in 1986 is an artifact of the reserve adjustment procedure used in this paper. In May 1986, reserve requirements on time and saving deposits were reduced substantially, leading to a considerable reduction in reserve demand. However, reserve requirements on demand deposits were not changed at the time, so the reserve adjustment procedure described above does not capture this change.

[21]The 0.12 magnitude exceeds the fraction of west German GDP represented by east Germany but is smaller than the analogous fraction in terms of domestic demand.

[22]The 1990 values of the GDP and base variables are averages of quarterly values. Two quarters of the year passed before unification; therefore, even if the full impact occurred in 1990, the appropriate adjustment to the annual average growth rates is to assign half to 1990 and half to 1991.

Chart 6. Italy: Monetary Impulse Measure, Monetary Base Growth, and Low-Inflation Band
(In percent)

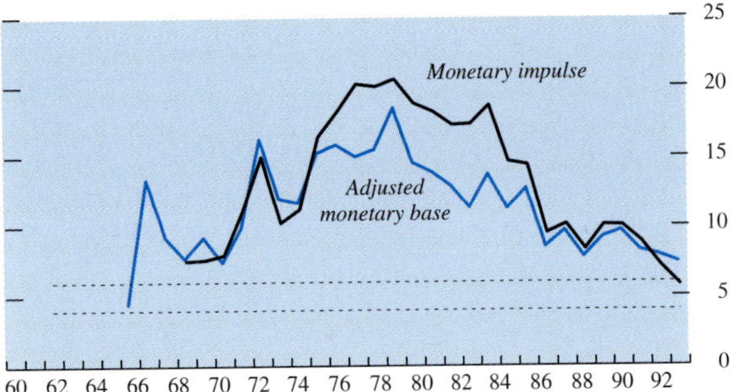

Sources: See appendix.

Chart 7. United Kingdom: Monetary Impulse Measure, Monetary Base Growth, and Low-Inflation Band
(In percent)

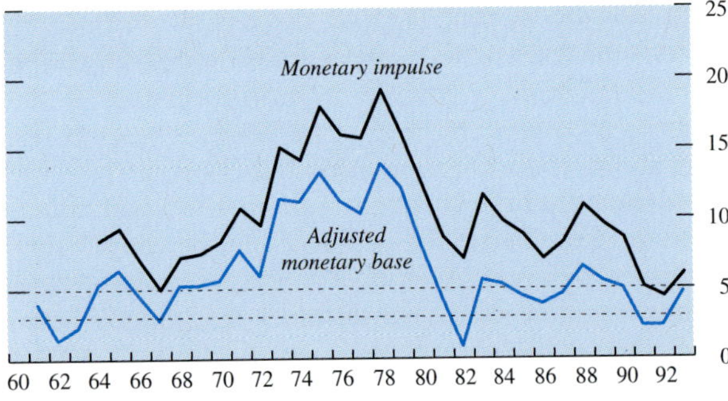

Sources: See appendix.

The Italian impulse measure in Chart 6 indicates a continuation of substantial monetary leniency until the mid-1980s. Its peak value is quite high, and the plot shows a substantially greater cumulative magnitude of excessive monetary impulse for Italy than for any of the other six countries. A sustained movement toward a low-inflation stance has dominated the record since the mid-1980s, however, despite a slight interruption in 1989–90.

The U.K. measure in Chart 7, by contrast, shows a sharp tightening as early as 1979–1982, but one that reached the low-inflation zone only in 1991.[23] The upward surge in 1987–88 presumably reflects a

---

[23]During 1979–82, the monetary aggregate then being targeted, sterling M3, grew very rapidly—well above its target range—thereby inappropriately signaling that monetary policy was loose. The instability of M3 velocity at that time was recognized and attributed to financial innovation and the removal in 1980 of the "corset" that had suppressed M3 growth.

Chart 8. Canada: Monetary Impulse Measure, Monetary Base Growth, and Low-Inflation Band
(In percent)

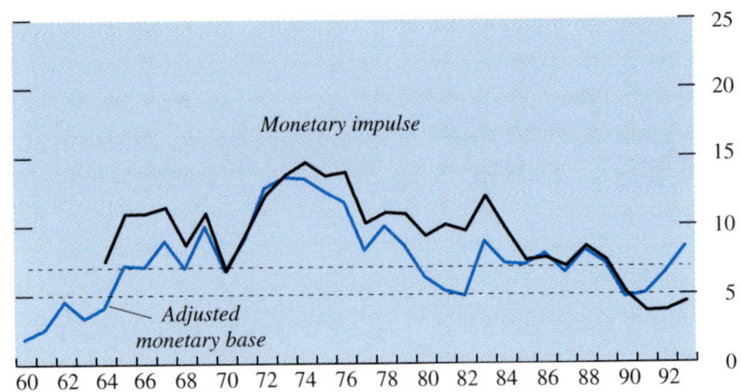

Sources: See appendix.

monetary loosening that was the consequence of Chancellor of the Exchequer Lawson's controversial device of "shadowing the deutsche mark" at a time that turned out, in retrospect, to have been inappropriate.

Finally, Chart 8 shows a predominantly downward path for Canada since 1974, with temporary upward blips in 1983 and 1988. The velocity adjustment term contributes to make this downward path less steep through 1982, indicating a smaller disinflationary impulse than would have been indicated by base growth alone. The drive toward a "zero inflation" target that began about a year after John Crow became Governor of the Bank of Canada in 1987 appears clearly in the diagram. For 1992, the Canadian monetary policy stance appears to have been quite tight, but policy shifted toward a more neutral stance in 1993.

It should perhaps be mentioned explicitly that, with one exception, Charts 1–8 use the same vertical axis range rather than modifying the range to reflect the *IM* values experienced by the country in question. This convention was chosen, despite a resulting slight loss of detail for the countries with lower inflation peaks, to reveal more clearly the comparative performance of the various countries in keeping their monetary policies close to a low-inflation range. The one exception is the chart for France, which uses the same scale as the other countries but a different range of values in order to accommodate the very low *IM* values in the 1990s.

Quarterly Measures and Alternative Monetary Indicators

This section examines impulse measures based on quarterly data. As quarterly values of the impulse measure *IM1* defined in equation (1) are very choppy in appearance, plots of a smoothed series are presented.[24] This series, denoted *IM1AVG*, is a four-quarter moving average of *IM1*, defined as (1/4) (*IM1* + *IM1*(−1) + *IM1*(−2) + *IM1*(−3)).[25] Plots are presented in the top panels of Charts 9–15, with magnitudes scaled to represent annual growth rates comparable to those in Charts 1–8.[26] The story told by the new charts is basically consistent with that of the plots utilizing annual data (Charts 1–8); however, the details are not identical because the two measures involve different timing.

A question that arises naturally in response to the foregoing presentation is whether there are other controllable variables that might be superior—in terms of reflecting more accurately the medium-term inflationary implications of current monetary policy—to the measures of monetary impulse used in this paper. Here, two such measures are considered, namely, the spread or difference between long- and short-term nominal interest rates, and growth in a broad monetary aggregate. Before looking at these series, however, it will be useful to consider time plots of the actual inflationary experiences of the countries in the sample. The second panels of Charts 9–15 show inflation rates in terms of consumer price indices for each of the countries in the sample. The charts are expressed in percent on an annualized basis and reflect four-quarter changes (rather than year-to-year values based on annual averages of price level indices).

In these inflation plots, several important aspects of the trajectories match parallel movements in the monetary impulse plots in the top panels and in Charts 1–8. For the United States, to begin with, Chart 9 reveals a fairly regular upward trend persisting from 1960 until 1980, with dips in 1971–72 and 1975–76 that show up two years earlier for the *IM* measure. The sharp decline in inflation in 1981–83 also has a corresponding decline in the *IM* measure roughly two years earlier. For Japan, a period of very high inflation rates in the mid-1970s is followed by an abrupt decline and a low-inflation record (Chart 10). For Germany, the inflation rate has stayed reasonably low throughout most of the period but surged about 1972,

corresponding to the 1969–73 buildup evident in the top panel of Chart 11 and in Chart 4.[27] In France, by contrast, inflation was more severe; despite a temporary slowdown in the late 1970s, inflation did not begin to fall steadily until after 1982 (Chart 12). The case of Italy is somewhat similar, but with even more severe inflation experienced in the 1970s (Chart 13). In the United Kingdom, inflation was also rather severe in the 1970s, but its elimination began somewhat earlier than in Italy. This downward trend was interrupted by an increase over 1987–89 (that follows the upward *IM* jump in Chart 7 and the top panel of Chart 14). In Canada, the main movement away from the moderate inflation of the 1970s came only after 1982 (Chart 15).

More generally, these plots of inflation rates based on consumer price indices are encouragingly similar to those of the monetary impulse measures. There are disagreements, of course, pertaining to timing and to brief movements. But in terms of broad tendencies, the profiles have many features in common.

With respect to the interest rate spread, the third panels of Charts 9–15 show values of the spread between long- and short-term interest rates. The precise series utilized are those listed in Table A18 of the October 1994 *World Economic Outlook*; ten-year government bonds and three-month treasury bills are fairly representative. Thus the plotted spread—like the impulse measure—is supposed to serve as an indicator of monetary ease rather than tightness. But, in general, these profiles do not agree to any significant extent with the inflation rate profiles. Most of these panels do show substantial dips in 1980–81, presumably reflecting policy movements toward an anti-inflationary posture. However, the story told by the pictures does not accord nearly as well with the inflationary experience as does the impulse measure.

Other measures could be examined, of course, especially if the criterion of controllability is sacrificed. Consideration of other measures is limited in this paper to growth rates of a broad monetary aggregate, plots of which appear as the final panels of Charts 9–15.[28] For the United States, Chart 9 shows a steady but irregular inflationary buildup from 1960 into the 1980s, but the date of the tightening of policy is not as clearly located as in Chart 1 (or the top panel of Chart 9). In particular, there is little evidence of sustained anti-inflationary efforts before 1986.

---

[24]The severe choppiness of the unsmoothed quarterly *IM1* measures that have not been reported comes primarily from the *DLB* series, rather than from *DLVBAR* (which is already smoothed), and presumably reflects the fact that the various central banks have not regarded stability of base growth rates as a desideratum. An exception to this statement is Germany, where central bank money was a target variable for a number of years.

[25]The *IM1AVG* measure is equivalent to one based on growth rates calculated for each quarter relative to the same quarter one year earlier.

[26]The adjustment made for German unification in the quarterly data was to subtract 7 percent from the growth rate of the monetary base in 1990:3, 3 percent in 1990:4, and 2 percent in 1991:1, which amounts to the adjustment of magnitude 0.12 made to the annual data. The caveats noted above in the discussion of the adjustment to the annual series apply here as well.

[27]The sharp increase in inflation in 1980–81 is not matched by a correspondingly large rise in the impulse measure in prior years. However, as the other panels in Chart 11 show, alternative measures of monetary conditions also do not seem to capture this episode.

[28]The choice of a broad aggregate differs across countries so as to conform somewhat with national preferences. The aggregates used are as noted in the charts.

Chart 9. United States: Inflation, Monetary Impulse, and Alternative Monetary Indicators

(Percent change from four quarters earlier, unless otherwise noted)

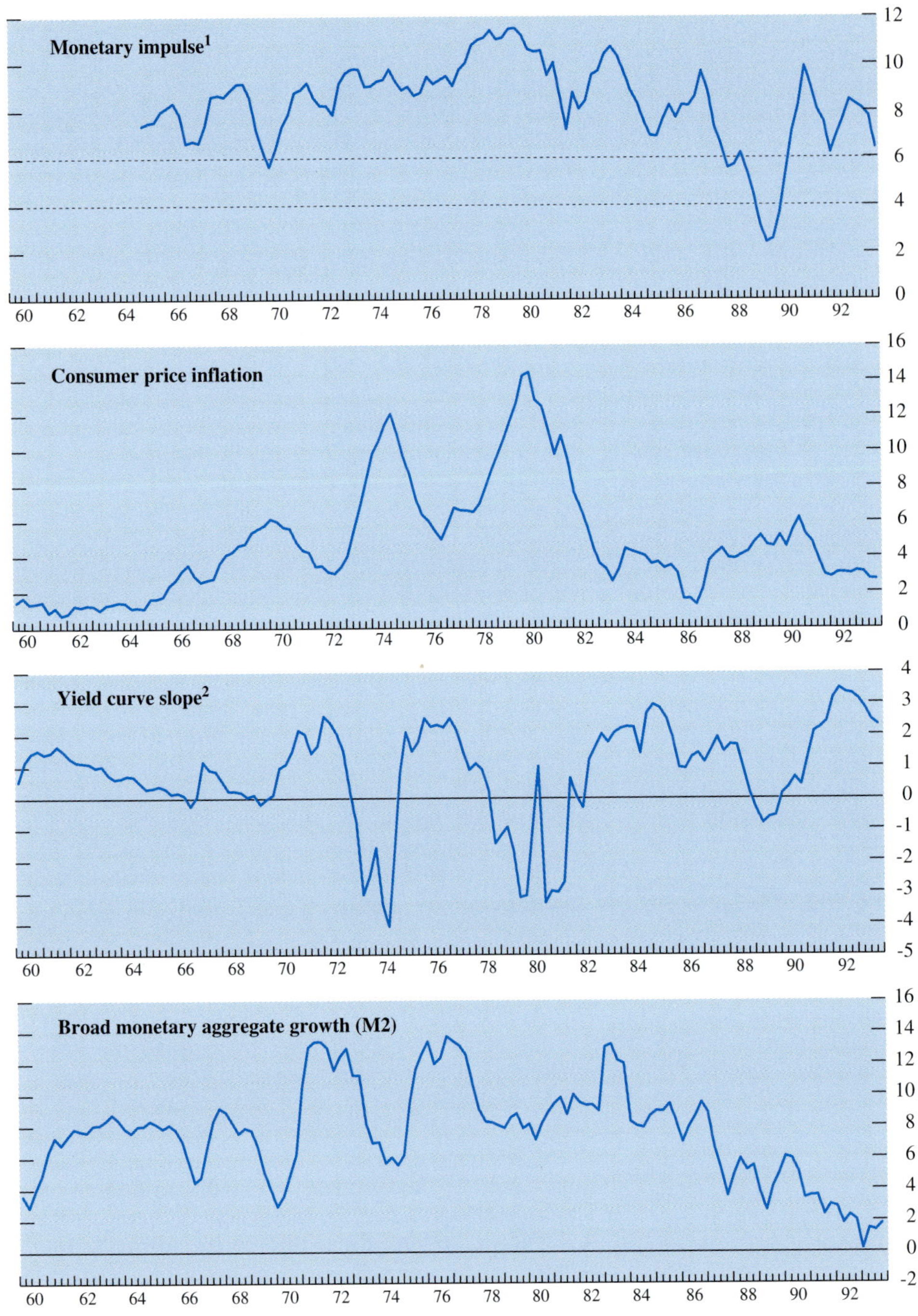

Sources: See appendix.
[1]Four-quarter moving average of quarterly impulse measure.
[2]Difference between ten-year government bond yield and three-month treasury bill rate.

Chart 10. Japan: Inflation, Monetary Impulse, and Alternative Monetary Indicators

(Percent change from four quarters earlier, unless otherwise noted)

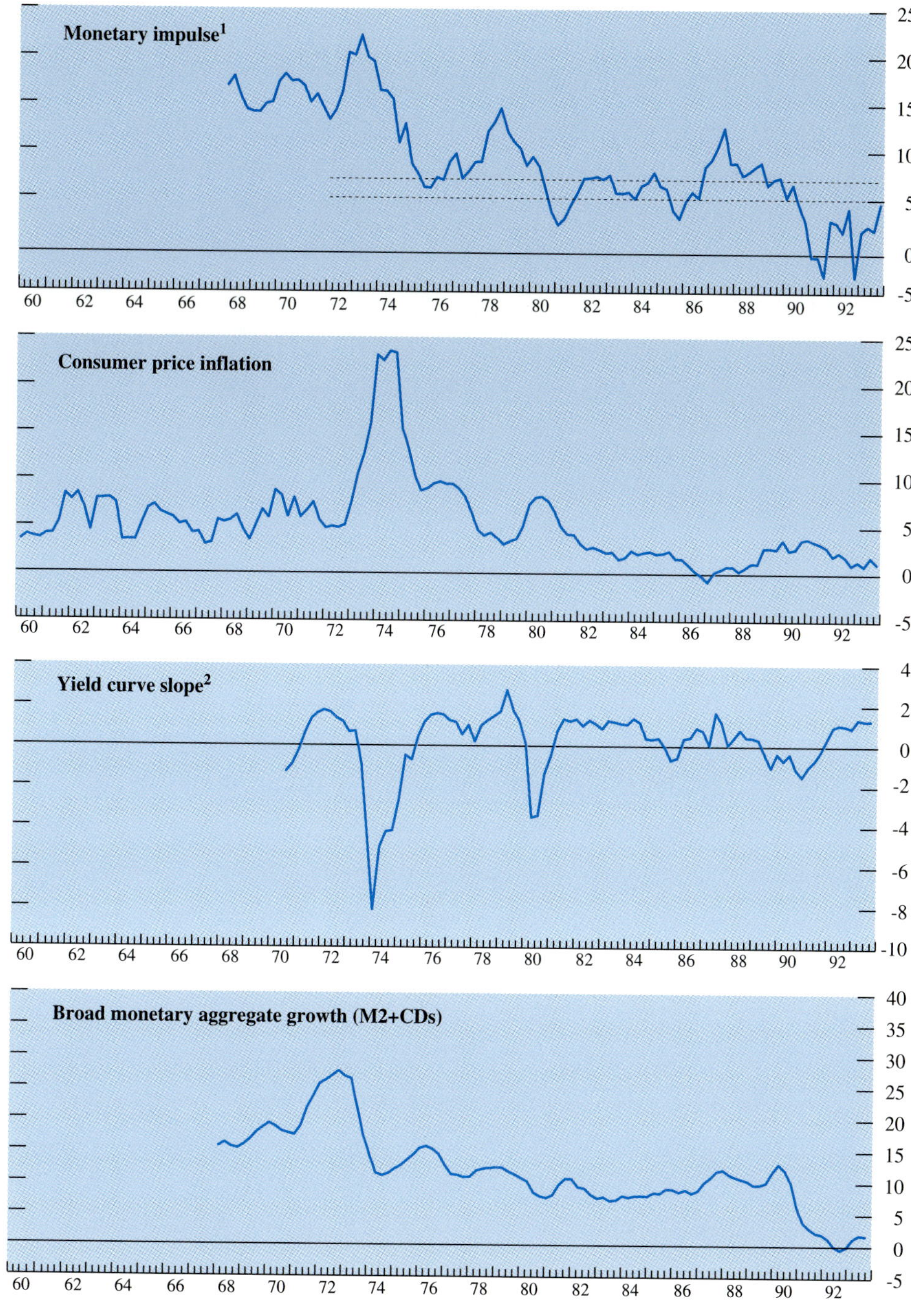

Sources: See appendix.

¹Four-quarter moving average of quarterly impulse measure. The low-inflation band is presented only from 1972 onward because average real growth was significantly higher during the 1960s than in the following decades.

²Difference between ten-year government bond yield and three-month repurchase (Gensaki) rate.

Chart 11. Germany: Inflation, Monetary Impulse, and Alternative Monetary Indicators

(Percent change from four quarters earlier, unless otherwise noted)

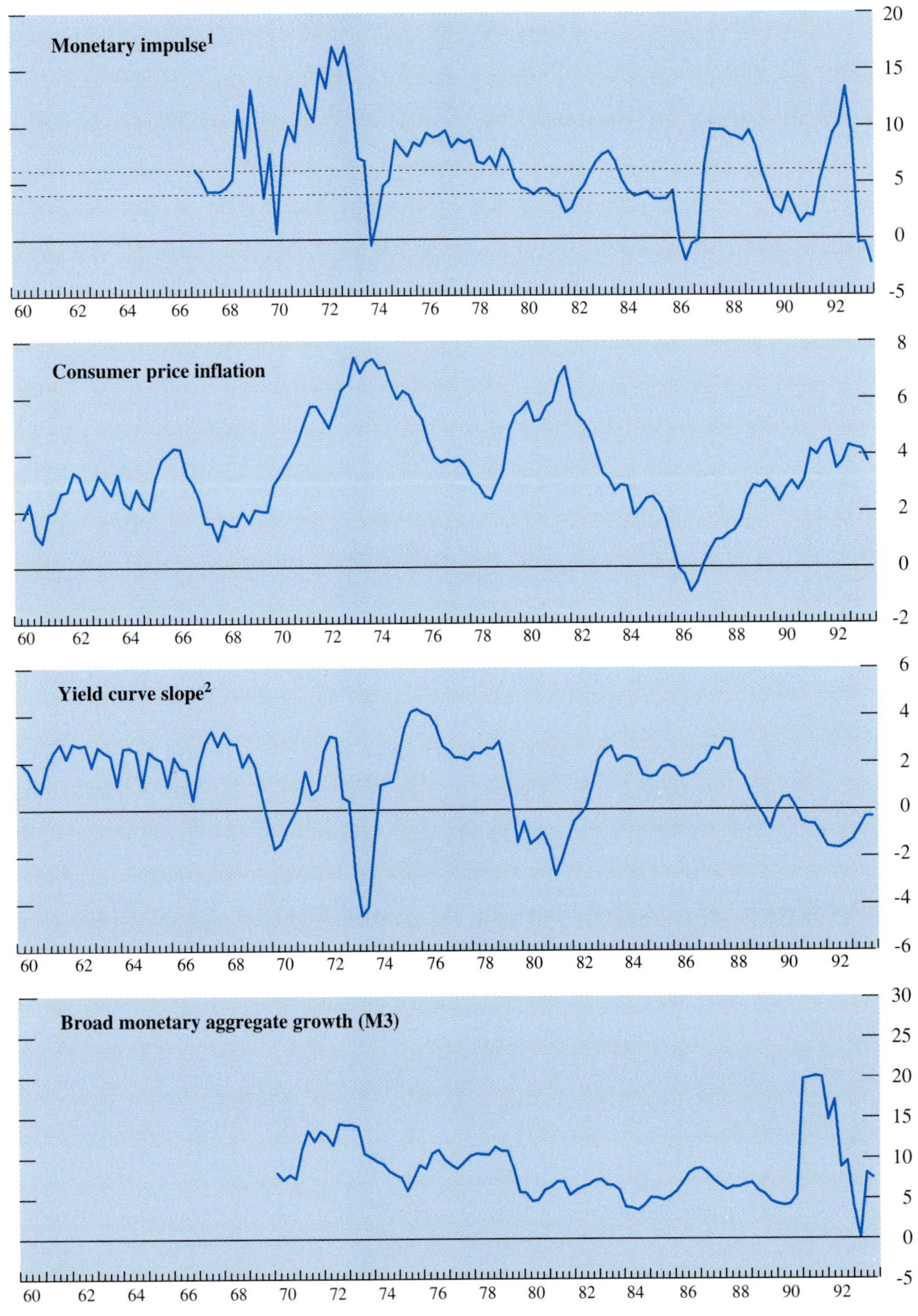

Sources: See appendix.
[1]Four-quarter moving average of quarterly impulse measure.
[2]Difference between ten-year government bond yield and three-month interbank rate.

Chart 12. France: Inflation, Monetary Impulse, and Alternative Monetary Indicators

(Percent change from four quarters earlier, unless otherwise noted)

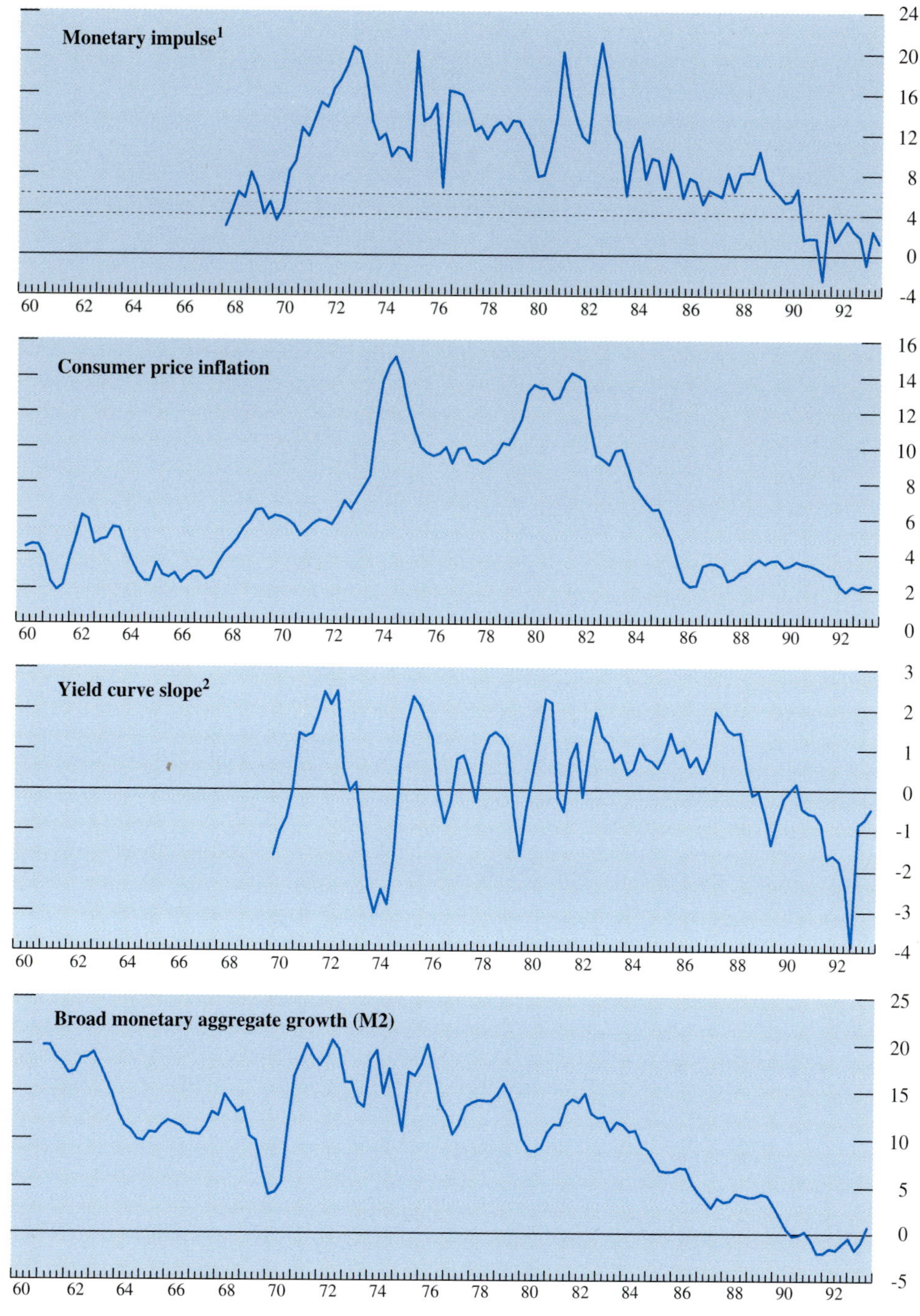

Sources: See appendix.
[1] Four-quarter moving average of quarterly impulse measure.
[2] Difference between ten-year government bond yield and three-month interbank rate.

Chart 13. Italy: Inflation, Monetary Impulse, and Alternative Monetary Indicators

(Percent change from four quarters earlier, unless otherwise noted)

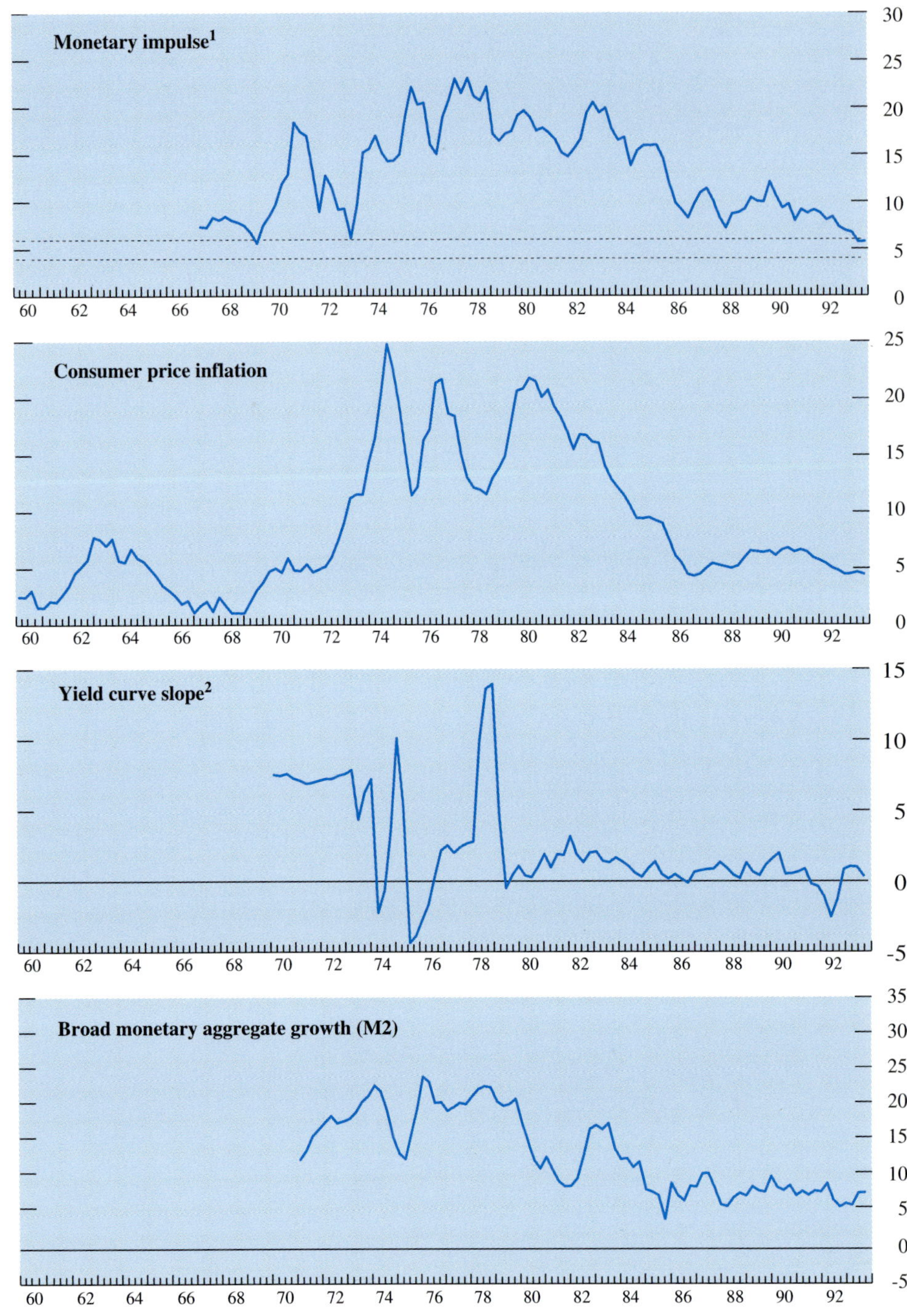

Sources: See appendix.
¹Four-quarter moving average of quarterly impulse measure.
²Before June 1991, difference between average yield on government bonds with two- to four-year residual maturity and three-month treasury bill rate; thereafter, yield on ten–year government bonds.

Chart 14. United Kingdom: Inflation, Moneatry Impulse, and Alternative Monetary Indicators

(Percent change from four quarters earlier, unless otherwise noted)

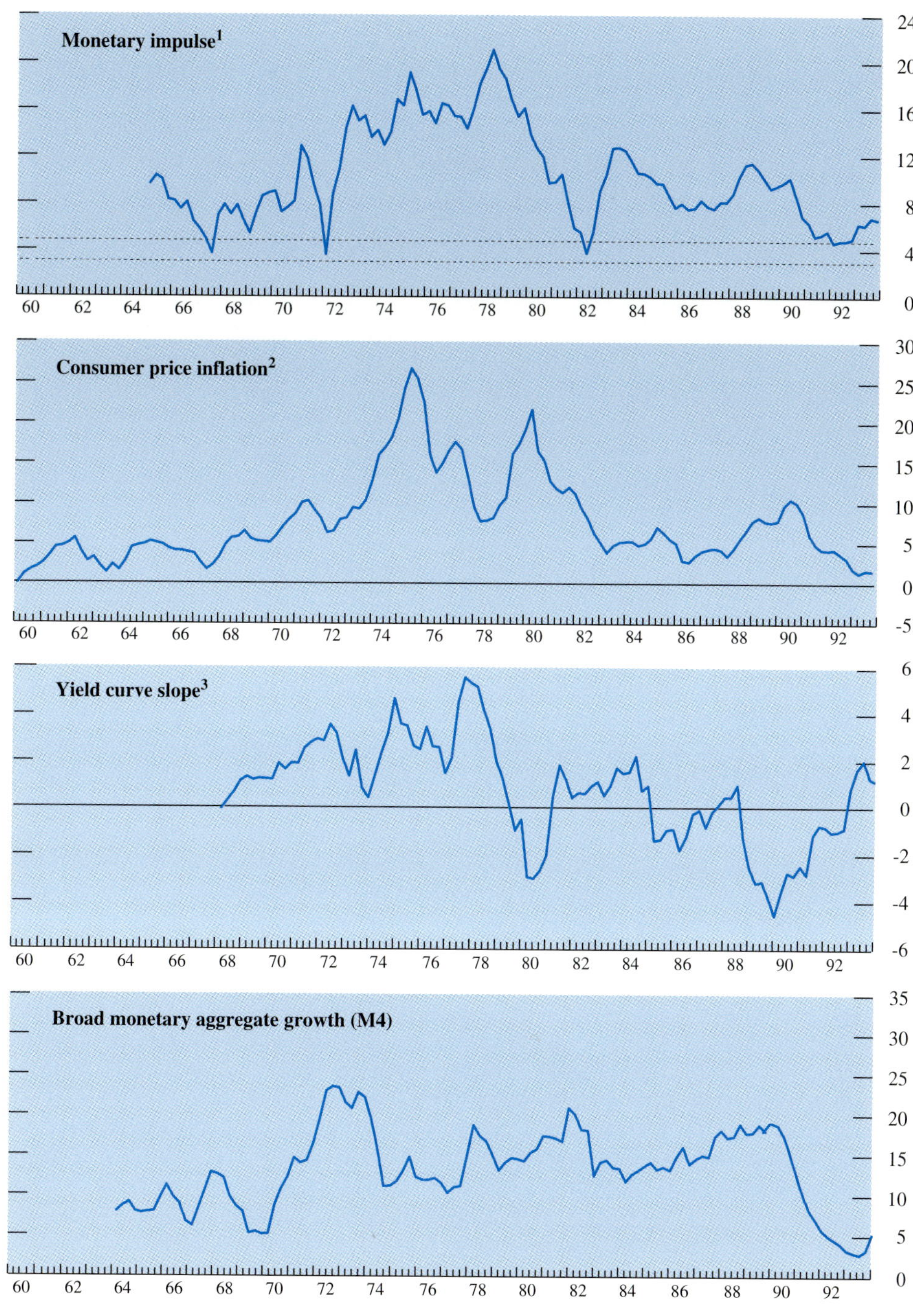

Sources: See appendix.
[1]Four-quarter moving average of quarterly impulse measure.
[2]Retail price inflation excluding mortgage interest.
[3]Difference between ten-year government bond yield and three-month interbank rate.

Chart 15. Canada: Inflation, Monetary Impulse, and Alternative Monetary Indicators

(Percent change from four quarters earlier, unless otherwise noted)

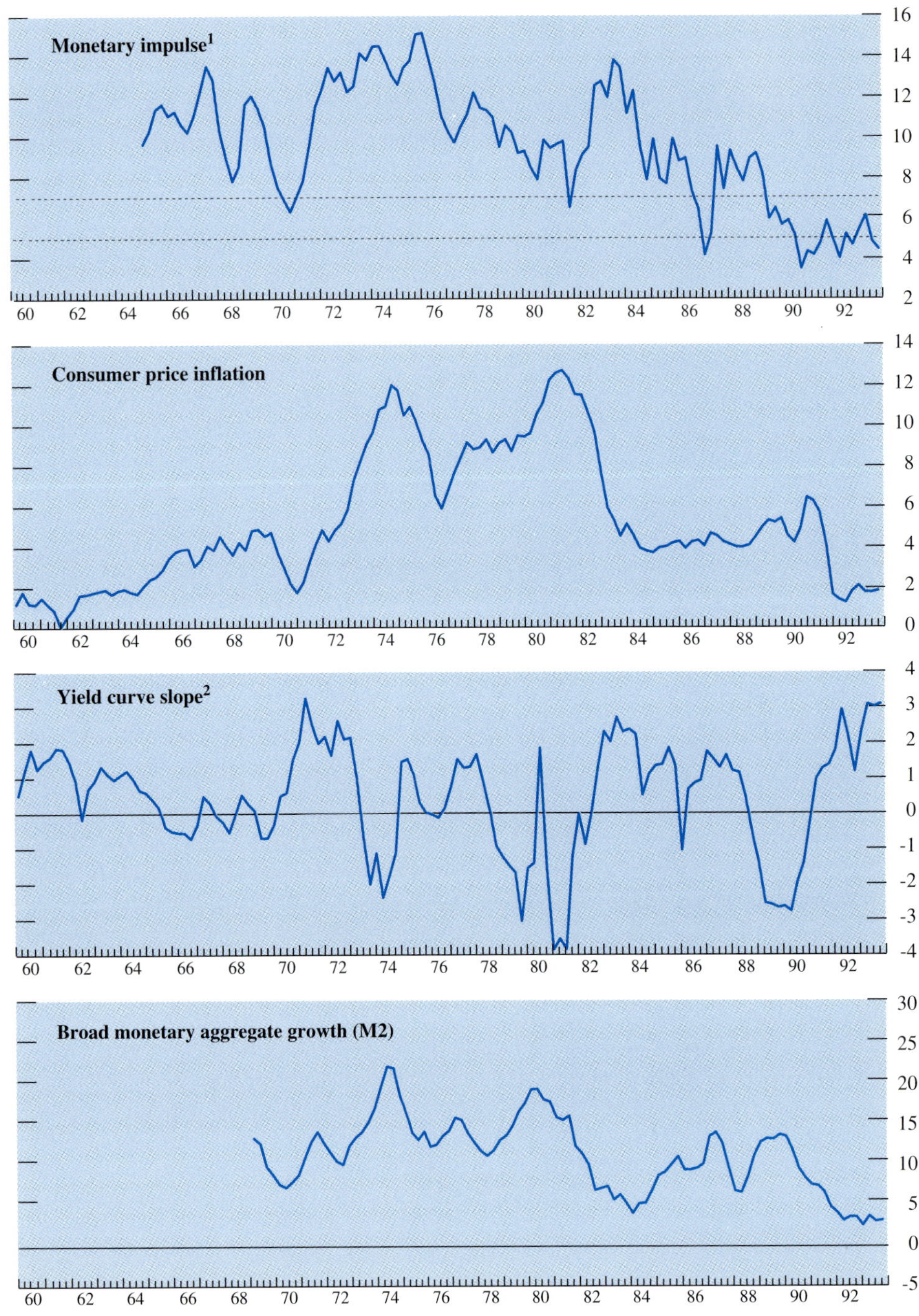

Sources: See appendix.

¹Four-quarter moving average of quarterly impulse measure.

²Difference between average yield on government bonds with ten or more years residual maturity and three-month corporate commercial paper rate.

For Japan, the behavior of the M2 + CD growth rate does provide a satisfactory picture of policy stance, one that is quite similar to that based on the impulse measure developed in this paper. For Germany, however, the inflationary stance of the early 1970s is not adequately signaled by the broad aggregate's growth rate. Broad money growth in France does not accord well with inflation performance in the 1960s; moreover, it seems to lag behind the downturn in inflation in the 1980s. In the case of Italy, the short time span covered by the data makes evaluation difficult; there appears to be some correspondence in the movements of M2 growth and inflation, although, in many instances, the lags appear to be extremely short.

For the United Kingdom, the growth of the broad aggregate indicates a generally increasing inflationary tendency from 1975 through the 1980s, followed by a sharp dip beginning in 1990. The impulse measure, by contrast, turns down in 1979 and remains comparatively low through the 1980s—a pattern that is significantly closer to that of the consumer price inflation rate. In the case of Canada, however, the impulse measure does not outperform the broad monetary aggregate as an indicator of inflationary pressures.

Overall, the impulse measure performs somewhat better than the broad monetary aggregates, even though the aggregates have been selected as the most reliable of various available candidates on a country-by-country basis. Besides having the same definition for all countries, the impulse measure has the additional advantage of being based on a variable that—unlike broad aggregates—is potentially controllable by central banks.

Conclusion

In this paper, a measure of monetary impulse has been proposed that is intended to reflect the medium-term inflationary implications of a country's current monetary policy. The measure consists of the growth rate of the monetary base, adjusted for reserve requirement changes and augmented by an implicit forecast of future growth rates of base velocity. As this forecast is based on past velocity growth—its average value over the previous four years—the impulse statistic reflects an easy-to-calculate measure of a variable that could be accurately controlled by any central bank that chose to do so.

Given the velocity growth feature of the proposed measure, its magnitude at a given time will reflect the implied medium-term growth rate of nominal GDP. The inflationary implications are readily obtained by comparing the monetary impulse with the trend growth rate of real GDP for the economy in question. Time series of the impulse measure have thus been plotted with low-inflation bands, centered around a rate of 2 percent, reflecting an appropriate average rate of annual real GDP growth plus 1–3 percentage points. These plots have then been used for a brief discussion of the 1965–93 inflationary experiences for each of the major industrial economies, and the paper has argued that the impulse measure provides a useful characterization of monetary policy behavior over those years. As the velocity adjustment term is designed to incorporate effects of technological and regulatory change in the payments and financial industries, the impulse measure should also be useful for analyzing policy stances in the future.

Appendix
Description of Data

All data on nominal and real GDP are seasonally adjusted quarterly series. These series, as well as the data on consumer prices, the yield curve, and broad monetary aggregates, are obtained from national sources compiled by IMF staff. For the monetary base, various sources were utilized. These are described for each of the seven major industrial countries in the following paragraphs.

United States

The series came from the "adjusted monetary base" series that was developed by the Federal Reserve Bank of St. Louis and is available on the WEFA database. Monthly (seasonally adjusted) values were averaged to obtain the quarterly series.

Japan

These figures were taken from McCallum (1993). The basic underlying data were provided by Bank of Japan end-of-month series on "cash currency issued" and "deposits from deposit-money banks." The latter series was adjusted for changes in reserve requirements, as explained in McCallum (1993). Then quarterly averages were calculated, added to the cash series, and the sum was seasonally adjusted to provide an adjusted monetary base series extending from 1963:1 to 1992:4. The extension through 1994:1 was based on Bank of Japan data available from Nikkei Services.

Germany

For 1960 to October 1968, the reserve series used was the sum of "total reserve required" and "excess reserves" published in the Bundesbank's *Monthly Report*, Table II.A.5. For November 1968 to February 1978, the reserve series used was "actual reserves," from Table IV.3(a) and then Table IV.2(a) of the *Monthly Report*. Beginning in March 1978, vault cash in banks began to count as reserves, so the reserve series became "actual reserves" plus "deductible cash balances" from Table IV.2(a) and then Table V.2 of

the *Monthly Report*. Beginning in August 1990, the reserve and vault cash data cover the entire deutsche mark currency area. In order to make the reserve data correspond to the data on currency in circulation (which cover unified Germany beginning in July 1990) the reserve and vault cash figures for July 1990 were scaled up by the respective series' average ratios of unified to west-only figures for the next three months.

The resulting (monthly) reserve series was adjusted for reserve requirements changes, converted to a quarterly average series, seasonally adjusted, and added to quarterly averages of the monthly seasonally adjusted "currency in circulation" series.[29] The latter series was provided by the Bundesbank and is reported in the Bundesbank's *Statistical Supplement* to the *Monthly Report*, Table I.2.

France

For 1960–77, data on notes and currency in circulation and bank reserves (quarterly averages), constructed by Sylvie LeCarpentier for a doctoral thesis, were provided by the Bank of France. For 1978–93, data on reserves and on coins and currency in circulation were obtained from the IMF's *International Financial Statistics*.[30] Data on vault cash (end of quarter) were obtained for 1990–93 from various issues of the following Bank of France publications: *Statistiques Monétaires et Financières Trimestrielles* (Tables 06 and 1.8); and *Bulletin de la Banque de France, Supplément Statistiques* (Table 1.1.1.8).

Basically, the monetary base series is the sum of these components, but the reserve series had to be adjusted for frequent major changes in reserve requirements. This adjustment procedure was necessarily

---

[29]Because of data limitations, one difference between the calculated base series for Germany and those for other countries is that currency held by banks is not counted in "currency in circulation."

[30]The quarterly series for coins is an end-of-period series. For 1978 to 1990:3, a quarterly series on reserves and currency was obtained by averaging monthly data. For 1990:4 to 1993, end-of-quarter values for currency and reserves were used because vault cash—which began to count toward reserve requirements in 1990:4—is published as an end-of-quarter series.

more complex than in the case of Japan and Germany because reserve requirements were nonexistent before 1967 and became extremely low in 1992—possibly low enough to be nonbinding. The adjustment was not calculated as the product of the unadjusted reserve figure and rr^o/rr (as is mentioned in the text and as was done for Japan and Germany); instead, the multiplicative adjustment factor for France was $rr^*/\max(rr,rr^*)$, where rr is the current required ratio for sight deposits and rr^* is the ratio that would be held voluntarily in the absence of requirements. This rr^* value was estimated to be 3 percent prior to 1967 and then to decline geometrically toward a value of 1.76 percent in 1994:1 (the value of each quarter is 0.9951 times the value of the preceding quarter).

The quarterly series for the adjusted monetary base is then equal to adjusted reserves plus the sum of notes and coins in circulation and those held by banks. After 1990:3, however, "reserves" includes currency in banks, and so the base is simply notes and coins outside banks plus adjusted reserves. The quarterly values of the monetary base were seasonally adjusted; annual values are averages of quarterly figures.

Italy

The basic sources were two monthly series, not seasonally adjusted but adjusted for changes in reserve requirements, provided by the Bank of Italy. The first series, from February 1962 to September 1990, presents end-of-month reserve holdings. Beginning in October 1990, reserve requirements have been specified instead in terms of average monthly reserve holdings, and the second series, from October 1990 to May 1994, is accordingly on a monthly average

basis.[31] The monthly values were averaged to yield quarterly figures, which were seasonally adjusted.

United Kingdom

For the United Kingdom, a quarterly series labeled "MO, break-adjusted, sa," beginning in 1969:3, was obtained from the Central Statistical Office database. For quarters before 1969:3, the monetary base series developed by Capie and Webber (1985) was utilized. It was seasonally adjusted by means of the (multiplicative) ratio-to-moving-average routine of the Micro TSP software package and spliced on to the later series using 1969:3 as the splice date.

Canada

A monthly adjusted monetary base series, seasonally adjusted, was obtained from the CANSIMS database, based on Bank of Canada data. Because reserve requirements are being phased out, the adjustment for reserve requirement changes was intended to determine what the monetary base would have been had reserve requirements been zero over the entire period. The resulting adjustment amounts to the noninclusion of required reserves. However, this method may be somewhat problematic, as quantities desired for transaction purposes will exceed quantities required when requirements are small.

---

[31]The Bank of Italy's *Statistical Bulletin* reports *growth rates* of its adjusted monetary base series; underlying level data were obtained from the Bank of Italy.

Bibliography

Capie, Forrest, and Alan Webber, *A Monetary History of the United Kingdom, 1870–1982* (London and Winchester, Massachusetts: Allen and Unwin, 1985).

Estrella, Arturo, and Gikas A. Hardouvelis, "The Term Structure as a Predictor of Real Activity," *Journal of Finance*, Vol. 46 (June 1991), pp. 555–76.

Fischer, Stanley, "International Macroeconomic Policy Coordination," in *International Economic Cooperation*, a National Bureau of Economic Research Conference Report, ed. by Martin Feldstein (Chicago: University of Chicago Press, 1988).

Friedman, Milton, and Anna J. Schwartz, *A Monetary History of the United States, 1867–1960* (Princeton, New Jersey: Princeton University Press, 1963).

Hargraves, Monica, and Garry J. Schinasi, "Monetary Policy, Financial Liberalization, and Asset Price Inflation," Annex I, *World Economic Outlook*, World Economic and Financial Surveys (Washington: International Monetary Fund, May 1993).

International Monetary Fund, "Price Stability," Box 2, *World Economic Outlook*, World Economic and Financial Surveys (Washington: International Monetary Fund, May 1993).

McCallum, Bennett T., "Specification and Analysis of a Monetary Policy Rule for Japan," *Monetary and Economic Studies*, Bank of Japan, Vol. 11 (November 1993), pp. 1–45.

IV

Evaluating Unemployment Policies: What Do the Underlying Theories Tell Us?

Dennis J. Snower[1]

This paper is motivated by a simple idea that has received lamentably little attention in the literature on unemployment policy: different unemployment policies are generally based on different theories of unemployment, and confidence in a policy should depend—at least in part—on the ability of the underlying theory to account for some prominent empirical regularities in unemployment behavior.

Some theories depict unemployment as the efficient outcome of market activity. These usually serve to rationalize a laissez-faire policy stance. Other theories depict unemployment as the product of market failures. Here, unemployment must be seen as the symptom of many possible diseases, as many different market failures can produce the same problem of joblessness. And just as different diseases require different treatments, so different market failures may call for different government policies.[2] It is because different theories of unemployment focus on different market failures that different policies are generally based on different theories.

It is difficult to evaluate the various unemployment policies through a direct empirical assessment of the market failures identified by the underlying theories. After all, market failures arise when people are not fully compensated for the costs and benefits that they impose on one another, and uncompensated costs and benefits are inherently difficult to measure. For this reason, it is natural to evaluate unemployment policies by investigating the predictive power of the underlying theories. A first step in this direction is to examine the degree to which these theories are able to account for some generally recognized regularities in the movement of unemployment rates in Organization for Economic Cooperation and Development (OECD) countries over the postwar period. This approach would perhaps be too obvious, were it not so frequently at variance with the standard rationalizations of unemployment policies.

Admittedly, the suggested criterion is highly simplistic. In practice, unemployment may generally be expected to arise from several different causes operating simultaneously, and it would not be reasonable to expect any single theory to explain all the salient empirical features of unemployment behavior in the OECD. All that this paper claims is that confronting unemployment policies with these empirical features can give a useful preliminary indication of how significant these policies are likely to be. It would surely be unwise to have a heavy stake in a policy whose underlying theory explains little of how unemployment has evolved in the postwar period.

The paper is organized as follows. The first section deals with the laissez-faire policy stance, based on theories of voluntary unemployment. The next section deals with demand-management policies, which rest on Keynesian theory. The following three sections consider, respectively, supply-side policies aimed at raising workers' productivity, the interaction between demand- and supply-side policies, and institutional policies designed to change labor market institutions. Concluding remarks are then presented.

Laissez-Faire

The laissez-faire policy stance—in which the government does little or nothing to influence unemployment—is based primarily on models in which swings in unemployment are viewed as the outcome of the optimizing decisions by job seekers and job providers in efficient markets. In this context, active unemployment policy is generally undesirable as it only disturbs the workings of well-functioning markets and interferes with people's free choices to accept or reject employment.

There are two main types of laissez-faire stances. One argues that government interventions aimed at influencing the long-run equilibrium unemployment

[1]The author wishes to thank David T. Coe and Bert Hickman for their perceptive comments and is particularly indebted to Robert P. Ford for his insightful suggestions. The paper was written while the author was a visiting scholar at the Research Department of the International Monetary Fund, and the research is part of the Labour Market Imperfections Program, funded by the U.K. Employment Department and organized by the Centre for Economic Policy Research.

[2]However, these failures need not call for government intervention at all, as it may not be feasible to correct some market failures through government unemployment policy. Even when it is possible to do so, the gains from correcting the market failures may fall short of the losses from the "government failures," namely, policy-induced inefficiencies.

rate would be ineffective or undesirable but acknowledges the possible effectiveness and desirability of policies to deal with cyclical swings in unemployment. In particular, it advocates the implementation of predictable policies, whose effects can be readily foreseen by economic agents. This view receives its most forceful expression in the market-clearing variant of the natural rate theory. The other laissez-faire stance discourages intervention not only with the long-run equilibrium unemployment rate, but also with cyclical unemployment swings. This stance rests primarily on intertemporal substitution theory and real business cycle theory.

Policy Predictability

The market-clearing variant of the *natural rate theory* is an obvious vehicle for rationalizing the importance of policy predictability. In this theory, unemployment is at its "natural rate" when people's expectations about wages and prices are correct. Under conditions of perfect competition and perfect information, this natural rate depends only on people's tastes, technologies, and resource endowments.[3] When wage-price expectations are out of line with actual wages and prices, unemployment deviates from its natural rate.

Provided that tastes, technologies, and endowments do not fluctuate cyclically, fluctuations in unemployment—according to this theory—must be explained by fluctuations in expected wages and prices around their actual values.[4] In order for this theory to have predictive power, it needs to be combined with a theory of how expectations are formed. The dominant one is the rational expectations theory, which asserts—quite plausibly—that people are not fooled in ways that they themselves could have predicted. To test this hypothesis, a description of people's "information sets" is required, from which expected wages and prices could be inferred. In practice, this is, of course, an impossible task, so empirical models generally assume that everyone has the same information as the authors of the models—except that the authors have more recent data.

The combination of the natural rate theory with this variant of rational expectations theory has a well-known implication: as people make no systematic expectational errors (errors that they could have predicted), unemployment cannot diverge systematically from its natural rate. Just as expected wages and prices will fluctuate randomly around their actual values, so unemployment will fluctuate randomly around the natural rate.

It is not hard to see why policy predictability is advisable in this context. With well-functioning markets, there is clearly no efficiency case to be made for interfering with the natural rate of unemployment. Policies that have no influence on this natural rate—monetary policies, for example—can affect unemployment only by driving a wedge between actual and expected wages and prices through unexpected policy variations, such as unexpected changes in the money supply. To put it simply, demand-management policies are effective only when they are deceptive. But deceptive policies are generally not in the public interest: if people were initially pursuing their own interests in well-functioning markets—and thereby promoting the public interest as well—unexpected changes in policy would only reduce individual and social welfare. Thus, stabilization policy is reduced to the limited task of being predictable.

The problem with this theory is that it fails to address many of the features of European unemployment over the past decade. In many OECD countries over the 1980s, union density remained constant or even declined, the expansion of unemployment benefits and other forms of welfare state support was arrested or even reversed, and deregulation, privatization, and liberalization of labor markets were not uncommon. On this account, it is difficult to argue that the natural rate of unemployment could have risen significantly. Some economists have maintained that the expansion of the welfare state in Europe over the 1950s, 1960s, and the first part of the 1970s may have been responsible for the growing unemployment in the 1980s, as people adjusted their behavior only gradually to the more generous social provision.[5] But it is hard to imagine that these lagged responses should have been so powerful and so delayed as to be responsible for the large, decade-long increases in European unemployment after most welfare states had ceased to expand.

Furthermore, given the stable rates of inflation over much of the decade, it cannot be argued that people's

---

[3]See, for example, Lucas (1972) and (1975). Some economists use the term "natural rate of unemployment" more broadly, letting it stand for any short-term equilibrium unemployment rate, regardless of whether the labor market clears (for example, Phelps (1970) and (1994)) and regardless of the underlying institutional structure (for example, Friedman (1968)). In that view, the natural rate clearly rests on much more than tastes, technologies, and endowments: it could also depend on the existence of credit constraints, the degree of competition in labor and product markets, the nature of wage-bargaining institutions, the level of labor turnover costs, and the size of the incumbent workforces, just to give a few examples. Then, however, the natural rate theory becomes so all-inclusive that it can no longer be distinguished from labor union, insider-outsider, efficiency wage, and other theories.

[4]Taking the wider view of the natural rate theory, as summarized in the previous footnote, it is worth observing that the degree of competition and the economic institutions governing behavior in the labor, product, credit, and international markets are generally not subject to cyclical fluctuations either. Thus, cyclical fluctuations in unemployment remain to be explained by fluctuations in expectational errors.

[5]See, for example, Grubb (1994) for a discussion of the lagged responses to changes in unemployment benefits.

wage-price expectations were getting further and further out of line with actual wages and prices; nor is it plausible to suppose that these misperceptions could have persisted for so long.

In short, there is nothing in the market-clearing variant of the natural rate theory that provides a clue to the massive rise in European unemployment through the 1980s. Nor does this theory shed useful light on why unemployment has been so much more persistent in Europe than in the United States, or why European unemployment rose with each major recession of the 1970s, 1980s, and early 1990s, while U.S. unemployment has always tended to return to its pre-recession level. Can it honestly be believed that Europeans are much slower than Americans to adjust their expectations, so that expectational errors are more persistent in Europe than the United States? Beyond that, theories based on expectational errors reveal little, if anything, about why unemployment spells tend to be longer in Europe than the United States (for given unemployment rates), why U.S. unemployment rates are more variable than most European ones, why unemployment falls unequally among different population groups, and why labor and product markets move so much more closely in tandem in the United States than Europe.

Noninterference with Business Cycles

The case against using stabilization policies in the labor market is made quite explicit in the intertemporal substitution and real business cycle theories.

As the name implies, the *intertemporal substitution theory*[6] is concerned with workers' desire to engage in intertemporal substitution of work for leisure in response to changing economic incentives. For example, if workers believe that real wages are temporarily depressed and will rise in the future, they may wish to take more leisure now and work harder later. The same may be true if they perceive real interest rates to be temporarily low, as that means that their current wage income cannot be transferred into the future at an advantageous rate.

The implication is that cyclical swings in employment may be the optimal response—by individual agents and society at large—to temporary shocks to tastes, technologies, and endowments.[7] Whereas most economists used to see business cycles as undesirable and needing to be damped through stabilization policies, the intertemporal substitution theory suggests that this is not so. It is not in the public interest to implement countercyclical monetary and fiscal policies, as these would prevent people from making their optimal dynamic responses to external shocks.

Although this theory can be used to generate an empirical account of much of the unemployment persistence and variability observed in the United States and other OECD countries,[8] it is hard to see how it could provide a reasonable explanation of European unemployment over the past 25 years. Is it plausible to believe that the many millions of Europeans who joined the unemployment register in the mid-1970s, early 1980s, and early 1990s were merely trying to take advantage of the high real wages or high real interest rates expected to occur in the future? Regarding the upward trend in European unemployment rates since the mid-1970s, is it plausible to believe that a very long-term intertemporal substitution is taking place, whereby workers have decided to enjoy considerable free time for two decades, perhaps with the intention of working very long hours for the next two decades? Furthermore, the available empirical evidence indicates that hours of work are unresponsive to real wage and real interest rate variations,[9] and that many of these variations tend to be permanent rather than temporary.

The *real business cycle theory*[10] builds on the intertemporal substitution theory and identifies technological shocks as the main source of macroeconomic fluctuations. Much effort has been expended attempting to establish that these fluctuations arise when perfectly informed individuals, all maximizing their utility subject to technological and resource constraints, respond to technological shocks by intertemporally substituting labor, leisure, and consumption. But beyond the predictive problems of the intertemporal substitution theory, it is hard to get an intuitive interpretation of the technological shocks. Whereas technological advances (which the real business cycle theory associates with the booms) are relatively easy to identify, the technological setbacks (which allegedly give rise to the recessions) are not.[11] It is hard to see how knowledge and expertise gets lost, particularly on the large scale that is necessary to account for the deep recessions that have been witnessed over the past two decades. Some economists argue that the negative

---

[6]See, for example, Barro (1981) and Lucas and Rapping (1969).

[7]The real business cycle theory, discussed below, incorporates this view in a model that emphasizes technological shocks.

[8]Intercountry differences in the persistence and variability of unemployment are motivated by differences in preferences and technological opportunities.

[9]However, measures of the elasticity of labor supply can be raised substantially if one assumes that the choice between work and inactivity is usually a discrete one. Then, to account for observed cyclical swings, the theory requires that decisions about whether to participate in the labor force be very sensitive to variations in real wages and real interest rates.

[10]See, for example, King and Plosser (1984), King, Plosser, and Rebelo (1988a) and (1988b), Kydland and Prescott (1982), and Long and Plosser (1983).

[11]The technological shocks in the real business cycle models are measured by Solow residuals, for example, the differences between the growth rate of output and a weighted average of the growth rates of factor inputs. But technological regress is not the only conceivable explanation of the negative Solow residuals; labor and capital hoarding is another.

technological shocks reflect such adverse macroeconomic events as oil price hikes or inappropriate investment (such as machinery that turns out not to work or that produces goods for which demand did not materialize). But the downturns in European labor market activity over the past two decades have lasted much longer than the price hikes for oil and other resources, and it would be strange—in the real business cycle world of rational expectations in clearing, perfectly functioning markets—for these shocks to generate investment fluctuations that are large enough to pull the massive OECD recessions in their wake. Beyond that, the long-term increase in European unemployment since the mid-1970s cannot plausibly be explained as the market-clearing outcome of technological shocks.

Demand-Management Policies

Demand-management policies to reduce unemployment fall into two broad categories: government employment policies, whereby the government stimulates employment directly by hiring people into the public sector; and product demand policies, which stimulate employment by raising aggregate product demand (for example, through tax reductions, increases in government spending on goods and services, or increases in the money supply).

For the "short run," in which wages and prices respond sluggishly to demand fluctuations, the main underpinning for both types of policies is Keynesian theory.[12] Here, recessions are characterized by deficient labor and product demand reinforcing one another: workers are unemployed because firms are not producing enough goods and services; firms are not doing so because there is too little demand; and demand is deficient because people are unemployed. In short, deficient demand in the labor market originates in the product market, and deficient demand in the product market originates in the labor market. Activity in these two markets thereby goes up and down together. The mechanism that couples these two markets is wage-price sluggishness. A fall in product demand will reduce labor demand if wages do not fall sufficiently; a fall in labor demand will reduce product demand if prices are sluggish downward.

This interaction between product and labor markets gives demand-management policy considerable leverage in the Keynesian theory. A rise in government employment will raise the purchasing power of the newly employed, who, in turn, will demand more goods and services, thereby inducing firms to employ yet more

people, and so on. In the same vein, a stimulus to product demand (resulting, say, from a tax reduction) gives firms the incentive to raise employment, which creates more purchasing power, which raises product demand even further, and so on. The more sluggish wages and prices are, the greater these multiplier effects become.

Of course, in practice wages and prices are not sluggish indefinitely, and thus the critical question is how short the Keynesian "short run" really is. Clearly, if it were shorter than the time it takes most firms to make and implement their employment and production decisions, the Keynesian employment repercussions of demand-management policies could not be expected to be significant. Wage-price sluggishness in excess of the relevant production and employment lags is required before Keynesian policies come into their own.

The Keynesian quantity-rationing theory[13] provides no guidance in this respect, as it merely *assumes* wages and prices to be indefinitely rigid. The New Keynesian theories of nominal sluggishness move beyond this primitive assumption. They seek to *explain* why wages and prices do not change sufficiently to obviate the need for substantial adjustments of output and employment in response to changes in demand. In shedding light on the degree of wage-price sluggishness, the ultimate aim is to help determine the length of time over which Keynesian policy effects are operative. The three dominant New Keynesian theories in this area are the "menu cost" theory, the theory of "near rationality," and the wage-price staggering theory.[14]

According to the *menu cost theory*, small fixed costs of changing prices induce firms to adjust quantities, instead of prices, in response to a sufficiently small change in demand. The same holds even in the absence of price adjustment costs if firms are "nearly rational," that is, changing their prices only when that has a substantial effect on profits. There are, however, a number of obstacles to using these theories to derive the degree of wage-price sluggishness. First, the existing menu cost models show how product demand variations affect employment when the costs of changing prices are the only adjustment costs. In practice, however, as employment adjustment costs (such as hiring, training, and firing costs) generally exceed the price adjustment costs by a large margin, it is not clear why product demand changes should have Keynesian effects on employment. Second, the menu cost theory implies that prices are either rigid or completely responsive to demand shocks, for the cost of

---

[12]See Keynes (1936). A microeconomic rationale for these effects, based on exogenously given wages and prices, was proposed by Barro and Grossman (1976) and others.

[13]For example, Barro and Grossman (1976), Malinvaud (1977), and Muellbauer and Portes (1978).

[14]Mankiw (1985) and Akerlof and Yellen (1985) develop the menu cost and near rationality theories, respectively; for the wage-price staggering theory, see, for example, Taylor (1979), Blanchard (1983), and Calvo (1983).

small price changes is generally no different from the cost of large ones. The theory is thus unable to explain an important feature of wage-price sluggishness in practice, namely, that many firms change their prices frequently, but not by sufficiently large amounts to make significant quantity adjustments unnecessary. These two difficulties make it difficult for the menu cost theory to predict the degree of wage-price sluggishness and the short-run effectiveness of Keynesian demand-management policy.

The *theory of near rationality* is subject to the first of these two difficulties: to explain the effectiveness of Keynesian demand-management policy, the deviation from complete rationality must be sufficiently large to outweigh the costs of adjusting employment and production. Moreover, as it is hard to see how this deviation could be measured empirically, this theory does not yield firm quantitative predictions on the degree of wage-price sluggishness.

The *wage-price staggering theory* demonstrates that, if wages and prices, once set, are fixed over substantial contract periods and if different wage-price decisions are staggered (rather than set simultaneously), a current change in aggregate product demand will affect production, employment, and unemployment well beyond the expiry of the current contract period. Several important lacunae in this theory, however, keep it from providing a firm basis to predict the degree of wage-price sluggishness. First, the theory does not identify the wage-price adjustment costs that keep wages and prices fixed over substantial intervals. Without a handle on these costs, the length of the contract periods—which plays such an important part in determining the degree of wage-price sluggishness in this context—cannot be derived. Second, the theory rests on the assumption that wages and prices are set in advance in nominal terms; it does not explain why rules for setting wages and prices generally do not involve indexing. If people have no "money illusion"—and therefore understand the difference between changes in value expressed in nominal and real terms—and if simple indexation schemes (such as making the wage depend on an aggregate price index) are easy to formulate and monitor, it remains an open question why so many wages and prices are set in nominal terms.[15] Third, the theory does not explain what determines the degree to which rules for setting wages and prices are time dependent (changing as a function of time) versus state dependent (changing as a function of external contin-

gencies).[16] This is an important issue because time- and state-dependent rules have very different implications for the degree of wage-price sluggishness following a change in product demand.[17] Fourth, little attention has been given to the question of why wage-price decisions are staggered rather than synchronized. Ball and Romer (1989) attribute it to firm-specific shocks, whereas Ball and Cecchetti (1988) suggest that staggering can arise from firms' incentives to set their prices after they have gained information about their rivals' price changes. As these examples show, the different sources of staggering imply radically different staggering structures and, presumably, radically different degrees of wage-price inertia. Finally, different sectors of the economy are characterized in practice by vastly different periods of nominal adjustment; the resulting patterns of staggering are enormously complex—perhaps too complex, at the requisite level of disaggregation, to be a convenient predictive tool.

Nevertheless, many economists agree that the Keynesian view sheds some light on unemployment behavior during deep recessions. When economies suffer from high unemployment and low capital utilization, increases in aggregate demand generally lead to declines in unemployment, and demand reductions usually lead to increases in unemployment. But the 1980s have exposed an important shortcoming of the Keynesian theory: for most of that decade, European labor and product markets did not move together at all. Product demand started to pick up toward the end of 1982, but unemployment did not start to fall until 1986 in the United Kingdom and even later in most other European countries. This gap is simply too large to be explained by inventory dynamics or lags between inputs and outputs in production processes; the Keynesian vision of tightly linked labor and product demand is called into question. The link was much stronger in the United States than in most European countries over the 1980s. This disparity is too large to be rationalized simply in terms of greater wage-price sluggishness in the United States than in Europe. Consequently, it becomes difficult to account for the serial correlation in OECD unemployment rates—and the greater degree of serial correlation in the European countries than in the United States—through the serial correlation in aggregate demand. Nor does

---

[15]See, for example, Carlton (1986), who finds significant price rigidities in manufacturing. Gordon (1990, p. 1150) has argued that, in the context of a complex input-output system, complete indexation may be difficult, owing to "the informational problem of trying to anticipate the effect of a currently perceived nominal demand change on the weighted average costs"; but it is hard to see why some (albeit imperfect) indexing should not be better than none.

[16]In practice, some rules for setting wages and prices appear to involve both time and state dependence, such as the provision in wage contracts to renegotiate at specified intervals but only under specified conditions—for example, if the inflation rate exceeds a certain magnitude. It has been suggested that, if the major cost is that of learning, a time-dependent rule is desirable; whereas, if the major cost is a menu cost, a state-dependent rule will be chosen. However, menu and learning costs are notoriously difficult to measure.

[17]Compare, for example, the nonneutrality of money under the time-dependent contracts of Taylor (1979) with the neutrality of money under the state-dependent contracts of Caplin and Spulber (1987).

the Keynesian theory explain readily why unemployment durations over the past two decades have been much longer in the European Community (EC) than in the United States or Japan, even after normalizing for differences in unemployment rates.

Lastly, the various New Keynesian theories of wage-price sluggishness can do no more than explain why unemployment can respond to variations in aggregate demand for a limited period of time. The long-run rise of European unemployment over the past two decades clearly cannot be rationalized on this basis. This does not mean that demand-management policies cannot conceivably influence unemployment over the longer run, but merely that such longer-term effectiveness must rest on something other than wage-price sluggishness. Several possibilities will be considered below in the discussion on the interaction between demand- and supply-side policies.

Supply-Side Policies

Job Search Support and Information Dissemination

This general policy approach covers such measures as counseling the unemployed, assisting them with personal problems, such as alcoholism and drug addiction, and alerting them to available training opportunities.[18] This approach also involves disseminating information about available labor services to firms and about available vacancies to workers.

Many of the market failures addressed by these policies can be analyzed effectively through the *theory of search and matching*.[19] In this theory, workers are not perfectly informed about the available jobs, and firms are not perfectly informed about the available workers. Thus, both sides of the market engage in search. Each agent acquires information up to the point at which the cost of searching for an additional job (or worker) is equal to the discounted stream of expected future returns from that job (or worker). Unemployment arises because jobless workers know that, although there are vacant jobs with wages sufficiently high to make the returns from the search exceed the costs, they do not know precisely where these jobs are and may not find them right away. The result is "frictional unemployment," which is never eliminated in aggregate since there are always some workers getting fired, some quitting, some entering the

labor force, and some retiring from it. At center stage in all search models lies a "matching function," which specifies how the expected number of matches is related to the number of unemployed workers and the number of vacant jobs.

It is not possible, of course, to attribute the rise in European unemployment to a deterioration of this matching technology, because the dissemination of labor market information has, if anything, improved with the passage of time. Nor are the recent periods of high unemployment related to comparatively high degrees of labor market "turbulence," that is, sectoral imbalances responsible for job creation and job destruction.[20]

Thus, if imperfect information about vacant jobs and unemployed workers were the only problem for job search support and information dissemination to overcome, its potential would probably be quite limited. However, this policy may also be useful in overcoming the discouragement and demoralization that prevent many long-term unemployed from seeking jobs effectively. The search and matching theory views this problem as the consequence of a decline in people's returns from job searches as their unemployment spells lengthen. The declining returns could be due to the depreciation or obsolescence of their skills and to a resulting fall in firms' efforts to attract these workers. Another reason why workers' search intensity may decline is that their preferences gradually change. In particular, the long-term unemployed can become accustomed and reconciled to remaining jobless, adopt it as a way of life, and stop searching seriously at all.[21] Counseling and personal assistance may help to mitigate these problems by restoring the attitudes and expectations necessary for successful job search strategies.

The potential importance of this policy approach may be highlighted by the recognition that the decline of search intensity with unemployment duration undoubtedly plays a significant role in explaining unemployment persistence (namely, the dependence of current unemployment rates on past unemployment rates).[22] This approach also helps explain why the burden of unemployment is distributed unequally. If the search intensity of workers falls the longer that they remain unemployed, and if the corresponding search intensity of potential employers falls as well, the expected future length of these workers' unemployment

---

[18]The European Community Commission laid stress on these measures in combating European unemployment. For example, the Council Resolution of May 29, 1990 recommended that counseling interviews be made available to all long-term unemployed. There is also wide recognition that these measures have a chance of being particularly effective only if they are combined with other active labor market policies, such as training programs.

[19]See, for example, Blanchard and Diamond (1989), Diamond (1982), Mortensen (1986), and Pissarides (1986).

[20]The turbulence hypothesis has been formalized by Lilien (1982) but has found no significant empirical support; see, for example, Abraham and Katz (1986).

[21]They have been said to become "addicted" to being unemployed. The theory of addiction provides some useful insights here. See, for example, Becker and Murphy (1988).

[22]This is, of course, not the only conceivable explanation of unemployment persistence. Other, comparably important, causes are employment adjustment costs, wage-price staggering effects, insider membership effects, and adjustment costs of labor force participation.

spells will depend positively on how long they have already been unemployed.

Aside from the search and matching theory, another rationale for supporting job searches and improving information dissemination—as well as for implementing various other policies to be discussed below—comes from the *efficiency wage theory*. Here, firms are assumed to have imperfect information about individual employees' productivities and are thus unable to make their wage offer contingent on their employees' performance. The firms, as wage setters, observe that by raising their wage offers they are able to increase the average productivity of their workforce, because higher wage offers enable a firm to recruit more highly qualified employees or motivate employees to work harder.[23] In other variants of the theory, higher wages discourage workers from quitting the firm, thereby reducing the firm's labor turnover costs.[24] Consequently, firms may have an incentive to keep wages above levels that would be necessary to ensure full employment. The unemployed are unable to get jobs by offering to work for less than the prevailing wage because it is not in the firms' interests to allow wages to fall.

In this context, policies that improve the dissemination of information about workers' ability, motivation, and quit behavior would enable firms to base their wage offers more closely on workers' individual productivities and potential labor turnover costs, thereby reducing the role of wages as an incentive mechanism and bringing down the associated level of unemployment.

The great strength of the efficiency wage theory is that it provides one conceivable explanation for why, even under perfectly flexible wages, people may be unemployed even though they would prefer to do the jobs of the current job holders at less than the prevailing wage.[25] Beyond that, however, it is not clear that the theory can shed much light on why EC unemployment has risen over the past two decades. It might be argued that with the decline in assembly line production, which is fairly easy to monitor, firms have placed increasing reliance on wages as an incentive mechanism. But if that were an important consideration, it would apply to both the EC and the United States, leaving the open question of why unemployment in the EC has risen so much relative to that in the United States. Moreover, the advance of computer technology has improved firms' monitoring capabilities in many sectors of the economy, making them less reliant on wages to motivate and attract employees.

It could also be argued that the use of wages as an incentive mechanism is more important in countries with more stringent job security legislation. After all, the more costly it is for firms to fire their employees, the lower are the chances a shirking or incompetent worker will be dismissed, and thus the greater the wages that firms have to pay (relative to unemployment benefits) in order to stimulate productivity. However, if this interaction between labor turnover costs and efficiency wages were significant in practice, it would be hard to explain why the EC unemployment rate averaged less than the U.S. unemployment rate over the 1950s and 1960s, given that job security legislation tended to be more stringent in the EC than in the United States over the entire postwar period.

Furthermore, the efficiency wage theory does not explain why the average duration of unemployment in Europe has significantly exceeded that in the United States and Japan since the mid-1970s, why labor and product market activities tend to move together in the United States but not in Europe, or why unemployment in many countries varies less within a business cycle than from one cycle to the next. These phenomena clearly cannot be ascribed to differences in monitoring technologies through time and across countries.

Of course, many efficiency wage models explain how unemployment may rise in response to a drop in labor productivity, a rise in the real interest rate, or a rise in the unemployment benefit. However, as with the search models, the efficiency wage models cannot lay unique claim to these predictions. The efficiency wage models do not add much to what other theories have to say in this respect. Similarly, the inclusion of labor turnover costs in an efficiency wage setting can explain why unemployment rates tend to be serially correlated, and differences in the magnitude of these costs can help account for intercountry differences in such serial correlation, as well as intercountry differences in duration of unemployment. But labor turnover costs are not an intrinsic building block of efficiency wage models. These models can rationalize the existence of unemployment even in the absence of labor turnover costs, and the addition of these costs to a wide variety of other theories would yield equivalent insights into unemployment dynamics.

---

[23]In Weiss (1980), a higher wage offer encourages workers of high skill, who were previously self-employed, to join the firm. In Shapiro and Stiglitz (1984), the firm randomly samples workers' effort and fires those who shirk; thus a higher wage offer raises effort by raising the expected penalty for shirking. In Snower (1983a), a higher wage offer discourages workers from searching on the job and thereby promotes productivity. In Akerlof (1982), workers agree to work more than is specified in their contract, and firms, in return, pay more than the minimum that would be necessary to attract them.

[24]See, for example, Salop (1979) and Stiglitz (1985).

[25]Sufficiently steep intertemporal wage scales or sufficiently large "exit fees" for employees may help firms stimulate productivity and discourage quitting, thereby giving firms less of an incentive to raise wages above market-clearing levels. It can be shown that, if these devices are practicable, they can eliminate some—but not all—sources of unemployment arising from the imperfect information analyzed by the efficiency wage theory.

Policies to Stimulate Worker Mobility

Some policies designed to reduce the burden of housing costs to the poor, such as rent control or low-cost public housing, reduce worker mobility by inhibiting workers from moving to available jobs and thereby create unemployment. This is a potentially significant problem in a number of OECD countries containing booming and slumping regions, as well as large differentials in house prices and rents across these regions.

These differentials may be incorporated in models of search and matching to provide an explanation for regional differences in unemployment rates. Although, as noted, there is little if any evidence that the rising European unemployment rates over the past two decades can be attributed to greater volatility of sectoral labor market shocks or to reduced availability of information about unemployed people or vacancies, differentials in house prices and rents can become an especially serious source of mismatch in the labor market, as they often expand when the degree of sectoral imbalance rises.[26] In particular, the greater the discrepancy between the excess of vacancies over unemployment in the booming regions and the excess of unemployment over vacancies in the slumping ones, the greater the differentials in house prices and rents are likely to be, owing to the greater discrepancy in excess demand across regions. Thus, as the degree of mismatch rises, the impediments to matching may rise in tandem.

Rent control and housing subsidies tied to the current place of residence give further leverage to these impediments to matching. Replacing these policy interventions by more efficient ways of redistributing income (such as conditional negative income taxes, which are discussed in the following section) could therefore help reduce unemployment. A similar argument can be made for implementing policies that increase the portability of health insurance and pensions between firms.

Policies Centering on Human Capital Formation

Policies that focus on human capital formation include government training programs and training subsidies to firms or workers,[27] as well as policies that reduce the rate of interest and thereby reduce the rate at which future returns to human capital formation are discounted.[28]

These policies may be analyzed through a special set of search and matching models that explain how unemployment can arise on account of market failures in the demand for, and supply of, training.[29] First, as unemployed people have few firm-specific skills, training them may involve a large "poaching externality." Specifically, if unemployed people were given training, a large share of the benefits from that training, in imperfectly competitive labor markets, would fall neither on the firms supplying the training nor on the workers receiving it, but on third parties, namely, firms that may poach the workers after they have been trained. In that event, the social benefit from training would exceed the private benefit, regardless of how the costs of training were distributed between the trainer and trainee. The market would then generate too few matches between firms and currently unemployed workers; with relatively few workers becoming productive and profitable through training, an inefficiently large number of them would remain jobless (see Snower (1994b)). This problem may become magnified considerably through the "low-skill, bad-job trap": a deficient supply of trained job seekers induces firms to create an excessive number of unskilled vacancies; these, in turn, further reduce workers' incentives to acquire training, leading to even more unskilled vacancies, and so on (see Snower (1994a)). These market failures are likely to be especially pronounced with regard to the long-term unemployed, who tend to be particularly poorly endowed with firm-specific skills and thus particularly prone to the poaching externality and the low-skill, bad-job trap.

Some of the rise in European unemployment over the past two decades might arguably be due to the interaction between these market failures, on the one hand, and the joint pull of skill-biased technological change and international trade, on the other. Technological developments that raise the productivity of skilled workers relative to unskilled workers, as well as rising trade with countries that have a comparative advantage in producing goods relatively intensive in unskilled labor, reduce the demand for unskilled labor relative to the demand for skilled labor. If the market failures discussed above are responsible for a deficiency in the acquisition of skills and an excessive number of unskilled workers without jobs, these two factors could lead to a rise in unemployment.

In addition, an expansion of trade or an increased rate of technological change could generate unemployment by raising the amount of labor market turbulence, particularly by increasing the rate of job

---

[26]See, for example, Bover, Muellbauer, and Murphy (1989).

[27]In general, training programs, whether in the public or private sector, may be divided into two broad categories: vocational training and "employability" training. In the latter category, a limited number of basic skills are developed that enable people to adjust to a worker environment and adapt to the requirements of semi-skilled jobs. In some countries, Germany in particular, vocational training is integrated within a formal system of basic education.

[28]Policies centering on physical capital formation are discussed in the next section.

[29]There are a variety of market failures in training provision that apply to all classes of workers. See, for example, Becker, Murphy, and Tamura (1990) and Booth and Snower (1995, forthcoming). Some of these market failures fall with particular severity on the unemployed and thus make the case for using training subsidies as an instrument to combat unemployment.

creation and destruction.[30] This, of course, is not an argument for the implementation of policies limiting the degree of technological change or international trade, for—as is well known—these two factors generally permit a given amount of goods and services to be produced with less labor input and thereby could improve the overall material standard of living, provided that the appropriate redistributions from the winners to the losers can be made without substantial loss of efficiency. Rather, the above diagnosis is an argument for job search support in order to improve the effectiveness of the matching process.

Thus, government training programs or training subsidies to the unemployed—particularly the long-term unemployed—may have a role to play in combating unemployment. Many government training programs, however, are ill-suited to firms' needs. This is scarcely surprising, as these needs are extremely diverse while government training programs are inevitably standardized and limited in variety. Training subsidies granted to firms thus appear preferable, for the firms then have the incentive to make the resulting training maximally appropriate to their available jobs. To keep firms from illicitly diverting the training funds to other purposes, it may be necessary to provide training subsidies only for programs leading to nationally recognized qualifications granted by institutions independent of the firms receiving the subsidies.[31]

The Interaction Between Demand- and Supply-Side Policies

Policies Centering on Physical Capital Formation

These policies range from government infrastructure investment to policies that raise the rate of capital utilization, stimulate the entry of firms, or promote physical capital formation by reducing the user cost of capital. What these policies all have in common is that they raise the level of capital services provided in the economy; consequently, if labor and capital are complementary in the production process, they increase the marginal product of labor, thereby raising employment and reducing unemployment. By simultaneously increasing investment demand and capital supply, these policies work on both the demand and supply sides. In so doing, they illustrate how demand-management policies can be effective in the "longer run," that is, over a time span long enough to permit full adjustment of wages and prices.

A growing number of economists have come to suspect that the effectiveness of demand-management policy is undersold by the short-run Keynesian mechanisms described above, which rest on wage-price sluggishness. Many believe that aggregate demand had a role to play in sustaining periods of prolonged low unemployment in the 1960s and prolonged high unemployment in the 1980s in Europe. However, for that to have been the case, the influence of aggregate demand on employment must extend well beyond the span over which wages and prices can be presumed sluggish.

The long-run effectiveness of demand-management policy may be analyzed through theories of imperfect labor market competition. In this vein, it is useful to picture labor market equilibrium in terms of the intersection of a downward-sloping aggregate labor demand curve and an upward-sloping wage-setting curve in real wage-employment space. The aggregate labor demand curve depicts the horizontal sum of firms' profit-maximizing relations between labor demand and the real wage under imperfect competition, and the wage-setting curve represents the real wage that emerges, at any given level of employment, from wage bargaining or efficiency wage minimization. Furthermore, the labor supply curve lies to the right of the wage-setting curve. The difference between labor supply and equilibrium employment is the equilibrium level of unemployment.

In this context, an increase in product demand can reduce unemployment by shifting the wage-setting curve or the labor demand curve outward. If only the wage-setting function shifted (along an unchanged labor demand curve), the real wage would move countercyclically. However, as real wage movements are often acyclic or even procyclical (particularly in the United States), it is important to explore how demand-management policy can shift the labor demand curve, thereby allowing for the possibility of procyclical real wage movements.[32] The most likely channels through which demand management can affect unemployment in the long run involve significant supply-side effects. Moreover, the interaction between demand- and supply-side policies becomes crucial in this regard.

Because the labor demand curve is the set of real wage-employment combinations at which the real

---

[30]As noted, however, there is little evidence that this has actually happened in advanced industrialized countries over the past two decades.

[31]The German apprenticeship system contains both of these ingredients.

[32]There are, of course, a number of other ways whereby changes in product demand can affect employment. These include income effects on labor supply (for example, Dixon (1987), Mankiw (1988), and Startz (1989)), increasing returns (for example, Cooper and John (1988) and Chatterjee and Cooper (1989)), search with strategic complementarities (for example, Howitt (1985) and Pissarides (1985)), union-induced labor immobilities, which make the employment level sensitive to the allocation of government spending across sectors (Dixon (1988)), and unemployment persistence mechanisms, which begin operation after a change in product demand temporarily reduces the real wage owing to a temporary nominal wage rigidity (for example, Lindbeck and Snower (1987c) and (1988b)).

marginal value product of labor is equal to the real wage, a change in product demand can shift the labor demand curve only if it affects the real marginal value product of labor at any given level of employment. It is easy to show that this shift occurs whenever the product demand change affects (i) the price elasticity of product demand, (ii) the imperfectly competitive interactions among firms, (iii) the degree of capital utilization, (iv) the user cost of capital, (v) the number of firms in operation, and (vi) the marginal product of labor.[33]

Of the channels through which product demand changes can be transmitted to employment, the first two do not appear to provide a firm foundation for the effectiveness of demand-management policies.

- With respect to the *price elasticity of product demand*, some authors have suggested that changes in government spending can affect employment by changing the composition of product demand, which, in turn, changes the associated price elasticity of aggregate demand (see, for example, the survey in Dixon and Rankin (1994)). There are, however, good reasons to believe that this hypothesis would be a tenuous basis for government policy. First, an increase in government spending would shift the labor demand curve outward through this channel only when the public sector price elasticity of demand exceeds that of the private sector, and there is no evidence that this is consistently the case across sectors and through time. Second, this transmission mechanism has the implausible implication that, if an increase in government expenditures shifts the labor demand curve outward, a tax reduction must shift that curve inward, as the former policy would raise public sector spending relative to private sector spending (thereby raising the aggregate price elasticity), while the latter policy would have the opposite effect. Moreover, affecting the price elasticity through changes in the composition of domestic versus foreign expenditures does not provide a firmer foundation for policy. In fact, if—as appears plausible—the foreign price elas-

ticity exceeds the domestic one, an increase in domestic demand would reduce the aggregate elasticity and thereby move the labor demand curve inward!

- As for *imperfectly competitive interactions among firms*, other economists have suggested that oligopolists might behave more competitively in a boom, so that a rise in product demand could shift the labor demand curve outward via its influence on competition.[34] However, Rotemberg and Saloner (1986) show that this effect holds only when firms are implicitly colluding oligopolists, and that this induced-competition channel is a weak foundation for demand-management policy.

That leaves the other four channels, which appear to be more promising avenues for transmitting demand-management policies to employment. All four of these channels make the employment impact of demand-management policies depend on their supply-side effects, which therefore ensures a special role for supply-side policies in enhancing the effectiveness of demand management.

- Lindbeck and Snower (1994) have shown that, when there is excess capital capacity, demand-management policy can affect the marginal product of labor by influencing the *degree of capital utilization*. To fix this idea, consider the following sequence of labor market decisions. First, each firm sets its supply of physical capital and determines from the range of its available technologies those that are to become accessible through its capital stock. Next, the nominal wage is determined (for example, through bargaining between the firm and its employees). Then, the firm observes the position of its product demand curve and makes its employment decisions. Under these circumstances, an unanticipated adverse product demand shock could make it unprofitable for a firm to operate at full capacity.[35] A subsequent favorable demand shock would induce a firm not only to hire more labor at the existing level of capital services, but also to raise the degree of capital utilization. When economies emerge from recessions in this way, with workers recalled to operate vacant machines and restart idle assembly lines, the capital brought back into use is often highly complementary to labor. Through this channel, expansionary demand-management policy may raise the marginal value product of labor, leading to procyclical movements of the real wage.

---

[33]Formally, the labor demand curve is given by $F \cdot (1-m) \cdot h_n = w$, where the left-hand term is the real marginal revenue product of labor and w is the real wage. Specifically, F is the number of firms, $h_n = h_n(n,k)$ is the marginal product of labor (where n and k are each firm's use of labor and capital, respectively), and m is Lerner's index of monopoly power, defined as $c/\eta F$ (where c is the conjectural variation coefficient and η is the price elasticity of product demand). Thus, channels (i) and (ii) work through the degree of monopoly power, channels (iii) and (iv) work through the effect of the capital stock on the marginal product of labor, channel (v) deals with shifts of the labor demand curve due to changes in the number of firms (which also affects the degree of monopoly power), and channel (vi) is concerned with the direct effect of product demand on the marginal product of labor. Lindbeck and Snower (1994) provide a formal analysis of all these channels of transmission.

[34]See, in particular, Rotemberg and Saloner (1986). This approach is in line with a long-standing tradition, characterized by Pigou (1927), Kalecki (1938), and Keynes (1939), all of whom asserted that firms' market power may vary countercyclically.

[35]In other words, the real marginal revenue product of labor at full capacity may fall short of the real wage.

- An increase in product demand that reduces the real interest rate will thereby also reduce the *user cost of capital*, increasing the size of the capital stock and shifting the labor demand curve outward, provided that labor and capital are Edgeworth complements in production (that is, the marginal product of labor depends positively on the capital stock). This could occur either through expansionary monetary policy, or, as Greenwald and Stiglitz (1988) indicate, through a decline in the risk premium on investment brought about by the expansion of demand. Naturally, if the rise in demand takes the form of an increase in government spending, the real interest rate may rise (rather than fall), shifting the labor demand curve inward through the mechanism described above. Moreover, even if the real interest rate falls, the labor demand curve still will shift inward when labor and capital are Edgeworth substitutes.

- With respect to the *number of firms in operation*, increases in product demand can (as demonstrated, for example, by Pagano (1990) and Snower (1983b)) induce entry of new firms, which shifts the labor demand curve outward, both directly and indirectly by increasing the degree of product market competition. Specifically, if nominal wages are temporarily rigid, a rise in product demand can reduce the real wage by raising prices, leading to the entry of new firms. Once nominal wages adjust, this entry ceases, but the recently entered firms remain operative. In this way, a temporary nominal wage rigidity can give product demand policy an influence on employment in the longer run (see Lindbeck and Snower (1987c)).

- If the increase in government spending takes the form of industrial infrastructure investment, there may obviously be a direct stimulus to the *marginal product of labor*. In this case, expansionary demand-management policy shifts the labor demand curve outward through its effect on the capital stock.

The policy implications regarding these four channels are potentially of considerable significance: the longer-term influence on employment of product demand policy depends on the availability of a limited number of supply-side channels of transmission. Supply-side policies—such as those that reduce barriers to the entry of new firms,[36] or those that augment industrial infrastructure—can help open these supply-side channels and thereby improve the long-term effectiveness of demand management. In the long run, therefore, demand- and supply-side policies are interdependent.

Although it is always difficult to assess the empirical importance of long-term policy effects, the above analysis does offer potentially interesting explanations of some long-run stylized facts about OECD unemployment. First, the relatively low unemployment rates experienced in Europe and the United States during the 1950s and 1960s came at a time of a significant buildup of industrial infrastructure, whereas the higher unemployment since the mid-1970s has been associated with a general rundown of industrial infrastructure in these areas. The analysis suggests that these two developments may bear some relation to one another. Second, the analysis also implies that the greater ease of entry and exit of firms in the United States, compared with European firms, may help in part to explain why the rise in aggregate demand in the aftermath of the recent recessions has had a greater impact in reducing unemployment in the United States than in Europe. Finally, the theory helps explain why the influence of demand management on unemployment appears to be particularly pronounced when this policy is associated with a decline in real interest rates and the availability of ample excess capital capacity.

Low-Wage Subsidies and Payroll Tax Reductions

This set of policies is designed to address the worsening of the relative position of workers at the bottom of the earnings distribution in many OECD countries over the past two decades.[37] This deterioration has taken the form of lower relative real wages in the United States (and, to a lesser degree, in the United Kingdom) and higher relative unemployment rates in many continental European countries. Providing subsidies or payroll tax reductions to low-wage workers is meant to raise firms' demand for these workers, thereby reducing their unemployment rates and raising their take-home pay.[38] It has been suggested that these policy measures be financed through a rise in value-added tax (VAT) or the "CO_2" tax. Econometric simulations, such as those reported in Drèze, Malinvaud, and others (1994), suggest that the expansionary employment effect of a drop in the payroll tax on low-wage earners may substantially outweigh

---

[36]These policies involve measures to dismantle government regulations restricting the creation of new firms; reform the system of profit, income, capital gains, and wealth taxes to put new firms at less of a disadvantage in comparison with established firms; increase competition among financial institutions so as to reduce credit constraints on new firms; and reduce the coverage of collective bargaining wage agreements so as to permit new firms to hire new recruits on competitive terms.

[37]See, for example, Drèze, Malinvaud, and others (1994) and Phelps (1995, forthcoming).

[38]The effectiveness of these policies clearly depends on the elasticity of labor demand. The greater the elasticity, the more the unemployment rates of the low-wage workers will fall, and the less their take-home pay will rise.

the contractionary effect of a corresponding rise in the VAT.

As these policies reduce unemployment by reducing employers' labor costs at the bottom of the wage spectrum, their effectiveness does not appear to be very sensitive to the precise underlying cause of the unemployment (in contrast to profit-sharing subsidies). Regardless of whether unemployment is generated by union pressures, efficiency wage considerations, or insider-outsider conflict, a drop in labor costs is bound to raise employment, as it permits firms to substitute labor for capital and enables them to reduce product prices and thereby create more demand.

However, three major factors limit the effectiveness of these policies: (i) "deadweight" (subsidies or tax reductions received by workers who would have become employed anyway); (ii) "displacement" (through which incumbent employees are displaced by the subsidized new recruits); and (iii) "substitution" (through which firms that benefit from these policies drive out of business firms that do not benefit). Clearly, the more closely the subsidies and the payroll tax reductions are targeted at the low-wage workers, the smaller are the effects of deadweight and substitution, and the larger that of displacement.

Another potential drawback of these policies is that, by raising the take-home pay of unskilled workers relative to skilled workers, they reduce the returns to training. Insofar as labor and capital are complementary in production, the resulting fall in human capital acquisition may also lead to a fall in physical capital formation. For this reason, it appears desirable that these policies be supplemented by subsidies to education and training. This additional element, however, would substantially increase the cost of the intervention. Another drawback is that these policies may encourage the excessive creation of unsatisfying, dead-end jobs providing little potential for advancement. In that event, the unemployment trap would be replaced by the "trap of the working poor." But even so, workers would experience a rise in their living standards: as the take-up is voluntary, workers and firms would avail themselves of these policy measures only if it were to their advantage.

Recruitment Subsidies

The case for implementing recruitment subsidies is similar to that for implementing low-wage subsidies and payroll tax reductions: they bring down labor costs and thereby promote employment and reduce unemployment.[39] In fact, they are better targeted because they are granted only to new recruits.

---

[39]See, for example, Bishop and Haveman (1979), Kaldor (1936), and Layard and Nickell (1980).

Once again, the effects of deadweight, displacement, and substitution limit the employment effect of recruitment subsidies. Obviously, the deadweight effect is generally smaller for recruitment subsidies than for low-wage subsidies or payroll tax reductions, but the displacement and substitution effects are likely to be larger. In any event, the aggregate employment impact of recruitment subsidies is invariably less than the number of jobs subsidized. Beyond that, their effectiveness is likely to be further reduced by the ways in which they are financed. Employer-based taxes will directly discourage employment, and income taxes will reduce product demand and thus indirectly discourage employment. In either case, however, the positive effect of the recruitment subsidies on employment will generally outweigh the negative effect of the taxes.

It is sometimes alleged that another deficiency of recruitment subsidies—one that is shared by low-wage subsidies and payroll tax reductions—is that they distort firms' decisions concerning factor composition, for example, by encouraging labor at the expense of capital. This matter is quite unlikely to have macroeconomic significance. The inefficiencies resulting from a distorted labor-capital mix are generally insignificant in comparison with the inefficiencies associated with long-term unemployment. Besides, as the efficiency wage, insider-outsider, and union theories suggest, free market activity may often be associated with market failures that give rise to excessive wages and deficient unemployment. In this context, recruitment subsidies may correct for existing distortions rather than create distortions themselves.

Benefit Transfers

"Benefit transfers" involve giving long-term unemployed the opportunity to use part of their unemployment benefits to provide vouchers for firms that hire them (see Snower (1995a)). The longer a person is unemployed, the larger is the voucher. Larger vouchers are also granted to firms that use them entirely on training. Workers provide vouchers on a regular basis to the firms that hire them, and the amount of the voucher gradually falls during the employment period. In this way, benefit transfers are a combination of several different structural policies: the vouchers are equivalent to a special type of recruitment subsidy; the voucher supplements for training are a special type of training subsidy; and the transfer of unemployment benefits amounts to a reform of the unemployment benefit system.

The reasons for using benefit transfers are various. First, they permit people to transfer funds out of a system that discourages employment in order to give firms an incentive to create employment. Second, benefit transfers extend the choice sets of workers and firms. Workers offer the vouchers to potential employers when their expected wage offers are sufficiently high; the employers accept the vouchers when the resulting labor costs are sufficiently low. Thus, benefit transfers are used only when both parties are made better off. Third, benefit transfer schemes are costless to the government because the vouchers are financed through the forgone unemployment benefits. Fourth, benefit transfers are not inflationary, as the long-term unemployed have no significant effect on wage inflation, and as the vouchers reduce labor costs and thereby exert downward pressure on prices. Fifth, benefit transfer schemes function as automatic stabilizers, as a fall in unemployment reduces the amount spent on unemployment benefits, which, in turn, reduces the funds available for the employment vouchers. Sixth, by providing generous vouchers to firms that use them for training, such schemes give these firms an incentive to maximize the productivity-enhancing effect of this training. Finally, the schemes could help to overcome regional unemployment problems. Regions with high unemployment would command a disproportionate share of training subsidies, which might give firms an incentive to relocate there and provide the unemployed with the requisite skills, even in the face of existing barriers to mobility.

In view of these advantages, benefit transfers appear desirable as a first line of attack against long-term unemployment. Once the employment-creating potential of unemployment benefits has been exploited in this way, further measures may well be necessary to bring European unemployment down to socially acceptable levels.

Institutional Policies

Institutional policies, as their name suggests, aim to change labor market institutions to reduce unemployment. These policies come in many guises, of which only the most prominent will be considered here.

Policies to Reduce the Power of Labor Unions

Policies to reduce the power of labor unions include, inter alia, restrictions on secondary picketing, laws prohibiting closed-shop agreements, and regulations restricting the coverage of union wage agreements. These policies may be analyzed straightforwardly through the theory of labor unions. In the traditional variants of this theory,[40] all union members are assumed to have identical preferences and an equal share in the available work. The union then represents the interest of its members by exerting its monopoly power in wage setting, much like sellers of goods or services exert their monopoly power in price setting. The resulting wages will be higher—and employment lower—than would otherwise be the case. If all workers in the economy belong to unions, aggregate employment will be less than it would be under full employment. The difference is unemployment (or underemployment).

More recent theories recognize that unions take greater account of the interests of their employed members than of the unemployed and that the employed workers have greater access to work than do the unemployed. The unemployment arising in this setting may be voluntary from the vantage point of the employed union members, but it is generally involuntary from the vantage point of the unemployed, as the latter could be made better off by a wage reduction associated with a rise in employment.

The main theoretical weakness of this theory lies not in what it explains, but in what it does not explain, namely, why the unemployed do not leave unions that do not represent their interests and start new unions making lower wage claims. Nor does this theory identify the basis of the unions' "clout." As union coverage in most market economies is far below 100 percent, it is not clear why employers do not simply throw out high-wage union members and hire low-wage nonmembers instead.[41]

On the empirical front, there is some evidence of an inverse relation between intercountry differences in unemployment rates, on the one hand, and intercountry differences in indexes of union power and union coverage, on the other, over the postwar period. Yet the union theories have not performed well in predicting movements of unemployment over the past decade. In the first part of the 1980s, for example, union membership in the United Kingdom and several other European countries fell while unemployment rose. For this reason, it is premature to say that unemployment policies designed to reduce union power are on a firm predictive foundation.

Reforming the Wage-Bargaining System

In recent years, there has been a growing call to strengthen firm-level and national-level bargaining at

---

[40]See, for example, McDonald and Solow (1981) and Oswald (1982) and (1985).

[41]This question is answered by the insider-outsider theory, discussed below. But if the answer of the insider-outsider theory is accepted, namely, that it is labor turnover costs that prevent firms from replacing union members by nonmembers, the traditional union theories must undergo substantial revision; see, for example, Lindbeck and Snower (1987a) and (1987b).

the expense of bargaining at the sectoral level.[42] This policy strategy is based on the analysis of Calmfors and Driffill (1988), who explore how the economic efficiency of wage bargaining depends on the number of independent agents engaged in bargaining. They argue that, when there is a high degree of centralization in bargaining—with few unions confronting few employers' confederations, such as in Austria and Sweden— the negotiating partners internalize most of the effects of their claims; in particular, the unions take account of the price increases associated with their wage claims, and the employers take account of the wage increases associated with their employment and pricing decisions. The resulting wage-employment outcome is therefore reasonably efficient. However, when there are large numbers of negotiating workers and firms, with each occupying a small portion of the market, the resulting activity is efficient for the standard competitive reasons. The United States approximates this setup. Calmfors and Driffill claim that it is only in the intermediate range, where the independent negotiators are sufficiently few in number to have market power but sufficiently numerous to ignore the external effects of their decisions, that gross inefficiencies arise. Calmfors and Driffill adduce some empirical evidence in favor of this thesis, and Layard, Nickell, and Jackman (1991, p. 55) provide cross-section evidence that the unemployment rates in 20 OECD countries tend to be inversely related to the degree of union and employer coordination in each country.

On this account, it has been argued, wage-bargaining systems need to be either highly centralized or highly decentralized.[43] Policies that reduce the power

of labor unions, reduce labor turnover costs, and promote international trade are all likely to strengthen decentralized, firm-level bargaining. Government sponsorship of "social pacts"—whereby unions accept targets for nominal wage growth (based on productivity growth and price inflation), firms accept targets for price increases (based on wage inflation), the central bank sets the growth of the money supply with a view to noninflationary growth, and the fiscal authority aims to control unemployment—encourages centralized, national-level bargaining. As a practical matter, however, wage-bargaining systems are very difficult to reform; thus, this should be seen more as a long-term structural policy desideratum than as a short-term policy instrument.

Reforming the Unemployment Benefit System

The main deficiency of all unemployment benefit systems is that, in helping to cushion the blow of unemployment, they worsen the underlying problem in two ways. First, unemployment benefits discourage job search because, when an unemployed person finds a job, the unemployment benefits are withdrawn and taxes are imposed. Second, unemployment benefits put upward pressure on wages by improving incumbent workers' negotiating positions. The first effect lies in the domain of search and matching theory, the second in the province of bargaining theory. Together, these effects make unemployment benefit systems inherently inefficient and inequitable.

In reforming unemployment benefit systems, it is important to distinguish carefully between the equity and efficiency objectives of these systems. The equity goal is simply to redistribute income from the rich to the poor. The efficiency goal is to respond to market failures in the provision of unemployment insurance.[44] However, unemployment benefits are generally a very poor tool to accomplish these objectives.

With regard to equity, it is worth keeping in mind that, for most poor people, employment is the best— and often the only—way to overcome poverty. Thus, it is particularly unfortunate that, by making the distribution of employment opportunities more unequal, unemployment benefits discourage employment. Clearly, a more effective way to redistribute income from rich to poor is to use income as the criterion of redistribution; the employment criterion is obviously a

---

[42]This issue can be addressed through labor-market-bargaining theory, which deals with the question of how employers and employees split the economic rent from employment activity. There are two broad approaches. In one approach, employers and employees bargain over wages, and, once the wages have been set, the employers make the employment decisions unilaterally. In the other approach, employers and employees bargain over wages and employment simultaneously. The former are called "right-to-manage" models (because the firms make the employment decisions by themselves), and the latter are usually known as "efficient bargaining" models. There are also models that straddle these two extremes (see, for example, Manning (1987)). It can be shown that the bargaining outcome from the right-to-manage models is inefficient, in the sense that it is possible to find wage-employment combinations that make one party to the negotiations better off without making the other party worse off. This is a common feature of institutional setups in which the price and quantity decisions are made by different agents. This inefficiency, of course, does not arise in the latter models, which are therefore called "efficient bargaining" models.

[43]However, in a more recent article, Calmfors (1993) distances himself somewhat from this simple policy conclusion. He acknowledges that centralization is a multifaceted feature of bargaining systems and that labor market performance is likely to respond quite differently to changes in the degree of centralization across occupations, sectors, unions, employers' confederations, and geographic regions. He also notes that the degree of centralization is likely to be particularly significant for labor market performance only in the nontradable sectors, where foreign competition is weak.

---

[44]Under free market conditions, the private sector generally has deficient incentives to provide unemployment insurance, owing to moral hazard and adverse selection problems: providing unemployment insurance increases the chances of being unemployed, and those with a greater chance of being unemployed will tend to purchase more insurance. Also, under free market conditions, credit constraints prevent workers from purchasing the optimal amount of insurance.

blunt instrument for this purpose because some employed are poor while some unemployed are well-off.

With regard to efficiency, the gains from provision of unemployment insurance must be set against the efficiency losses that arise when unemployment benefits discourage employment and encourage unemployment. It is by no means a foregone conclusion that the efficiency gains will exceed the associated losses. In any case, the unemployment benefit schemes that predominate in Europe—characterized by either flat-rate components or ceilings on benefits that depend on past wages—have much less in common with optimal unemployment insurance schedules than with standard redistributive schemes. In short, the unemployment benefits encountered in practice are not designed to yield major efficiency gains by correcting for failures in the unemployment insurance market.

These deficiencies, however, are not the only problems arising from unemployment benefits. The efficiency wage, labor union, and insider-outsider theories identify failures associated with free market activity that tend to yield excessively high wages and excessively low employment. Unemployment benefit systems exacerbate these market failures by further driving up wages and discouraging employment. Furthermore, these market failures are perpetuated through various dynamic effects. As noted above, the longer people are unemployed, the more their skills depreciate and become obsolete, the more discouraged and ineffective they become in the job search process, and the more wary firms become of hiring them. When governments reward unemployment through unemployment benefits and penalize employment through income taxes, they amplify these dynamic effects by discouraging unemployed from competing for jobs and becoming "enfranchised" in the wage determination process. As a result, unemployment becomes less effective in moderating wages or raising firms' returns from searching for new recruits. In this way, unemployment benefit systems make unemployment more persistent and put the long-term unemployed at a greater disadvantage in competing for jobs.

For all these reasons, unemployment benefit reform has become a topic of growing policy interest throughout Europe. But while it is relatively easy to recognize the need for reform, it is very difficult to agree on its content. The critical question is how to provide a safety net for the disadvantaged and the unfortunate without dramatically reducing people's incentives to fend for themselves and thereby creating more disadvantaged and unfortunate.

A growing number of European economists argue that unemployment benefits should be generous but made available for only a limited period of time (see, for example, Layard, Nickell, and Jackman (1991)). The generosity is allegedly required to give people the opportunity to make judicious job matches, which

credit constraints might otherwise keep them from doing. Limited benefit duration, it is claimed, is necessary to induce people to find work quickly, before they become discouraged and stigmatized, and lose their skills. This advice sounds eminently sensible, but little attempt has been made thus far to explore whether the theory behind it captures empirically important determinants of unemployment. It seems doubtful that workers' credit constraints are an important aspect of the European unemployment problem. If they were, the problem would be that unemployment duration was too short, resulting in overemployment. This, it appears, is the least of Europe's worries.

Beyond that, the prescription to shorten benefit duration characteristically becomes vague on the subject of how to deal with people who remain jobless after their unemployment benefits have expired. Some economists recommend that these people be given training, while others put more emphasis on job counseling. However, that still leaves the question of how to treat those left unemployed even after completion of the training and counseling. Many European economists still hold the popular European opinion that the social safety net—in the form of income support and a range of welfare state benefits—is required to keep these hapless individuals from destitution. However, a nominally short benefit duration may cease to give unemployed people an effective incentive to find jobs promptly.

This is, in fact, the problem that the current, unreformed European benefit systems face. Many European countries—such as Germany, France, Greece, Ireland, and the Netherlands—grant some form of unemployment insurance of limited duration, followed by unemployment assistance that is frequently unlimited. It is hard to see how the disincentive effects generated by these systems could be overcome simply by shortening the time span for unemployment insurance and inserting a period of training and counseling prior to the receipt of open-ended unemployment assistance.

Overall, it is safe to say that unemployment benefit reform should be guided by the objective to overcome its two biggest deficiencies, namely, the disincentive effects and the imperfections in targeting the poor. It is arguable that both deficiencies could be mitigated simply by replacing unemployment benefit systems by a conditional negative income tax program,[45] whereby receipt of negative income taxes is made to depend on the applicants' ability to pass stringent tests on their willingness and readiness to work.[46]

---

[45]See, for example, Coe and Snower (1995) and Snower (1995b, forthcoming) for more details on this policy approach.

[46]Handicapped people and those who are likely to be more productive in the household sector than in the labor market (such as single mothers with several infants) would be exempted from this condition; see Snower (1994c).

Work Sharing and Early Retirement

Work sharing and early retirement have begun to look attractive to an increasing number of European policymakers, particularly in Germany. It is based on the view that, as there is a fixed amount of work to be done in an economy in any given period of time, it is the job of the policymakers to decide how this work is to be distributed across the available workforce. If it is currently distributed unequally, with most people in the workforce working full time and some remaining unemployed for prolonged periods, work sharing and early retirement could spread the job opportunities more equitably.

But to call this a "theory" is an overstatement. Most economists would rather call it the "lump-of-labor fallacy," as it is well understood that the amount of work to be done in an economy is not a fixed number of hours that is beyond the influence of policymakers.[47] Keynesian theory drives this point home particularly forcefully: the more people are employed, the more they earn, the greater their purchasing power, the more they spend, and—completing the cycle—the more people firms will seek to employ.

In addition to their nonexistent theoretical foundation, job sharing and early retirement schemes suffer from a number of serious problems. First, they tend in practice to increase nonwage labor costs, particularly those associated with hiring, screening, training, and administration. Thus, these schemes may be expected to discourage employment and create more unemployment. Second, insofar as they are successful in reducing the pain from unemployment by distributing it among more people, they lessen the political pressure on governments to address the unemployment problem through more promising means. Third, in reducing the number of unemployed people competing for jobs, job sharing and early retirement schemes may well drive up wages and stimulate price inflation. These results may, in turn, induce governments to implement restrictive macroeconomic policies, which would raise unemployment, possibly creating a further perceived need to redistribute job opportunities through yet more work sharing and early retirement. The main advantage of work sharing and early retirement schemes is that they may enfranchise a larger number of people in the wage determination process and thereby moderate the insiders' wage demands. It appears unlikely, however, that this advantage would dominate the disadvantages discussed above.

Policies Centered on Labor Turnover Costs

Policies to reduce unemployment by mitigating the harmful effects of labor turnover costs are as varied as the turnover costs themselves. Some involve dismantling job security legislation (for example, by passing laws reducing statutory severance pay or simplifying mandated firing procedures); others reduce the ability of incumbent workers to exploit existing labor turnover costs in order to boost their wages (by imposing, for example, legal restrictions on strikes and picketing); yet others help the unemployed surmount the obstacles created by turnover costs (by implementing training subsidies, recruitment subsidies, profit-sharing schemes, policies to reduce the barriers to the entry of new firms, and the reform of wage-bargaining systems). This section focuses attention on the first two groups of policies; policies in the third group have been discussed in the preceding section.

What the first two groups of policies have in common is that they reduce the market power of the "insiders" (incumbent employees whose jobs are protected by significant labor turnover costs) and thereby strengthen the position of the "outsiders" (who are either unemployed or have jobs that are not protected in this way). In the process, insiders become less insulated from the forces of labor demand and supply, and firms find it easier to hire and fire employees. The upshot is that insiders' wages face downward pressure, as insiders now face greater competition from outsiders, and employment becomes more responsive to variations in revenue and cost conditions. The first effect stimulates employment[48] because insiders' wages fall and firms raise their demand for new recruits, who eventually turn into insiders. The second effect reduces the degree of employment and unemployment persistence.

This policy approach lies in the domain of the insider-outsider theory (see, for example, Lindbeck and Snower (1986) and (1988a)). According to this theory, labor turnover costs, falling at least in part on firms, give market power to the insiders, who know that their employers would find it costly to replace them. The insiders are assumed to use this power to pursue their own interests in the wage-setting process. Although the resulting insider wages are higher than they otherwise would be, the labor turnover costs discourage firms from firing the insiders. Of course, firms are also discouraged from hiring new entrants by the excessive wages.

---

[47]Of course, economies may generate something like a "lump of labor" over the very short run, that is, over a time span short enough to preclude readjustments in the size of firms' workforces. But this time span is of little interest for the design of unemployment policy.

[48]Of course, a reduction in labor turnover costs also has a direct effect on employment. This effect could be either positive (when a reduction in hiring costs stimulates hiring) or negative (when a reduction in firing costs leads to more firing). See, for example, Bentolila and Bertola (1990).

Some of the labor turnover costs (such as training costs) are an intrinsic part of the production process; others (such as severance payments) are primarily associated with rent-seeking activities. The rent-related turnover costs give the insiders preferential conditions of employment over the outsiders. Unemployment can then arise on account of the outsiders' inferior employment opportunities. In this context, policies that reduce labor turnover costs or check insiders' ability to exploit them in wage setting will generally lead to a reduction in unemployment.

The insider-outsider theory is able to account for a variety of empirical regularities in unemployment behavior. The relatively high labor turnover costs in Europe—both in their own right and through their influence on insiders' wages—play a role in making European unemployment more persistent (serially correlated) than U.S. unemployment. Because high labor turnover costs make firms reluctant both to hire and to fire employees, they raise the duration of unemployment. In this way, Europe's high labor turnover costs can lead to its high unemployment durations and low unemployment variability, in comparison with the United States. Furthermore, because labor turnover costs raise insiders' job retention rates relative to outsiders' job acquisition rates, they imply that unemployment falls more heavily on population groups whose work patterns are relatively unstable (with high entry and exit rates in the job market), such as young people.

Insofar as many of the full-time unskilled jobs in the traditional industrial sectors are associated with significant labor turnover costs, the insider-outsider theory also explains why wages in these sectors have not fallen with falling demand. It also helps explain why much service sector and temporary employment—associated with relatively low turnover costs—has been buoyant in comparison with industrial employment in OECD countries.

When business cycles are short-lived and mild, most European countries—facing higher labor turnover costs—may be expected to do relatively little hiring or firing, hoarding labor in the slumps and bringing it back into use in the booms. But in the face of deep, prolonged recessions, these countries will stop hoarding and start firing labor. In the subsequent recovery, firms will be comparatively slow to rehire, fearing that they may incur further firing costs should the recovery not materialize. Investment in labor-saving capital equipment may then take the place of new employment. This helps explain why unemployment rates in Europe, which were significantly lower than in the United States in the 1950s and 1960s (when business cycles were short-lived and mild), have been significantly higher since the mid-1970s; why U.S. unemployment has been more variable than European unemployment; and why production and employment move together to a greater degree in the United States than in Europe.

Profit Sharing

Under profit-sharing contracts, a part of workers' remuneration is paid as a fraction of the profits earned by their firms (see Weitzman (1983) and (1984)). For a given level of remuneration, it is clear that a firm's marginal cost of employment is lower under profit sharing than under a fixed wage because (under diminishing returns to labor) the profit share declines as employment rises, whereas a fixed wage, by definition, does not. Consequently, it is alleged, profit-sharing contracts lead to lower unemployment than do wage contracts. Weitzman has suggested that, in a world where wages seldom involve profit sharing, government subsidies for profit sharing are called for because firms have insufficient incentives to offer profit-sharing contracts.

The claim that profit-sharing contracts reduce unemployment is less general than it may appear at first sight. The effectiveness of profit sharing depends crucially on what is generating the unemployment. If, for instance, the unemployment is an efficiency wage phenomenon, the switch from wage contracts to profit-sharing ones will do little, if anything, to reduce unemployment, as workers' incentives to shirk and quit depend on the total amount of remuneration, not on how this amount is divided between wages and profit shares. Similarly, firms' ability to attract workers of relatively high productivity would not be affected by a switch from wage to profit-sharing contracts.

However, if the unemployment is predominantly generated by insider-outsider considerations, profit sharing may have an effective role to play. In the insider-outsider theory, the outsiders are unable to "bribe" insiders to forgo the rent-seeking activities that keep the outsiders from getting jobs. The insiders may, for example, boost their wages and protect themselves from competition with outsiders by refusing to cooperate with them in the process of production, thereby creating an insider-outsider productivity differential; or they may harass outsiders who offer to work for less than the prevailing wages and thereby make the available jobs more disagreeable for those outsiders. Alternatively, the insiders may be involved in determining the wages of new entrants and may use their market power to drive entrant wages up, thereby discouraging the employment of entrants, which would drive down the marginal product of insiders.

In this context, profit-sharing contracts may be construed as a device that permits the outsiders to bribe the insiders to stop these activities, so that everyone— the insiders, the outsiders, and their employers—can be made better off. In particular, if insiders were given a bonus for consenting to profit-sharing contracts for new entrants, the firm's marginal cost of hiring new entrants would fall, the entrants would receive more than they did when they were unemployed, and the firm's profits would rise. In the process, of course, unemployment would fall.

Although profit-sharing schemes are promising in this context, it is important to be aware of some potential difficulties. First, it may be impossible to induce the insiders to consent because their rent-seeking activities—like their harassment activities—may not be objectively monitorable. Second, to make profit sharing operational may require implementing costly monitoring procedures that enable workers to gain access to profit information.[49] Third, the extra profit generated through the introduction of profit sharing may be insufficient to compensate the insiders for their loss of market power resulting from the inflow of new entrants. Fourth, the extra profit generated may be insufficient to pay the premium that the new entrants would require to induce them to bear the income risk associated with profit sharing. Finally, the insiders may refuse to be bribed because that would create a two-tier remuneration system that would give firms an incentive to lay off the insiders and retain the entrants, once the latter had been fully trained.

Concluding Remarks

It has become a platitude to say that every sensible piece of economic policy advice rests on a reasoned analysis of the underlying policy problem, and that every reasoned analysis is based on a theory of how the economy functions. Politicians may believe that their policy proposals rest simply on "common

sense"; but if there is any sense underlying this common sense, it exists in the form of a coherent, self-contained theory. As Keynes (1936) put it:

> The ideas of economists and political philosophers, both when they are right and when they are wrong, are more powerful than is commonly understood. Indeed, the world is ruled by little else. Practical men, who believe themselves to be quite exempt from any intellectual influences, are usually slaves of some defunct economist.

Because this is obvious, it is surprising that so little is done to explore the predictive power of a theory before using it as a basis for policy formulation. This survey is a tentative first step toward evaluating unemployment policies in this light.

It goes without saying that such an evaluation alone is not sufficient for the design of unemployment policies, but, as has been demonstrated, it can provide a variety of useful insights about where promising policy approaches are to be found. For example, this paper has examined how differences in labor turnover costs across sectors (such as services versus manufacturing) and regions (such as Europe versus the United States) may help account for differences in the level, variability, duration, persistence, and distribution of unemployment. This analysis suggests that policies to reduce the harmful effects of these labor turnover costs—such as reductions in statutory severance pay, training and recruitment subsidies, benefit transfers, and policies to lower the barriers to the entry of new firms—may have a significant role to play in combating unemployment. These and the variety of other insights adduced above show why it is important to evaluate unemployment policies through the predictions of the underlying theories.

---

[49]Firms may not wish to disclose this information in order to preserve the confidentiality of their business strategies.

Bibliography

Abraham, Katharine G., and Lawrence F. Katz, "Cyclical Unemployment: Sectoral Shifts or Aggregate Disturbances?" *Journal of Political Economy*, Vol. 94 (June 1986), pp. 507–22.

Akerlof, George A., "Labor Contracts as Partial Gift Exchange," *Quarterly Journal of Economics*, Vol. 97 (November 1982), pp. 543–69.

_____, and Janet L. Yellen, "A Near-Rational Model of the Business Cycle, with Wage and Price Inertia," *Quarterly Journal of Economics*, Vol. 100 (Supplement, 1985), pp. 823–38.

Ball, Laurence, and Stephen G. Cecchetti, "Imperfect Information and Staggered Price Setting," *American Economic Review*, Vol. 78 (December 1988), pp. 999–1018.

Ball, Laurence, and David Romer, "The Equilibrium and Optimal Timing of Price Changes," *Review of Economic Studies*, Vol. 56 (April 1989), pp. 179–98.

Barro, Robert J., "Intertemporal Substitution and the Business Cycle," *Carnegie-Rochester Conference Series on Public Policy*, Vol. 14 (Spring 1981), pp. 237–68.

_____, and Herschel I. Grossman, *Money, Employment and Inflation* (Cambridge and New York: Cambridge University Press, 1976).

Becker, Gary S., and Kevin M. Murphy, "A Theory of Rational Addiction," *Journal of Political Economy*, Vol. 96 (August 1988), pp. 675–700.

_____, and Robert F. Tamura, "Human Capital, Fertility, and Economic Growth," *Journal of Political Economy*, Vol. 98 (October 1990), S12–S37.

Bentolila, Samuel, and Giuseppe Bertola, "Firing Costs and Labor Demand: How Bad Is Eurosclerosis?" *Review of Economic Studies*, Vol. 57 (July 1990), pp. 381–402.

Bishop, John, and Robert Haveman, "Selective Employment Subsidies: Can Okun's Law Be Repealed?" *American Economic Review*, Vol. 69 (Papers and Proceedings, May 1979), pp. 124–30.

Blanchard, Olivier Jean, "Price Asynchronization and Price Level Inertia," in *Inflation, Debt, and Indexation*, ed. by Rudiger Dornbusch and Mario H. Simonsen (Cambridge, Massachusetts: MIT Press, 1983).

_____, and Peter A. Diamond, "The Beveridge Curve," *Brookings Papers on Economic Activity*, No. 1 (1989), pp. 1–60.

Booth, Alison, and Dennis J. Snower, eds., *Acquiring Skills: Market Failures, Their Symptoms, and Policy Responses* (Cambridge, Massachusetts: Cambridge University Press, 1995, forthcoming).

Bover, Olympia, John Muellbauer, and Anthony Murphy, "Housing, Wages, and U.K. Labour Markets," *Oxford Bulletin of Economics and Statistics*, Vol. 51 (March 1989), pp. 97–136.

Calmfors, Lars, "Centralization of Wage Bargaining and Macroeconomic Performance: A Survey," *OECD Economic Studies*, No. 21 (Winter 1993), pp. 161–91.

_____, and John Driffill, "Bargaining Structure, Corporatism and Macroeconomics Performance," *Economic Policy*, Vol. 6 (April 1988), pp. 13–61.

Calvo, Guillermo A., "Staggered Prices in a Utility-Maximizing Framework," *Journal of Monetary Economics*, Vol. 12 (September 1983), pp. 383–98.

Caplin, Andrew S., and Daniel F. Spulber, "Menu Costs and the Neutrality of Money," *Quarterly Journal of Economics*, Vol. 102 (November 1987), pp. 703–25.

Carlton, Dennis W., "The Rigidity of Prices," *American Economic Review*, Vol. 76 (September 1986), pp. 637–58.

Chatterjee, Satyajit, and Russell W. Cooper, "Multiplicity of Equilibria and Fluctuations in Dynamic Imperfectly Competitive Economies," *American Economic Review*, Vol. 79 (Papers and Proceedings, May 1989), pp. 353–57.

Coe, David T., and Dennis J. Snower, "Fundamental Labor Market Reform" (unpublished; Washington: International Monetary Fund, 1995).

Cooper, Russell W., and Andrew John, "Coordinating Coordination Failures in Keynesian Models," *Quarterly Journal of Economics*, Vol. 103 (August 1988), pp. 441–63.

Diamond, Peter A., "Aggregate Demand Management in Search Equilibrium," *Journal of Political Economy*, Vol. 90 (October 1982), pp. 881–94.

Dixon, Huw, "A Simple Model of Imperfect Competition with Walrasian Features," *Oxford Economic Papers*, Vol. 39 (March 1987), pp. 134–60.

_____, "Unions, Oligopoly and the Natural Range of Employment," *Economic Journal*, Vol. 98 (December 1988), pp. 1127–47.

_____, and Neil Rankin, "Imperfect Competition and Macroeconomics: A Survey," *Oxford Economic Papers*, Vol. 46 (April 1994), pp. 171–99.

Drèze, Jacques, Edmond Malinvaud, and others, "Growth and Employment: The Scope of an European

Initiative," *European Economic Review*, Vol. 38 (April 1994), pp. 489–504.

Friedman, Milton, "The Role of Monetary Policy," *American Economic Review*, Vol. 58 (March 1968), pp. 1–17.

Gordon, Robert J., "What Is New-Keynesian Economics?" *Journal of Economic Literature*, Vol. 28 (September 1990), pp. 1115–71.

Greenwald, Bruce C., and Joseph E. Stiglitz, "Examining Alternative Macroeconomic Theories," *Brookings Papers on Economic Activity*, No. 1 (1988), pp. 207–60.

Grubb, David, "Unemployment and Related Welfare Benefits," in *OECD Jobs Study: Evidence and Explanations* (Paris: Organization for Economic Cooperation and Development, 1994).

Howitt, Peter, "Transactions Costs in the Theory of Unemployment," *American Economic Review*, Vol. 75 (March 1985), pp. 88–100.

Kaldor, Nicholas, "Wage Subsidies as a Remedy for Unemployment," *Journal of Political Economy*, Vol. 44 (December 1936), pp. 721–42.

Kalecki, Michal, "The Determinants of the Distribution of the National Income," *Econometrica*, Vol. 6 (April 1938), pp. 97–112.

Keynes, John Maynard, *The General Theory of Employment, Interest, and Money* (London: Macmillan, 1936).

______, "Relative Movements of Real Wages and Output," *Economic Journal*, Vol. 49 (March 1939), pp. 34–51.

King, Robert G., and Charles I. Plosser, "Money, Credit and Prices in a Real Business Cycle," *American Economic Review*, Vol. 74 (June 1984), pp. 363–80.

King, Robert G., Charles I. Plosser, and Sergio Rebelo (1988a), "Production, Growth and Business Cycles I: The Basic Neoclassical Model," *Journal of Monetary Economics*, Vol. 21 (March/May 1988), pp. 195–232.

______ (1988b), "Production, Growth and Business Cycles II: New Directions," *Journal of Monetary Economics*, Vol. 21 (March/May 1988),pp. 309–41.

Kydland, Finn E., and Edward C. Prescott, "Time to Build and Aggregate Fluctuations," *Econometrica*, Vol. 50 (November 1982), pp. 1345–70.

Layard, P. Richard G., and Stephen J. Nickell, "The Case for Subsidizing Extra Jobs," *Economic Journal*, Vol. 90 (March 1980), pp. 51–73.

______, and Richard Jackman, *Unemployment: Macroeconomic Performance and the Labour Market* (Oxford and New York: Oxford University Press, 1991).

Lilien, David M., "Sectoral Shifts and Cyclical Unemployment," *Journal of Political Economy*, Vol. 90 (August 1982), pp. 777–93.

Lindbeck Assar, and Dennis J. Snower, "Wage Setting, Unemployment, and Insider-Outsider Relations," *American Economic Review*, Vol. 76 (May 1986), pp. 235–9.

______ (1987a), "Union Activity, Unemployment Persistence, and Wage-Employment Ratchets," *European Economic Review*, Vol. 31 (February/March 1987), pp. 157–67.

______ (1987b), "Strike and Lock-Out Threats and Fiscal Policy," *Oxford Economic Papers*, Vol. 39 (December 1987), pp. 760–84.

______ (1987c), "Transmission Mechanisms from the Product to the Labor Market," Institute for International Economic Studies Seminar Paper No. 403 (Stockholm, Sweden: University of Stockholm, December 1987).

______ (1988a), "Cooperation, Harassment, and Involuntary Unemployment," *American Economic Review*, Vol. 78 (March 1988), pp. 167–88.

______ (1988b), "Long-Term Unemployment and Macroeconomic Policy," *American Economic Review*, Vol. 78 (Papers and Proceedings, May 1988), pp. 38–43.

______, "How Are Product Demand Changes Transmitted to the Labor Market?" *Economic Journal*, Vol. 104 (March 1994), pp. 386–98.

Long, John B., Jr., and Charles I. Plosser, "Real Business Cycles," *Journal of Political Economy*, Vol. 91 (February 1983), pp. 39–69.

Lucas, Robert E., Jr., "Expectations and the Neutrality of Money," *Journal of Economic Theory*, Vol. 4 (April 1972), pp. 103–24.

______, "An Equilibrium Model of the Business Cycle," *Journal of Political Economy*, Vol. 83 (December 1975), pp. 1113–44.

______, and Leonard A. Rapping, "Real Wages, Employment, and Inflation," *Journal of Political Economy*, Vol. 77 (No. 5, 1969), pp. 721–54.

Malinvaud, Edmond, *The Theory of Unemployment Reconsidered* (Oxford: Blackwell, 1977).

Mankiw, N. Gregory, "Small Menu Costs and Large Business Cycles: A Macroeconomic Model of Monopoly," *Quarterly Journal of Economics*, Vol. 100 (May 1985), pp. 529–37.

______, "Imperfect Competition and the Keynesian Cross," *Economics Letters*, Vol. 26 (No. 1, 1988), pp. 7–13.

Manning, Alan, "An Integration of Trade Union Models in a Sequential Bargaining Framework," *Economic Journal*, Vol. 97 (March 1987), pp. 121–39.

McDonald, Ian M., and Robert M. Solow, "Wage Bargaining and Employment," *American Economic Review*, Vol. 71 (December 1981), pp. 896–908.

Mortensen, Dale T., "Job Search and Labor Market Analysis," in *Handbook of Labor Economics*, Vol. 2, ed. by Orley Ashenfelter and P. Richard G. Layard (Amsterdam and New York: North-Holland, 1986).

Muellbauer, John, and Richard Portes, "Macroeconomic Models with Quantity Rationing," *Economic Journal*, Vol. 88 (December 1978), pp. 788–821.

Oswald, Andrew J., "The Microeconomic Theory of the Trade Union," *Economic Journal*, Vol. 92 (September 1982), pp. 576–95.

______, "The Economic Theory of Trade Unions: An Introductory Survey," *Scandinavian Journal of Economics*, Vol. 87 (No. 2, 1985), pp. 160–93.

Pagano, Marco, "Imperfect Competition, Underemployment Equilibria and Fiscal Policy," *Economic Journal*, Vol. 100 (June 1990), pp. 440–63.

Phelps, Edmund S., "Money Wage Dynamics and Labor Market Equilibrium," in *Microeconomic Foundations of Employment and Inflation Theory*, ed. by Edmund S. Phelps (New York: Norton, 1970).

______, *Structural Slumps: The Modern Equilibrium Theory of Unemployment, Interest, and Assets* (Cambridge, Massachusetts: Harvard University Press, 1994).

______, "Wage Subsidy Programs: Alternative Designs," in *Unemployment Policy*, ed. by Guillermo de la Dehesa and Dennis J. Snower (Cambridge: Cambridge University Press, 1995, forthcoming).

Pigou, A.C., *Industrial Fluctuations* (London: Macmillan, 1927).

Pissarides, Christopher A., "Short Run Equilibrium Dynamics of Unemployment, Vacancies, and Real Wages," *American Economic Review*, Vol. 75 (September 1985), pp. 676–90.

______, "Unemployment and Vacancies in Britain," *Economic Policy*, Vol. 1 (October 1986), pp. 499–559.

Rotemberg, Julio J., and Garth Saloner, "A Supergame-Theoretic Model of Price Wars During Booms," *American Economic Review*, Vol. 76, (June 1986), pp. 390–407.

Salop, Steven C., "A Model of the Natural Rate of Unemployment," *American Economic Review*, Vol. 69 (March 1979), pp. 117–25.

Shapiro, Carl, and Joseph E. Stiglitz, "Equilibrium Unemployment as a Worker Discipline Device," *American Economic Review*, Vol. 74 (June 1984), pp. 433–44.

Snower, Dennis J. (1983a), "Search, Flexible Wages and Involuntary Unemployment," Birkbeck College Discussion Paper in Economics No. 132 (London: Birkbeck College, University of London, January 1983).

______ (1983b), "Imperfect Competition, Under- employment and Crowding-Out," *Oxford Economic Papers*, Vol. 35 (November 1983, Supplement), pp. 245–70.

______ (1994a), "The Low-Skill, Bad-Job Trap," IMF Working Paper, WP/94/83 (Washington: International Monetary Fund, July 1994).

______ (1994b), "Poaching and Unemployment" (unpublished; 1994).

______ (1994c), "Converting Unemployment Benefits into Employment Subsidies," *American Economic Review*, Vol. 84 (Papers and Proceedings, May 1994), pp. 65–70.

______ (1995a), "The Simple Economics of Benefit Transfers," IMF Working Paper, WP/95/5 (Washington: International Monetary Fund, January 1995).

______ (1995b), "Unemployment Benefits versus Conditional Negative Income Taxes," IMF Working Paper (Washington: forthcoming, 1995).

Startz, Richard, "Monopolistic Competition as a Foundation for Keynesian Macroeconomic Models," *Quarterly Journal of Economics*, Vol. 104 (November 1989), pp. 737–52.

Stiglitz, Joseph E., "Equilibrium Wage Distributions," *Economic Journal*, Vol. 95 (September 1985), pp. 595–618.

Taylor, John B., "Staggered Wage Setting in a Macro Model," *American Economic Review*, Vol. 69 (Papers and Proceedings, May 1979), pp. 108–13.

Weiss, Andrew, "Job Queues and Layoffs in Labor Markets with Flexible Wages," *Journal of Political Economy*, Vol. 88 (June 1980), pp. 526–38.

Weitzman, Martin, "Some Macroeconomic Implications of Alternative Compensation Systems," *Economic Journal*, Vol. 93 (December 1983), pp. 763–83.

______, *The Share Economy: Conquering Stagflation* (Cambridge, Massachusetts: Harvard University Press, 1984).

V

Institutional Structure and Labor Market Outcomes: Western Lessons for European Countries in Transition

Robert J. Flanagan[1]

Slow growth of total factor productivity limited the economic achievements of centrally planned economies, and central planning itself produced many of the distortions that thwarted economic growth. Most observers presume that the substitution of market for planning processes should ultimately remove the distortions inherited from central planning and, in particular, produce improved labor allocation and effort. In contrast, the discussion of economic policy during the transition accords much less attention to an issue that occupies the research agenda of many western economists: the distortions and inefficiencies that may result from the institutional structure of labor markets in market economies. The outcome of this research is a conviction that labor market performance is not independent of the institutional structures governing pay determination and the regulation of employment relationships.

Changes in economic systems provide a unique opportunity to redesign basic institutional structures. The opportunity includes significant risks, however, as change is costly and, once chosen, institutions tend to remain frozen for long periods of time (North (1990)). Given the inertia and path dependence of institutions, a crucial challenge facing economies in transition is to develop institutional structures that facilitate or at least do not interfere with the labor market adjustments needed to improve economic performance. The challenge is all the more difficult because centrally planned economies in Central and Eastern Europe implemented much of their commitment to greater economic equality through administered wage structures and other benefits delivered through enterprises. The legacy of central planning makes a regime in which greater wage differentiation secures labor reallocation and related efficiency goals while taxes and transfers secure distributional goals more difficult to accept than in western market economies.

This paper attempts to provide guidance for such institutional choice, drawing on research and evidence from western market economies on the relationship between institutional structure and labor market performance. The paper is primarily concerned with the economies in transition in Central and Eastern Europe, although much of the discussion may also be relevant to the Baltic countries and the other countries of the former Soviet Union. Unemployment has been the main performance indicator considered in the western research, and the paper begins by considering whether this research is relevant to the different setting of transition labor markets—notably, the greater emphasis on labor reallocation. After concluding that the research findings are compatible with transition objectives, the rest of the paper examines the relationship between various institutional structures and labor market performance. The following section considers wage determination mechanisms—bargaining structure, minimum wages, and indexation. Succeeding sections examine the effects of employment security regulations and review alternative approaches to passive and active labor market policies. Conclusions and policy implications appear in the final section.

Distinctive Features of Transition Labor Markets

An assessment of the potential role of institutional structures in transition economies must reflect the differences in the labor market setting between transition economies and market economies. The key difference is the magnitude of the resource reallocation needed in transition economies in Central and Eastern Europe.[2] The inherited economic structure reflects the emphasis under central planning on production of goods over services and most intellectual work, and, within the production sector, heavy industry over consumer goods. To support these preferences with appropriate human capital, planners also encouraged vocational training over most varieties of university education. The implementation of national wage structures reduced overall wage dispersion (Atkinson and Mick-

---

[1]The author is Professor of Economics at the Graduate School of Business, Stanford University.

[2]A survey of labor markets in transition economies is presented in Flanagan (1994a).

lewright (1992)), although certain wage differentials were widened to encourage investment in vocational training and a reallocation of labor into heavy industry. Returns to university education fell drastically following the introduction of central planning (Adam (1984) and Flanagan (1994b)). By the late 1980s, the industrial structure and the distri-bution of human capital in the centrally planned and market economies of Europe differed markedly.

As a consequence, most countries entering the transition process face three interrelated dimensions of the problem of the reallocation of labor. First, the transitions require large-scale reallocations of labor from the state to the private sector. Only some of this shift will occur through changing governance arrangements—the privatization process. Second, there will be major interindustry resource shifts away from the heavy manufacturing industries emphasized by central planning toward consumer goods and services. Third, the first two changes should reduce the demand for workers with vocational education and increase the demand for workers with university education. The scale and the desired speed of these reallocations are larger and faster, respectively, than the norm in market economies. Moreover, with slow prospective labor force growth, little of the reallocation is likely to occur through the job choices of new labor force entrants.

Facing these challenges requires sharp changes in the pattern of wage differentials inherited from central planning and implies more dispersed wage structures for transition economies. Initially, large wage differentials will be necessary to reverse the industrial preferences of central planners and to overcome historical biases against highly educated labor. Some of the increased wage differentiation will be transitory, however, as supply responses to larger differentials will eventually reduce subsequent wage dispersion, although not to the central planning level.[3] Increased wage dispersion is already evident in Eastern European labor markets. In the Czech Republic and the Slovak Republic, earnings inequality increased substantially between 1988 and 1992, with the most rapid earnings increases occurring in the upper deciles of the income distribution (Vecernik (1994)). Polish data reveal similar general patterns but provide more detail. Wage dispersion has increased mainly for white-collar workers and particularly for relatively high-paid white-collar workers in the private sector (Rutkowski

(1994)). All indications are that the privatization process will increase earnings inequality. The inherent tendency toward increasing wage dispersion and its role in the labor reallocation process in transition economies is crucial in the assessment that follows of the relationship between institutional structure and economic performance.

The increasing wage differentiation in transition labor markets serves two purposes. First, it provides signals that facilitate the reallocation of labor from low-productivity to high-productivity sectors, a process that raises the aggregate productivity level. Second, with sufficiently flexible relative wages, and in the absence of constraints on labor mobility, such as insufficient housing, little structural unemployment need emerge from the transition process. Much of this paper considers the interaction of greater wage dispersion with various labor market regulations, based on experience in western market economies.

The setting of industrialized market economies in Europe, North America, and Japan during the postwar period has been quite different, and this has been reflected in the labor market research emphasis in these countries. In particular, during the 1970s and 1980s, structural unemployment in European countries—whose labor market institutions are distinctly different from those in North American countries and Japan—increased relative to the other industrial economies. Labor market analysts soon discovered that the character of European unemployment differed as well. Most notably, a declining probability of exiting unemployment characterized most European labor markets, producing comparatively long unemployment durations. Labor market research turned to the relationship between institutional structure and unemployment persistence.

How useful are the findings of this research for solving the labor market problems facing transition economies? Would transition economies draw different conclusions regarding the consequences of implementing alternative institutional structures depending on whether they were focusing on improving the reallocation of labor or reducing structural unemployment? In fact, the reallocation and structural unemployment objectives merge, for institutions that thwart the reallocation of labor tend to produce structural unemployment. The key issue is whether labor market institutions prevent the adjustment of relative wages. If they do not, serious reallocation and structural unemployment problems are unlikely to arise, absent significant barriers to mobility. However, to the extent that institutions prevent market-driven changes in relative wages, quantity responses dominate labor market adjustments, and structural unemployment emerges.

The corollary is that the effects of institutional structures are not independent of the market environment

---

[3]The initial size of wage differentials may be exacerbated by limitations on labor mobility. Although quit rates under central planning were at least as high as in most western market economies, the geographical dimension of labor mobility remains circumscribed by housing shortages, which prevent most workers from ranging outside commuting distances from their current residences. As a result, it seems likely that geographical wage differentials will be the last to disappear via supply adjustments.

in which they operate. Regulations or other labor market institutions that have a benign impact in an environment characterized by low, market-driven pay dispersion may thwart labor reallocation and produce structural unemployment in an environment characterized by high, market-driven pay dispersion. An evaluation of the effects of alternative institutions must consider the environment in which they will operate. The growth of European unemployment since the 1970s illustrates this point. While some cross-country analyses show links between unemployment and labor market institutions, including bargaining arrangements, active labor market policies, and characteristics of unemployment insurance systems (Layard, Nickell, and Jackman (1991)), the rise in European unemployment over time cannot in general be explained by institutional change. Indeed, some institutional changes that occurred since the 1970s should have produced a reduction in unemployment. Instead, the interaction of the growing market pressures for greater wage inequality with pre-existing institutional structures appears to have contributed to the rise of unemployment.

Wage Determination

Collective bargaining and minimum wage and indexation legislation provide the main direct institutional influence on wage levels and structure. As such, the exact institutional arrangements may influence both the speed of labor reallocation and the amount of cyclical unemployment. The main issues of institutional design are discussed below.

Collective Bargaining

Labor unions, which were little more than extensions of the Communist Party under central planning, have only recently been able to assume more of the traditional responsibility for collective bargaining of wages and working conditions in transition economies. The former union organizations have been transformed or displaced, and the new organizations have begun collective bargaining, although the exact institutional arrangements continue to evolve. Five years into the transition, union representation rarely reaches beyond the state sector, and it is far from complete there.[4] As wages tend to be higher in the private sector than in the state sector, union members on average appear to earn less than nonmembers, and there is little evidence of significant union wage impact within the state or private

sectors (Flanagan (1995)). Unions do not appear to have introduced significant wage distortions into labor markets during the early years of the economic transition. Nonetheless, research in western market economies indicates that the relationship between collective bargaining and economic performance in the longer term may depend on the structure of collective bargaining.

Collective bargaining may produce three types of outcomes influencing general labor market performance. First, unions can be a source of allocational distortions to the extent that they alter competitive wage structures. Second, collective bargaining can have macroeconomic impacts through its effects on aggregate real wage levels, the adjustment of real wages in the face of unemployment, and the inertia of inflation (for example, through indexation arrangements). Finally, collective bargaining contracts may regulate employment security, work rules, and other nonwage aspects of the employment relationship.

None of these outcomes is likely to be independent of the structural features of industrial relations systems, and the wide variety of structures in place in western countries provides a range of experience for assessing links between structure and performance. What lessons from research into the effects of collective bargaining institutions in market economies are most pertinent for transition economies?

A key characteristic of an industrial relations system is its bargaining structure, whether bargaining occurs at the level of the plant, firm, industry, or nation. During the postwar period, market economies have provided examples of both decentralized bargaining (for example, at the plant and company levels, as in the United States) and centralized bargaining (for example, at the national level, as has occurred at times in some Scandinavian countries). Despite the range of bargaining structures that have survived in market economies, many economists have argued that some structures produce superior labor market performance. Most of these arguments rest on macroeconomic performance measures.

Bargaining structure influences wage pressure through its effects on the externalities of the collective bargaining process, on the one hand, and through union bargaining power, on the other. With respect to the first kind of influence, each union when pressing wage demands under decentralized bargaining tends to consider only the interests of its members and to ignore the effect of the resulting price increases (for the output of the union's members) on other worker groups. The real wage gains of each union's members are accompanied by modest real wage losses for workers who are unorganized or represented by other unions. In contrast, centralized bargaining arrangements should create incentives and means to

---

[4]For example, in the Czech Republic in November 1994, about 75 percent of employees of state enterprises—but only 8 percent of workers in private firms—were union members (Flanagan (1995)). World Bank surveys of private manufacturing firms in other Eastern European countries found little or no evidence of unions in the private sector (Webster (1993a) and (1993b)).

internalize the externality by pursuing more moderate wage demands.[5]

Working against this effect is the relationship between bargaining structure and bargaining power. To the extent that there are more substitutes available for output produced in decentralized bargaining units, there will be greater elasticity of labor demand and less bargaining power than in centralized units. Taking into account both of these effects, some economists have hypothesized a hump-shaped relationship between bargaining structure and power, with industry-level bargaining arrangements (such as are found in many continental European countries) yielding the greatest wage pressures (Calmfors and Driffill (1988)).

While some authors have produced evidence supporting the superior performance of centralized bargaining, and others, citing the hump-shaped hypothesis, have argued for the superior performance of decentralized bargaining, most of the evidence is crude, amounting to little more than correlations between rough measures of centralization or "corporatism" and measures of macroeconomic performance (for example, unemployment and inflation). Moreover, these correlations have not remained stable over time. A cross-country regression of unemployment on several measures of labor market structure found a significant negative relation with bargaining coordination and a significant positive relation with union coverage for 1983–88 (Layard, Nickell, and Jackman (1991)). When the regression was run on 1993 data, however, the signs on these variables reversed, and the statistical significance disappeared (Forslund and Krueger (1994)). The fragility of estimated links between bargaining structure and macroeconomic performance reflects many factors, including severe measurement difficulties and inattention to the endogeneity of bargaining structures. Overall, empirical work has ignored important qualifications to the basic arguments noted above. Virtually all of these qualifications go in the direction of raising doubts about the advantages of centralized bargaining structures.

First, the internalization of externalities that can produce wage restraint in centralized bargaining structures depends crucially on whether different unionized work groups are substitutes or complements. When they are complements, the original argument in support of centralized bargaining holds. When different work groups are substitutes, however, employment under centralized bargaining is redistributed within the bargaining unit rather than lost, and wage pressure increases. In contrast, a wage increase by one decentralized union reduces the demand for its members while increasing the demand for substitutes represented by other unions—a consideration that would tend to moderate wage pressure. The advantage of centralized bargaining therefore depends on the pattern of union jurisdictions. Centralized bargaining will produce less wage pressure when unions establish a nationwide system of complementary jurisdictions. Otherwise, decentralized bargaining may be more advantageous. Recommendations concerning bargaining structure should thus consider the prevailing pattern of union jurisdictions.

Second, the international openness of an economy influences the macroeconomic consequences of different bargaining structures. Notably, the adverse effect of industry-level bargaining in a closed economy is tempered as that economy is opened to foreign trade. By providing a substitute for domestic production, import competition increases the elasticity of demand facing employers in industry-wide bargaining units and circumscribes their ability to pass on wages into prices. The higher risk of employment loss in the face of international competition should also mitigate wage demands. At the same time, increased foreign competition may exacerbate the wage pressures arising from centralized bargaining structures. As nominal wages increase, the weight of import prices will keep consumer prices from rising as fast as producer prices, with the result that the real consumption wages of union members will advance more rapidly than real product wages.

Third, experience in western countries has illustrated certain practical difficulties connected with the operation of so-called centralized bargaining systems. In most countries, the practical issue is: At how many levels will collective bargaining occur? In a decentralized bargaining system, bargaining will occur only at the lowest (firm or company) level. However, centralized bargaining always includes intermediate (industry) or local bargaining over the "implementation" of the central agreement. When there are several levels of bargaining, lower levels rarely restrict themselves to distributing the central wage agreement: they also exercise their bargaining power to influence wage levels, producing wage drift. In the most centralized systems, the impact of this wage drift is far from trivial, ranging from 30 to 60 percent in Scandinavian countries, for example (Flanagan (1990)).

A related issue concerns the relationship between bargaining structure and the scope of collective bargaining agreements. Central agreements tend to be skimpy. Bargainers tend to negotiate a set of issues that are common to all covered places of employment. Issues that tend to be unique to individual workplaces,

---

[5]Price spillovers are only one externality that may be internalized under centralized bargaining. Others include input price externalities (when wage increases in one bargaining unit raise the price of inputs to other sectors, thereby reducing output and employment in other bargaining units), fiscal externalities (when wage increases in one unit reduce employment and the tax base, requiring tax increases elsewhere), and unemployment externalities (when unemployment resulting from wage increases in one sector make it more difficult for all workers to find jobs). For further details, see Calmfors (1993) and Moene, Wallerstein, and Hoel (1993) and the references therein.

such as work rules, safety, and technical change, are unlikely to be addressed. This situation also explains the presence of multiple levels of bargaining in purportedly centralized systems. Lower levels of bargaining emerge not only to implement (and possibly add to) the wage provisions of the central agreement, but also to address pressing issues on which the central agreement is mute. To the extent that these issues involve flexibility of work assignments and other factors influencing productivity, the overall effect on labor costs may not be superior under centralized bargaining. In summary, substantial transactions costs can develop in centralized bargaining systems.

In fact, increased global competition and tensions within centralized bargaining units produced considerable decentralization of bargaining structures in western market economies during the 1980s and early 1990s (Hartog and Theeuwes (1993)). Notable decentralization occurred at both extremes of bargaining structures, as some Scandinavian countries abandoned centralized bargaining arrangements and some industry-wide and multicompany arrangements in the United States gave way to additional company- and plant-level bargaining (Organization for Economic Cooperation and Development (1994a)).

A fourth qualification to the empirical work produced thus far pertains to the importance of the reallocation of the labor force in transition economies in Central and Eastern Europe. Narrow wage distributions often accompany centralized bargaining institutions.[6] Pay compression policies can be reliably delivered only by centralized bargaining arrangements that overcome the relative wage comparisons that inevitably enter decentralized collective bargaining. Among market economies, the relatively compressed wage structures in countries with centralized bargaining most closely resemble wage structures in the former Soviet bloc countries under central planning and, in some cases, are even less dispersed (Boeri and Keese (1992)). Thus, a further concern with centralized bargaining in transition economies is that it might retard adjustment of relative wage structures and, hence, the reallocation of labor. One can see this development in the experience of western market economies since 1980. Countries that had decentralized bargaining structures at the beginning of the period (for example, the United Kingdom, the United States, Canada, Australia, and Japan) experienced substantial increases in earnings dispersion and small increases in unemployment in comparison with countries with more centralized structures (Organization for Economic Cooperation and Development (1994b), Vol. 1, p. 19).

There are important implications in this literature for the transition economies in Central and Eastern Europe. First, influencing the framework in which collective bargaining occurs is likely to be more useful for long-run economic performance than efforts to influence outcomes of the collective bargaining process. To date, transition economies have mainly adopted the latter approach through the application of incomes policies. Such policies have a poor record in market economies and appear particularly unsuitable for economic transition purposes (Flanagan (1994a)). Second, for transition economies, applying the empirical evidence from western market economies is less important than developing collective bargaining structures that fit the unique economic contexts of the former economies. This is partially because of the importance of ensuring relative wage adjustments in transition economies—an objective largely ignored in empirical studies in market economies—and partially because the evidence does not adequately capture how bargaining structures change in the face of changing economic circumstances.

Forty years of central planning may incline transition economies toward corporatist bargaining arrangements that facilitate dialogue between the government and major economic interest groups. However, several features of transition economies suggest that relatively decentralized bargaining structures will provide better long-run economic performance. To a large extent, the birth of new small private enterprises has led the transitions in Central and Eastern Europe. It is particularly important that the collective bargaining system permit the wage dispersion necessary to accommodate the considerable dispersion of productivity across these new business units. (This same consideration argues against the adoption of legal rules extending the terms of collective bargaining agreements to firms not involved in the negotiations, a common practice in continental Europe.) Moreover, a major reorientation of international trade has accompanied the economic transitions. The expansion of trade with the western market economies weakens the attractiveness of centralized bargaining structures, for reasons noted above. Evidence from western market economies also warns against the transactions costs of the multiple levels of bargaining that accompany so-called centralized bargaining systems.

Minimum Wages and Indexation

Most market economies have established statutory minimum wages covering some (but usually not all) groups in the labor force. Although these minimum wages have generally been adopted as an antipoverty policy, economic analysis has suggested a long list of potential impacts that would tend to counter any effects that such legislation might have to reduce poverty in competitive labor markets. Minimum

---

[6]Indeed, narrow wage dispersions have occasionally been proposed as indications of centralization (Freeman (1988)).

wages may reduce employment, induce substitution between covered and uncovered employment categories, raise unemployment, lower labor force participation, reduce training opportunities for unskilled workers (by precluding the use of training wages sufficiently low to cover the costs of general training), and raise prices. In addition, the correlation between low wages and low family income may be weak: in the United States, many workers subject to the minimum wage are youths from families with incomes well above the poverty line (Gramlich (1976)). In short, limited distributional benefits appear to be purchased with significant allocational costs and deadweight losses. Only in monopsonistic labor markets would a carefully set minimum wage raise both wages and employment.

Empirical research has largely focused on the employment effects of minimum wages, drawing on evidence from several countries. Time-series studies using data for the entire economy have documented the negative employment effects of increases in the minimum wage and extensions of coverage (Brown, Gilroy, and Kohen (1982)). Recently, however, more disaggregated studies in the United States and the United Kingdom have found quite different employment impacts. Some studies have examined how firms in low-wage, seemingly competitive industries respond to minimum wage increases that require a substantial adjustment in their wage scales. Contrary to the predictions of the competitive model, (1) employment appears to increase in the firms experiencing the largest statutory shock to their wage structure and (2) most employers do not make available a special subminimum wage to teenage employees, whose productivity is presumably relatively low (Katz and Krueger (1992), and Card and Krueger (1994)). Studies contrasting teenage employment changes in the United States between states that increase their minimum wage and states that do not also fail to find negative employment effects (Card (1992)). Examining policy change in the other direction, a study found that the failure of British Wage Councils to raise minimum wages as rapidly as average wages during the 1980s did not increase adult employment and may even have reduced it in a few sectors (Machin and Manning (1994)).

The results from these studies have not been fully reconciled with the time-series findings. Not all of the adjustments included in the time-series measurements are captured in the industry case studies, for example. The relationship between higher minimum wages and the closing of firms or the discouragement of new entrants into the industry are generally not captured. The effect of the policy on school enrollment (Neumark and Wascher (1994)) and the substitution of part-time for full-time employment opportunities—an empirically important impact in some past studies (Gramlich (1976))—is also not captured. The studies also vary in their ability to control for non-minimum-wage influences on the employment of low-wage groups. Finally, it is difficult to assess the role of noncompliance in these results. While prior work has shown noncompliance to be empirically important, the case studies have generally relied on wage data provided by managers, who are unlikely to report clearly illegal wages. Nonetheless, these studies suggest that the effects of moderate changes in minimum wages on employment levels may be much smaller than originally believed, perhaps reflecting the presence of employer monopsony power in labor markets with limited information.

Most minimum wage policies place a floor under the nominal wages of covered workers. The real effects of such policies are therefore "repealed" over time by inflation. Some countries effectively place a floor under real wages by indexing the nominal minimum wages to a measure of inflation, thereby preserving both low-paid workers' higher relative wages and the real effects of those wages over time. In countries with high and variable inflation rates, a broader range of wages may be indexed to inflation via collective bargaining agreements or political action. Such wide-ranging efforts to protect the living standards of workers can have undesirable macroeconomic consequences, however.

The effects of mandated indexation depend on the nature of inflation. Inflation resulting from demand shocks does not imply downward real wage adjustments, and widespread indexation of wages does not adversely affect the adjustment of the economy. When inflation results from supply shocks, however, as in the case of transition economies in Eastern Europe, real wages should fall. Efforts to preserve real wages, whether through collective bargaining or widespread wage indexation, will produce a wage-price spiral and increase unemployment. Experience in Italy during the 1970s and 1980s provides an example. The adverse consequences are strongest for indexation arrangements linking wages to consumer price indices. Indexation linking wages to producer prices instead would connect wages more directly to profits, thereby mitigating the effects discussed above. The lessons learned from the effects of indexation during the supply shocks of the 1970s, as well as of the lower inflation rates in recent years, have resulted in a relaxation of indexation arrangements in most industrial countries.

Concluding Comments on Wage Determination

This section has considered the effects of institutions that influence the level and dispersion of wages. The impact of institutionally determined wage floors, whether established by collective bargaining or by minimum wage legislation, is likely to depend on the economic environment to which they are applied. Wage floors will have more adverse effects when they are established in real—rather than nominal—terms and when market forces call for increased—rather than decreased—wage dispersion. For reasons discussed in the previous section, transition economies require greater wage differentiation, so that the potential for harmful effects from the establishment of wage floors is great. To date, this potential has not been realized in the countries of Central and Eastern Europe, where the impact of unions on wages has been small. Most of these countries have set minimum wages well below average wages, avoided rigid indexation arrangements, and allowed the minimum wage to fall as a percent of average wages to levels well below those in industrialized market economies.

In contrast, the transition process in eastern Germany was accompanied by a commitment, negotiated by the west German unions, to equalize wages between the eastern and western parts of Germany over a brief period despite large productivity differences between the two regions. A recent analysis of employment adjustments in "two-digit" manufacturing industries in eastern and western Germany between 1991 and 1993 indicates that high-wage policies are very costly in transition economies. FitzRoy and Funke (1995) demonstrate that employment elasticities are higher in eastern Germany, and that employment losses from the high-wage policy were largest for unskilled workers in the east.

Central planning regimes appeared to deliver income equality through narrow administrative wage structures. Yet support of institutional arrangements permitting greater wage dispersion and flexibility need not abandon equity objectives. Government tax and transfer programs offer more powerful—and, according to recent research (Saint-Paul (1994)), more efficient—means of redistribution. In contrast, the effect of minimum wage regulation and other pay compression policies on the distribution of individual earnings is to a considerable extent undone by the mobility available to individuals through the earnings structure. Changes of employers, promotions, layoffs, and variation in effort under incentive payments systems all tend to rearrange the relative earnings of individuals. With so many workers changing their relative earnings position during even short periods of time, policy-induced changes in the earnings structure are not powerful influences on overall equality.

Employment Security Regulation

Dismissal legislation may provide procedures for addressing either arbitrary dismissals that lack good cause or dismissals in response to economic conditions, or both. This section considers experience with the regulation of economic dismissals. The discussion focuses on labor market effects of such legislation. Statutory dismissal legislation exists in most industri-

alized economies. Dismissal statutes most frequently require advance notice of economic dismissals and may also require severance payments. Although requirements vary across countries, dismissal costs are generally highest in Southern Europe and for white-collar workers. Statutory severance payments are compensatory, requiring salary payments ranging up to one year for blue-collar workers and two years for white-collar workers. Penalties for unfair dismissals are somewhat higher but do not exceed four years' salary (Organization for Economic Cooperation and Development (1993), Chapter 3).

Outside Europe, dismissal legislation is less common. In countries without statutes, such as the United States, similar protections may arise through two methods. First, collective bargaining contracts often include advance notice or severance payments similar to European legislation. Second, judicial decisions can set standards for wrongful dismissals through reinterpretations of the common law (Mendelsohn (1990)). In the United States, the financial consequences of wrongful dismissals can be more severe than in Europe because the courts permit punitive damages and place less stringent limitations on the period of compensatory damages than do European statutes.

Dismissal regulations may retard but not stop the release of workers from declining firms and industries. The effect on the reallocation of labor input should be more muted, if it exists at all, as variations in hours of work per employee can offset lack of variation in the number of employees. Relative to an unregulated labor market, dismissal costs should produce larger reductions in average weekly hours in declining sectors and larger increases in average weekly hours in expanding sectors, tending to offset the employment transfers inhibited by dismissal regulations. The initial response to changes in demand is a change in hours worked. If the change in demand is eventually perceived as permanent, employment will subsequently adjust. Eventually, the total adjustment in labor input is approximately the same in countries with and without formal dismissal regulations (Houseman and Abraham (1993)). That is, the regulations tend to encourage work sharing, rather than layoff regimes. Moreover, with sufficiently rapid labor force growth, new labor force entrants can compensate to some extent for a lack of interindustry transfers.

The relationship between dismissal rules and labor reallocation in advanced market economies has received little empirical attention. The study that addresses the link with reallocation most explicitly finds only weak effects, tending to confirm the foregoing analysis. Burgess (1994) develops several measures of speed of labor adjustment at the two-digit industry level (including the cross-industry variance of employment growth, the deviation between actual and equilibrium employment, and the persistence of employment disequilibrium), but most of these measures are not significantly related to the strength of employment protection regulations. (The study does not control for other factors that might be influencing the cost or speed of adjustment during the period, however.) More broadly, several analyses of European labor markets (reviewed in Flanagan (1987)) found no indication of increasing mismatches between job vacancies and the unemployed during periods of change in dismissal regulations.

Dismissal restrictions can reduce the overall level of employment and alter the duration structure of unemployment, however. By raising the cost of employment, dismissal regulations will tend to reduce the level of employment (while increasing the cyclical variance in weekly hours worked), and there is some rough evidence that higher severance pay requirements are associated with lower employment-population ratios (Lazear (1990)). The effect on unemployment is theoretically ambiguous, because in raising the cost of dismissals (a flow into unemployment), the legislation also discourages hiring (a flow out of unemployment). That is, dismissal regulations tend to raise the employment security of the employed and reduce the employment prospects of those who are not employed. Whatever the effect on overall unemployment, the increased reluctance of employers to hire new workers contributes to longer unemployment durations, which can have detrimental effects on the quality of the labor force. This relationship is confirmed in a study by the Organization for Economic Cooperation and Development (OECD), which found that countries requiring higher individual severance payments tended to have higher long-term (greater than one year) unemployment rates (Organization for Economic Cooperation and Development (1993)).

The recent history of dismissal legislation in OECD countries cautions against simple extrapolations of cross-section evidence to time-series developments. Since 1980, European countries that have altered their dismissal legislation have tended to lower the protections accorded workers. During this same period, European structural unemployment has increased. In the United States, judicial restrictions on terminations increased during the 1980s while the equilibrium unemployment rate apparently fell. In broad outline, these observations are the opposite of the implications drawn from cross-country analyses.

To summarize, research on western labor markets indicates that employment security regulations (1) influence both layoff and hiring behavior, (2) have an ambiguous effect on the level of unemployment, (3) influence the character of unemployment by contributing to longer durations of unemployment, and (4) influence the method rather than the scope of adjustments of labor input to demand shocks. In contrast, the key issue for economies in transition is whether dismissal legislation inhibits the reallocation of labor. The scale of reallocation required in mature

market economies is much smaller than in transition economies in Central and Eastern Europe, where, in principle, even small regulatory effects could retard the recovery of productivity. Interindustry employment transfers have been a key source of private sector growth during the early stages of the transitions. The size of the labor force has declined, and private firms have expanded mainly by hiring employees from state enterprises, rather than from the pool of unemployed. (This may reflect a tendency to associate the unemployed with low productivity.) There is evidence that private sector employers in the Czech Republic pay workers with recent unemployment experience less than they pay other workers with observationally equivalent human capital (Flanagan (1994b)). As long as the private sector grows less rapidly than the state sector declines, however, it is hard to view dismissal legislation as a restraint on the reallocation of labor. Western research on this issue, although slim, tends to cast doubt that employment security policies are a major barrier to labor reallocation.

Labor Market Policies

Market economies pursue both "active" and "passive" labor market policies. Passive measures, such as unemployment insurance and incentives for early retirement, provide a cushion or safety net to support the unemployed during periods of job search or to facilitate withdrawal from the labor force. Active measures seek to raise the odds of re-employment by improving the matching process, raising the productivity of the jobless, or subsidizing the employment of low-skill workers. With no official unemployment under central planning, the economic transition began without even rudimentary job-matching institutions and social safety nets, except those still provided by large state-owned enterprises. By 1992–93, most transition economies in Central and Eastern Europe had higher unemployment rates than most OECD countries but spent smaller percentages of their GDP on labor market policies. Moreover, public expenditures on labor market policy were concentrated on passive measures (Organization for Economic Cooperation and Development (1993)). This section considers lessons from research in market economies for the development of unemployment insurance systems and active labor market policies in transition economies.

Unemployment Insurance

Unemployment insurance exists in virtually all market economies to address the problem of risk aversion—a preference for a certain income stream over an uncertain income stream for a given expected income. Labor markets are notorious sources of income uncertainty; however, the efficiency gains from unemployment insurance systems are to some extent countered by the efficiency costs of moral hazard. These systems reduce the cost of unemployment, and workers can adopt behavior that influences the amount of unemployment that they incur. More specifically, unemployment insurance effectively raises the reservation wage—and also the wage aspirations—of unemployed workers. With a higher reservation wage, the unemployed reject more low-wage job offers and search longer before accepting jobs.[7] As a result, unemployment insurance should raise unemployment durations, as well as the wages of jobs ultimately accepted by covered workers. The existence of this insurance may also increase wage pressure in collective bargaining by reducing the economic losses of unemployment.

The scope of the potential moral hazard problem is governed by several parameters of an unemployment insurance system. The replacement ratio—the fraction of prior earnings replaced by this insurance—places a floor under the reservation wage, and benefit duration rules establish the effective period that the floor is in place. Eligibility rules determine how much of the work force is subject to unemployment insurance protection and incentives, thereby influencing the impact on aggregate unemployment.

After almost two decades of active research, there is now considerable evidence of the relationship between the parameters of the unemployment insurance system, unemployment, and wages in North America and Europe.[8] Unemployment benefits clearly extend the duration of unemployment by increasing the reluctance of the unemployed to accept a job. Most estimates of the elasticity of the expected duration of unemployment with respect to the replacement ratio ranged between 0.2 and 0.9. There is evidence that unemployment was more sensitive to the design of insurance systems in the early 1990s than in the 1980s (Forslund and Krueger (1994)). Moreover, the unemployment of younger workers and low-skill workers seems particularly responsive to changes in unemployment benefits. Related to this evidence are findings in the U.S. data that job acceptance rises dramatically just as unemployment benefits expire. (Most U.S. studies also find that more generous unemployment benefits raise the re-employment wage.) Long-duration unemployment itself discourages em-ployment through the depreciation of skills, reduced effectiveness of the job search, and the hiring reluctance of employers.

These findings have two implications for transition economies trying to cushion the blow of unemployment. The first is that relatively high replacement ratios, long benefit durations, and broad eligibility rules will produce higher unemployment. The second is that, because of the different labor market environment in transition economies, the elasticity of unemployment with respect to unemployment insurance parameters may be higher than estimated by research on market economies. Ultimately the moral hazard costs of an unemployment insurance system will depend on the interaction between the parameters of the system and the economic environment. Periods of growing wage dispersion should increase the unemployment produced by unemployment insurance, as an increasing fraction of wage offers are rejected by the unemployed because they fall below the reservation wage.

How can transition economies design unemployment compensation systems that address the demand for insurance while minimizing the costs of moral hazard? One approach is to limit the period of joblessness for which benefits are collected. Benefits are available for much shorter periods in the United States than in Europe, for example, and the incidence of long-duration unemployment is much lower in the United States. As noted above, however, this situation creates a notch that tends to concentrate job acceptance at the expiration date.

An alternative approach to stimulating greater search intensity is to combine unemployment insurance benefits with a re-employment bonus. The amount of the bonus could be fixed (for example, some multiple of a job seeker's weekly unemployment insurance payment) or could decline with the duration of unemployment. Field experiments of the effects of a fixed bonus held in three states of the United States found that such bonuses reduce the average spell of insured unemployment and, hence, unemployment payments. The magnitude of the effect depends on the size of the bonus, and the smallest experimental bonuses produced no effect. For more generous bonuses, reduced unemployment duration ranged from one half of a week to over one week.

The evidence on the net benefits of a re-employment bonus policy to the unemployment insurance system is more mixed, however. In one U.S. state, unemployment payments were reduced by more than the direct and administrative costs of the re-employment bonus program (Woodbury and Spiegelman (1987)), but the net benefits were negative in two other states because the bonus produced much smaller reductions in the spells of insured unemployment (Decker and O'Leary (1994)). The financial shortfall was modest, however, and net social benefits may well be positive

---

[7]Unemployment insurance may therefore interact importantly with other policies. In economies in which generous unemployment benefits establish high reservation wages, reducing wage floors established by collective bargaining or minimum wage legislation may have less effect on employment than in economies with less generous benefits.

[8]The research is too voluminous to cite, but extensive reviews of the evidence can be found in Atkinson and Micklewright (1992), Layard, Nickell, and Jackman (1991), and Bjorklund and Holmlund (1991), from which the material in this paragraph is freely drawn.

when reduced skill depreciation and other detrimental effects of long-term unemployment are considered.

A third proposal for encouraging unemployed job search would replace unemployment benefits with a negative income tax that is conditional on job search (Snower (1995, forthcoming)). This proposal improves search incentives because workers who find and accept jobs would lose only part of their negative income tax payments, in contrast to losing all of their unemployment benefits. By targeting low income directly, rather than one of its causes, the negative income tax also provides a more efficient approach to income redistribution. To date, no western country has adopted this approach, so there is no evidence on its effects.

Active Labor Market Policies

The goals of active labor market policies, which include public employment services, labor market training, youth employment measures, subsidized private employment, job creation in the public or nonprofit sectors, and vocational rehabilitation and work for the disabled, are to raise skills and improve job matching in the labor market. In principle, public investment in active labor market policy is an attractive approach to facilitating the reallocation of labor and reducing structural unemployment in transition economies. Unlike some of the institutions discussed above, active labor market policies are unlikely to interfere with the adjustment of relative wages (although to the extent that such programs provide an alternative to unemployment, they may stimulate more upward pressure on wage levels). Indeed, if classical market mechanisms for reallocating labor worked sufficiently rapidly, there would be little rationale for implementing active labor market policies. In principle, such policies can supplement the role of relative wage changes by accelerating the quantity responses to wage signals.

In practice, active labor market policies work through a variety of channels; like other policies, they can have unintended side effects. The potential effects are sufficiently diverse and complicated that the net policy impact cannot be predicted a priori (Calmfors (1994)). Virtually all industrialized market economies have experimented with active labor market policies over the past 30–35 years, and there is considerable cross-country variation in both the ratio of active to passive policies and the mix of active policies. The research strategy in the macroeconomic evaluations is to relate international variations in public expenditures on active labor market policy to international variations in macroeconomic performance. Unfortunately, these studies reach no consensus on the effects of active labor market policies. Some studies find that an increase in such expenditures reduces unemployment by more than the amount of program participation, re-

sulting in a net increase in employment (Layard, Nickell, and Jackman (1991)). Other studies find that the estimates of policy influence are quite fragile. For example, Forslund and Krueger (1994) find that the significant negative relationship between active labor market policy expenditures and unemployment reported by Layard, Nickell, and Jackman (1991) for 1983–88 turned positive (but insignificant) for 1993. Moreover, an OECD study found that the level of expenditure on active labor market policy had a negative effect on employment, although employment appeared to adjust more rapidly to output changes in countries with relatively high expenditures on active labor market policy (Organization for Economic Cooperation and Development (1993)). Most of the macroeconomic evaluations are subject to potentially serious methodological problems.[9]

Even if there were a consensus that expenditures on active labor market policies tend to produce favorable macroeconomic outcomes, practical policy questions remain. In particular, how should money for active labor market policy be spent, given the many varieties of active labor market policy? Which policies in the active labor market policy arsenal produce superior outcomes? The macroeconomic evaluation studies will not answer such questions. One must turn instead to the microeconomic evaluations of individual programs. Such evaluations now constitute a modest cottage industry, whose size tends to be inversely related to the scale of active labor market policy expenditures in the country under study.

The large body of microeconomic evaluation literature is not easily summarized because its results are so diverse. One review of U.S. policies noted a tendency for programs to work better for women and less educated individuals but also found little evidence of effective employment and training policies for seriously disadvantaged males (Haveman and Hollister (1991)). Reviews of the few Swedish evaluations of training programs conclude that there is little evidence of the effectiveness of government training programs (Bjorklund (1991), and Forslund and Krueger (1994)). In summary, microeconomic evaluations of labor market policies in western market economies do not support a reliable prediction that public training programs will improve either the earnings or the employment prospects of the unemployed.

In transition economies, this conclusion is also likely to hold true for the vocationally oriented training that has comprised many programs in market economies. As noted earlier, the former economies have begun their transitions with an excess supply of

---

[9]The cross-country studies generally do not address the endogeneity of active labor market policy expenditures. As these typically increase with unemployment, the appropriate interpretation of the correlations between policy expenditures and unemployment is somewhat uncertain.

vocational training. A major task is to increase the proportion of the labor force with a university education—more of a task for the formal education system than active labor market policy.

Wage subsidies appear to be an attractive policy alternative to training or job matching—or both—in a full-information labor market; by driving a wedge between the wage that employers pay and the wage that workers receive, subsidies can increase employment. Moreover, subsidy programs can be targeted toward particular groups, such as new entrants into the labor force (to provide work experience and on-the-job training), or to the long-duration unemployed (to prevent skill depreciation). However, experience with wage subsidies in market economies also illustrates certain behavioral responses that can undermine the overall effectiveness of active labor market policies. These (and other) programs contain deadweight losses to the extent that some people hired under the program would have been hired without it. In addition, employers clearly face financial incentives to substitute members of targeted groups for members of nontargeted groups. While deadweight losses and substitution effects are often ignored in evaluation studies, these losses, when considered, tend to be large.[10]

Evidence from the United States also indicates that the effect of programs depends on the information structure of labor markets. Subject to deadweight losses and substitution effects, wage subsidies should theoretically provide more jobs in a full-information world. When employers are imperfectly informed about workers' productive potentials, however, workers with superior abilities have an interest in signaling their superiority in a credible manner, that is, in a way that would be more costly for less-qualified workers to imitate. Remaining outside labor market programs can provide such a signal, as this option is not available to low-quality workers, who would be subject to dismissal once their productivity was observed. Those who participate in the programs are thus effectively stigmatized as low-quality workers. This is a serious practical concern in some wage subsidy programs. Employer participation in targeted wage subsidy programs in the United States has been low, for example, and there is evidence that employers prefer to hire unsubsidized workers.[11]

One lesson of the various behavioral responses to active labor market policies is that design features may have a crucial influence on program impact. For example, although many supporters of active labor market policies believe that targeting policies toward specific groups raises the effectiveness of the policies, targeting under conditions of asymmetric information may, by stigmatizing the targets, harm the employment prospects of groups that need help. It may be more effective to provide wage subsidies directly to employers (rather than giving workers subsidy vouchers), but targeting the groups for which a subsidy can be used tends to raise the signaling issue again.

With the low level of involuntary labor market transitions under central planning, Eastern European countries had little need for the labor market policy apparatus common to most western industrial countries. The transition from central planning has produced a greater emphasis on passive over active labor policies than is typical of mature market economies, although traditional discussions of labor market policy often presume that active labor market policies are more likely to facilitate the labor reallocation required in transition economies. The experience in market economies reviewed in this section suggests that the ratio of passive to active labor market policy expenditures may be less important than the features of policy design. Although passive policies that support the unemployed without providing strong incentives to seek and accept work are not well suited for the transition, effective job-seeking incentives clearly can be embedded within passive policies. At the same time, evaluations of active labor market programs in market economies provide little evidence that they have fulfilled their promise in practice. Moreover, the effectiveness of each approach to labor market policy is limited in conditions of deficient demand, when the problem is one of insufficient job vacancies rather than of matching the unemployed to unfilled vacancies.

Conclusions

Transition economies face a relatively short window of opportunity to establish new institutional forms, which, once in place, are slow to change. The long-run purposes of their transitions would be better served if the development of long-run institutional structures that contribute to good labor market performance were encouraged over the implementation of short-run wage restraint policies that actually interfere with the objectives of the transitions and have a poor track record in western labor markets.

Unfortunately, research in industrialized market economies offers an unwelcome message. Efforts to provide the level of social welfare and low pay differentiation that were customary under central planning through direct labor market interventions will thwart the needed reallocation of labor resources and produce relatively high equilibrium unemployment. The unintended side effects of labor market interventions are particularly severe when market conditions

---

[10]In a review of the international evidence, Calmfors (1994) reports combined effects of deadweight and substitution losses of approximately 70–90 percent of the total cost of subsidy programs for several countries.

[11]For a more extended discussion of the evidence and consequences of asymmetric information in labor markets, see Flanagan (1993).

dictate wide pay dispersion. Labor market adjustments in the transition economies in Central and Eastern Europe would be better served if equity objectives were pursued through general tax and transfer policies rather than through labor market interventions.

Of the specific institutional structures reviewed, the conditions facing transition economies appear to provide a case for establishing relatively decentralized bargaining units. Minimum wages appear to be a particularly weak redistributional policy, as efficiency costs remain uncertain after 45 years of spirited research. There is a clear danger in placing a floor under wages in economies whose markets require greater wage differentiation; thus far, however, the floors established in transition economies have been well below the floors found in market economies. Employment security regulations appear to have a minor impact on the reallocation of labor input but contribute to long unemployment durations. The evidence on active labor market policies from industrialized market economies is very mixed and tends to support the conclusion that they have been more "promise than performance" thus far. Passive labor market policies do not directly encourage skill development and are subject to moral hazard; however, the redesign of such policies can reduce the moral hazard problems.

Bibliography

Adam, Jan, *Employment and Wage Policies in Poland, Czechoslovakia and Hungary Since 1950* (New York: St. Martin's Press, 1984).

Atkinson, Anthony B., and John Micklewright, *Economic Transformation in Eastern Europe and the Distribution of Income* (Cambridge and New York: Cambridge University Press, 1992).

Boeri, Tito, and Mark Keese, "Labour Markets and the Transition in Central and Eastern Europe," *OECD Economic Studies*, No. 18 (Spring 1992), pp. 133–63.

Bjorklund, Anders, "Comment on Haveman and Hollister," in *Labour Market Policy and Unemployment Insurance,* ed. by Anders Bjorklund and others (Oxford: Clarendon Press, 1991).

Bjorklund, Anders and Bertil Holmlund, "The Economics of Unemployment Insurance: The Case of Sweden," *Labour Market Policy and Unemployment Insurance*, ed. by Anders Bjorklund and others (Oxford: Clarendon Press, 1991).

Brown, Charles, Curtis Gilroy, and Andrew Kohen, "The Effect of the Minimum Wage on Employment and Unemployment," *Journal of Economic Literature*, Vol. 20 (June 1982), pp. 487–528.

Burgess, Simon M., "The Reallocation of Employment and the Role of Employment Protection Legislation," LSE Centre for Economic Performance Discussion Paper No. 193 (London: London School of Economics, April 1994).

Calmfors, Lars, "Centralisation of Wage Bargaining and Macroeconomic Performance: A Survey," *OECD Economic Studies*, No. 21 (Winter 1993), pp. 161–91.

______, "Active Labour Market Policy and Unemployment: A Framework for the Analysis of Crucial Design Features," OECD Labor Market and Social Policy Occasional Paper No. 15 (Paris, Organization for Economic Cooperation and Development, 1994).

______, and John Driffill, "Bargaining Structure, Corporatism and Macroeconomic Performance," *Economic Policy*, Vol. 3 (April 1988), pp. 13–61.

Card, David, "Using Regional Variation in Wages to Measure the Effects of the Federal Minimum Wage," *Industrial and Labor Relations Review*, Vol. 46 (October 1992), pp. 22–37.

______, and Alan B. Krueger, "Minimum Wages and Employment: A Case Study of the Fast Food Industry in New Jersey and Pennsylvania," *American Economic Review*, Vol. 84 (September 1994), pp. 772–93.

Decker, Paul T., and Christopher J. O'Leary, "Evaluating Pooled Evidence from the Reemployment Bonus Experiments," W.E. Upjohn Institute Staff Working Paper No. 94–28 (Kalamazoo, Michigan: Upjohn Institute, July 1994).

FitzRoy, Felix, and Michael Funke, "Skills, Wages, and Employment in East and West Germany," IMF Working Paper, WP/95/4 (Washington: International Monetary Fund, January 1995).

Flanagan, Robert J., "Labor Market Behavior and European Economic Growth," in *Barriers to European Growth: A Transatlantic View*, ed. by Robert Z. Lawrence and Charles L. Schultze (Washington: Brookings Institution, 1987).

______, "Centralized and Decentralized Pay Determination in Nordic Countries," in *Wage Formation and Macroeconomic Policy in the Nordic Countries*, ed. by Lars Calmfors (Oxford: Oxford University Press, 1990).

______, "Can Political Models Predict Union Behavior?" in *Trade Union Behaviour, Pay Bargaining, and Economic Performance,* ed. by Robert J. Flanagan, Karl O. Moene, and Michael Wallerstein (Oxford: Clarendon Press, 1993).

______ (1994a), "Labor Market Responses to a Change in Economic System," in *Proceedings of the World Bank Annual Conference on Development Economics*, 1994 (Washington: World Bank, 1994).

______ (1994b), "Were Communists Good Human Capitalists?" Working Paper, Graduate School of Business, Stanford University (Stanford, California: June 1994).

______, "Wage Structure in the Transition of the Czech Economy," IMF Working Paper, WP/95/36 (Washington: International Monetary Fund, March 1995), and *IMF Staff Papers*, forthcoming.

Forslund, Anders, and Alan B. Krueger, "An Evaluation of the Swedish Active Labor Market Policy: New and Received Wisdom," NBER Working Paper No. 4802 (Cambridge, Massachusetts: National Bureau of Economic Research, July 1994).

Freeman, Richard B., "Labor Market Institutions and Economic Performance," *Economic Policy*, Vol. 3 (April 1988), pp. 64–80.

Gramlich, Edward M., "Impact of Minimum Wages on Other Wages, Employment, and Family Incomes," *Brookings Papers on Economic Activity*, No. 2 (1976), pp. 409–61.

Hartog, Joop, and Jules Theeuwes, *Labor Market Contracts and Institutions: A Cross-National Approach* (Amsterdam, London, New York, and Tokyo: North-Holland, 1993).

Haveman, Robert, and Robinson Hollister, "Direct Job Creation: Economic Evaluation and Lessons for the United States and Western Europe," in *Labour Market Policy and Unemployment Insurance*, ed. by Anders Bjorklund and others (Oxford: Clarendon Press, 1991).

Houseman, Susan N., and Katharine G. Abraham, "Labor Adjustment Under Different Institutional Structures: A Case Study of Germany and the United States," NBER Working Paper No. 4548 (Cambridge, Massachussets: National Bureau of Economic Research, October 1993).

Katz, Lawrence F., and Alan B. Krueger, "The Effect of the Minimum Wage on the Fast-Food Industry," *Industrial and Labor Relations Review*, Vol. 46 (October 1992), pp. 6–21.

Layard, P. Richard G., Stephen J. Nickell, and Richard Jackman, *Unemployment: Macroeconomic Performance and the Labour Market* (Oxford and New York: Oxford University Press, 1991).

Lazear, Edward P., "Job Security Provisions and Unemployment," *Quarterly Journal of Economics*, Vol. 105 (August 1990), pp. 699–726.

Machin, Stephen, and Alan Manning, "The Effects of Minimum Wages on Wage Dispersion and Employment: Evidence from the U.K. Wage Councils," *Industrial and Labor Relations Review*, Vol. 47 (January 1994), pp. 319–29.

Mendelsohn, S., "Wrongful Termination Litigation in the United States and Its Effect on the Employment Relationship," OECD Labor Market and Social Policy Occasional Paper No. 3 (Paris: Organization for Economic Cooperation and Development, September 1990).

Moene, Karl O., Michael Wallerstein, and Michael Hoel, "Bargaining Structure and Economic Performance," in *Trade Union Behaviour, Pay Bargaining, and Economic Performance,* ed. by Robert Flanagan, Karl O. Moene, and Michael Wallerstein (Oxford: Clarendon Press, 1993).

Neumark, David, and William Wascher, "Minimum Wage Effects on Employment and School Enrollment," NBER Working Paper No. 4679 (Cambridge, Massachusetts: National Bureau of Economic Research, March 1994).

North, Douglass C., *Institutions, Institutional Change, and Economic Performance* (Cambridge and New York: Cambridge University Press, 1990).

Organization for Economic Cooperation and Development, *Employment Outlook* (Paris: Organization for Economic Cooperation and Development, 1993).

______ (1994a), *Employment Outlook* (Paris: Organization for Economic Cooperation and Development, 1994).

______ (1994b), *The OECD Jobs Study: Evidence and Explanations* (Paris: Organization for Economic Cooperation and Development, 1994).

Rutkowski, Jan, "Changes in Wage Structure and in Returns to Education During Economic Transition: The Case of Poland," Working Paper, Center for International Studies (Princeton, New Jersey: Woodrow Wilson School, Princeton University, 1994).

Saint-Paul, Gilles, "Do Labor Market Rigidities Fulfill Distributive Objectives? Searching for the Virtues of the European Model," *IMF Staff Papers*, Vol. 41 (December 1994), pp. 624–42.

Snower, Dennis J., "Unemployment Benefits Versus Conditional Negative Income Taxes," IMF Working Paper (Washington: forthcoming, 1995).

Vecernik, Jiri, "Changing Earnings Inequality Under the Economic Transformation: The Czech and Slovak Republics, 1984–92," Working Paper, Institute of Sociology, Academy of Sciences (Prague, 1994).

Webster, Leila M. (1993a), "The Emergence of Private Sector Manufacturing in Hungary: A Survey of Firms," World Bank Technical Paper No. 229 (Washington: World Bank, 1993).

______ (1993b), "The Emergence of Private Sector Manufacturing in Poland: A Survey of Firms," World Bank Technical Paper No. 237 (Washington: World Bank, 1993).

Woodbury, Stephen A., and Robert G. Spiegelman, "Bonuses to Workers and Employers to Reduce Unemployment: Randomized Trials in Illinois," *American Economic Review*, Vol. 77 (September 1987), pp. 513–30.

VI

How Large Was the Output Collapse in Russia? Alternative Estimates and Welfare Implications

Evgeny Gavrilenkov and Vincent Koen[1]

Since the onset of economic transition in Russia, the perception has become increasingly widespread that output and living standards are highly unlikely to have dropped as much as the official numbers indicate.[2] Many observers find it hard to believe that the size of the Russian economy really halved between the late 1980s and 1994. This judgment, however, remains very much an impressionistic one, relying on anecdotal or partial evidence rather than on a documented set of alternative estimates. The ambition of this paper is to show that the output decline was much less than what is recorded in the national accounts data published by the Russian State Committee for Statistics (Goskomstat). The paper also discusses some of the welfare implications of the fall and recomposition of output. It concludes that too many tears have been shed on measured output losses, and that the transition process itself should not be blamed for the dismal heritage with which it was endowed.

Output, of course, really did collapse in many sectors, owing, inter alia, to the breakdown of internal and external trading arrangements; the contraction in demand (for example, military procurement and investment programs); the compression of imports of some intermediate goods; price liberalization, insofar as changes in relative prices rendered some activities inviable; the archaic financial system, which limited enterprises' ability to engage in intertemporal substitution and hampered settlements; and domestic and cross-border "domino" or contagion effects. It cannot be ruled out a priori that the cumulative fall in production was even larger than the one experienced in the United States during the Great Depression of 1929–33 (Table 1)[3] and larger than any downturn registered in Russia during the previous seventy years.[4]

There are a number of reasons, however, to suspect that the official real GDP statistics are overstating the output collapse.[5] The traditional statistical apparatus, based on a census rather than a sampling approach, is obviously missing an increasingly large portion of economic activity, as publicly acknowledged by both the former head of Goskomstat (Guzhvin (1992)) and his successor (Yurkov (1994)).[6] Furthermore, the official data show an increasing discrepancy between output and consumption in many sectors, with the latter falling much less (or rising more) than the former.[7] Likewise, the official data imply a puzzling divergence between the huge decline in output and the much more resilient behavior of household incomes, which have tended to recover and by late 1994 had reverted to the level of the late 1980s.

Other indications supporting the presumption that output is higher than reported by Goskomstat include evidence from other transition economies. For example, Rajewski (1993) shows that the cumulative fall in real GDP in Poland from 1989 to 1991 was probably of the order of 5–10 percent, in stark contrast to the officially registered 18 percent drop, and that actual consumption also fell less, a result consistent with the reestimation of the decline in 1990 carried out earlier by Berg and Sachs (1992). According to the "Czech Economic Monitor" (1994) and the "Slovak Economic

---

[1]Evgeny Gavrilenkov is Acting Director of the Center for Economic Analysis under the Government of the Russian Federation. This paper was written while he was a visiting scholar at the Research Department of the IMF. Vincent Koen is an Economist in the Research Department. Comments from Anders Åslund, Andrew Berg, David T. Coe, François Lequiller, Bryan Roberts, Doris Ross, Mark Schaffer, and participants in an IMF seminar are gratefully acknowledged. However, the authors remain responsible for any judgments formulated in the paper, as well as for any remaining errors.

[2]See, for example, "Russian Agency Tracks Soviet-Style Economy as Free Market Thrives," *Wall Street Journal*, July 6, 1994, and "Services Take Lead in Russia," *Financial Times*, July 14, 1994.

[3]In Table 1, published yearly rates of change are chained to derive cumulative declines. As these rates of change are computed in different ways across countries, the resulting cumulative declines are not strictly comparable, but they are nevertheless relevant as a first approximation.

[4]See Gavrilenkov (1994b). Consumption, however, fell much more in 1941–42 than output, and much more than in the course of the transition.

[5]There are also reasons to doubt the accuracy of real GDP data, which for the past few years have been published two weeks after the end of the monthly period to which they relate, without any subsequent revisions. The only revision published so far was for 1991 as a whole, in which the decline originally estimated at 9 percent was adjusted to 13 percent.

[6]See also Koen (1994) and the references therein.

[7]The same divergence was noted for Poland by Berg (1993).

Table 1. Selected Countries in Transition: Cumulative Officially Registered Real Output Declines

(Percent change compared to base year)

Country	Output Measure	1990	1991	1992	1993
			Base year = 1989		
Albania	GDP	−10	−35	−41	upturn
	Industry[1]	−13	−50	−65	upturn
Bulgaria	GDP[2]	−12	−32	−36	−39
	Industry	−15	−37	−47	. . .
Czech Republic	GDP	−1	−15	−21	−21
	Industry	−3	−27	−37	−42
Slovak Republic	GDP	−2	−17	−22	−26
	Industry	−4	−21	−32	−39
Poland	GDP	. . .	−12	−18	upturn
	Industry	. . .	−24	−33	upturn
Romania	GDP	−6	−18	−29	upturn
	Industry	−18	−34	−49	. . .

Country	Output Measure	1991	1992	1993	1994
			Base year = 1990		
Belarus	GDP	−1	−11	−19	−36
	Industry	−2	−11	−21	−33
Estonia	GDP	−12	−28	−31	upturn
	Industry	−10	−45	−65	. . .
Kazakhstan	GDP	−12	−23	−33	−50
	Industry	−1	−14	−28	−48
Latvia	GDP	−8	−42	−49	upturn
	Industry	−1	−35	. . .	. . .
Lithuania	GDP	−13	−46	−55	upturn
	Industry	−5	−54	. . .	. . .
Russia	GDP	−13	−30	−38	−47
	Industry	−8	−25	−37	−50
Ukraine	GDP	−12	−27	−37	−50
	Industry	−5	−11	−18	−41

Memorandum items

United States (Great Depression)	GNP	1930	1931	1932	1933
			Base year = 1929		
		−10	−17	−29	−31

U.S.S.R. (World War II)	Industry	1941	1942	1943	
			Base year = 1940		
		−2	−23	upturn	

Sources: Central Statistical Administration of the U.S.S.R.; Statistical Committee of the Commonwealth of Independent States; Goskomstat of the Russian Federation; Rajewski (1993); United States Bureau of the Census (1975); World Bank (1994); statistical offices of Albania, Poland, Romania, Bulgaria, the Czech Republic, and the Slovak Republic; and authors' calculations.

Note: In some cases, pretransition output peaked before 1989–90.

[1]Gross sales used for Albania; for the other countries, gross output used.

[2]The figures shown for Bulgaria do not reflect the large upward revision of the real GDP series for 1990–91 implemented by the statistical authorities in 1992.

Monitor" (1994), similar results obtain for the Czech Republic and the Slovak Republic. Finally, it could be conjectured that, if half of the economy had genuinely evaporated, major social upheavals would already have been observed.

Some of these reasons may be less than fully compelling. If underground activities represent a broadly constant share of the officially measured economy, as they do in many countries, ignoring the shadow sector will not bias growth rates. However, underrecording is most blatant in those sectors that are expanding, particularly the new private entities, reflecting the highly plausible motivation of tax evasion, as well as the attempt to avoid all kinds of government regulations. Consumption may be declining less than output because less of the latter is wasted on the way to the final user, because the share of investment goods is falling, or because of destocking. Also, the monetization of transactions associated with the move to a market economy would in itself increase household money incomes and expenditures. Lastly, the Russian population has endured so much hardship in the past that it may be showing more patience than outsiders would expect.

This paper focuses on the size of the output collapse and on its welfare implications but will not dwell on its causes. Much of the discussion is relevant for the other countries of the former Soviet Union, where large declines in output have analogously been recorded (Table 1).[8] The paper proceeds as follows. The first section discusses the extent to which pre-transition output is overstated by the official statistics, and what the magnitude of the understatement of economic activity may have been in the course of the transition. In the process, alternative real GDP estimates are proposed. The next section discusses the benefits of moving away from a teratogenetic system. Some of the tremendous inefficiencies characterizing the centrally planned economy lost their prominence as the latter was dismantled, but the associated welfare gains are often overlooked—even though they should be part and parcel of any analysis of the output collapse. Finally, some concluding remarks on welfare are offered.

Quantities

Growth rates were probably overstated in the old regime, as argued by Khanin and others.[9] While, under central planning, incentives were mostly geared toward overreporting, they are now reversed, suggesting that the rates of output decline since the onset of transition are likely to be overstated.

Overstatement of the Base

Official output data under the Soviet regime suffered from manipulations by the statistical agency and from falsification by the reporting units themselves. Perversely, cheating was sometimes necessary for the reporting firms to overcome the inefficiencies of central planning and meet plan targets. A variety of tricks were used to document the achievement or over-achievement of the objectives laid out in the Plan, ranging from sheer tampering with the raw data to the inclusion in finished goods totals of *brak* (spoilage, rejects, and substandard goods) and incompletely assembled articles.[10]

Insofar as the resulting officially recorded pretransition output levels were artificially high, a portion of

the decline recorded for 1990–94 could constitute a belated recognition of earlier overstatements. Khanin (1992), for example, argues that actual output in the late 1980s has been vastly overstated by Goskomstat. If, indeed, part of the measured output around 1989 was essentially fictitious, part of the subsequent collapse may also have been an illusion. Importantly, this would imply that the centrally planned economy had exhausted its growth potential well before the start of radical reforms.

It should be recognized, however, that enterprise managers in the centrally planned economy also faced incentives to underreport, not least to conceal the illegal appropriation or diversion of production. Another incentive to underreport was related to the so-called ratchet effect: as firms' targets were set on the basis of registered performance, it was prudent not to advertise success too boldly. Managers perhaps also underreported unintentionally, owing to prior theft or pilferage of the product. Nevertheless, on balance, the overall impression was that traditionally the underreporting bias was smaller than the overreporting one (Grossman (1960)).

It should also be acknowledged that the overstatement of activity in the official sector in the late 1980s was offset to some extent by the understatement of the growing activity in the "informal" sector, notwithstanding the attempts initiated by the U.S.S.R. Goskomstat at that time to include estimates of the second economy in the computation of GDP.[11]

On the whole, it seems fair to conclude that, although the pretransition peak of output in the registered economy was overstated by Goskomstat, the actual size of overall GDP in the late 1980s, including the shadow economy, may have been smaller or larger than indicated by the official statistics.

Understatement of Output Since the Onset of the Transition

Reform of the statistical apparatus used by Goskomstat, which had originally been set up as a central planning instrument, has lagged the breakdown of the command economy. In particular, exhaustive reporting of production outcomes, as opposed to business surveys, has so far continued to be a key data collection tool.[12] As a result, whole

---

[8]In those countries, unlike in Central Europe, officially measured GDP fell as much as or more than industrial output, thus contradicting the presumption that the share of industry shrinks during the transition.

[9]See Ericson (1989), Kostinsky and Belkindas (1990), and, for an official recognition, Guzhvin (1992).

[10]Grossman (1960) provides a wealth of examples.

[11]See Treml (1994) and, for more general references, Grossman (1990). It may be no coincidence that such methodological innovations were undertaken as growth in the state sector could on some measures be seen to be coming to a halt. The effort to measure underground activity collapsed, however, with the dissolution of the Soviet Union in 1991 and resumed only slowly. It should be noted that the *System of National Accounts 1993* (Secs. 6.30–6.36) recommends that underground and illegal production of goods and services be included in GDP.

[12]Surveys are admittedly difficult to implement in a context of high rates of exit from, and entry into, any pool of enterprises.

Table 2. Russia: Measured Output and Consumption of Selected Items
(Percent change)

	Production in 1994 Compared to				Consumption in 1994 Compared to		
	1990	1991	1992	1993	1991	1992	1993
Meat	−60	−52	−37	−23	. . .	. . .	. . .
Sausages	−35	−29	−2	2	. . .	. . .	. . .
Meat and meat products	. . .	. . .	. . .	. . .	−7	6	2
Milk	−68	−64	−30	−17	. . .	. . .	. . .
Cheese	−40	−31	−27	−11	. . .	. . .	. . .
Milk and milk products	. . .	. . .	. . .	. . .	−14	−5	−2
Flour	−30	−30	−27	−13	. . .	. . .	. . .
Bread	−31	−34	−27	−18	. . .	. . .	. . .
Bread products	. . .	. . .	. . .	. . .	13	18	5

Sources: Goskomstat of the Russian Federation (production); and Center for Economic Analysis (consumption).

chunks of economic activity have vanished from the official statistics even as many new entities escape recording. Moreover, reporting incentives are presumably inversely correlated with output expansion, as enterprises would readily report sharp output declines in order to justify claims for subsidies, tax exemptions, cheap credits, or other favors but would be reluctant to advertise relatively buoyant performances, which would imply substantial tax liabilities. Thus, the official rates of decline in production tend to depict what is happening in the shrinking state sector more than the movements in overall economic activity.

A number of inconsistencies between the official data collected from various sources point to a significant understatement of output. One of the most prominent inconsistencies is the sharp divergence between the output and consumption of various food items (Table 2). Changes in net imports, dishoarding, and declines in waste are unlikely to account for the full discrepancy between the very large drop in production and the small decrease—or, in some cases, the increase—in consumption. As the underreporting bias is less of a problem for consumption data, the odds are that output is substantially understated.

In the case of bread, it is reasonable to believe that, as indicated by household budget surveys, household consumption increased because bread is a typical inferior good. Imports and exports are virtually nil, implying that changes in foreign trade flows cannot be invoked to reconcile changes in output and consumption. Similarly, the scope for intertemporal substitution in the form of hoarding and dishoarding is negligible. One rationale for the observed divergence could be that the quantity of bread used as fodder declined considerably, thus presumably offsetting to some extent the increase in household consumption. However, as the price of bread did not rise more than that of grain, and as privately owned livestock increased, this is unlikely to be a plausible explanation, given that

feeding bread to animals was done only by households, not state or collective farms. Indeed, Goskomstat seemingly continues to rely exclusively on production figures collected from factories, even though small-scale bakeries have sprung up in many cities.

In the case of meat and milk, imports represented no more than 10–15 percent of consumption in 1994. Again, changes in net imports cannot account for the gap between production and absorption. Most probably, the missing output of milk and meat is produced but either not reported or underreported by privatized enterprises, new small farms, or even collective farms equipped with their own processing facilities.

More generally, published Goskomstat national accounts data (Goskomstat of the Russian Federation (1994), for example) suggest that the decline of real GDP based on end-use categories is smaller than the drop derived from the production side. These data indicate, inter alia, that Goskomstat has started to make upward adjustments to better measure consumption but has not correspondingly amended its techniques to measure the production side. This discrepancy will be exploited below to produce an alternative GDP series.

A second type of inconsistency pertains to financial stocks and flows by main sectors, as compared to these sectors' shares in value added (Table 3). It appears that a major portion of the credits (50 percent) go to the category "other sectors," which contributes only marginally to GDP (about 12 percent). Similarly, current accounts with the banking system are predominantly held by these same "other sectors." In all likelihood, these sectors comprise entities that either are not registered with or do not report to Goskomstat, or both.[13]

---

[13]Admittedly, this phenomenon could also reflect an inability or unwillingness on the part of banks to classify enterprises in well-defined categories.

Table 3. Russia: Sectoral Shares in Credits, Current Accounts with Banks, and GDP

(In percent)

	Bank Credits[1]	Current Accounts with Banks[1]	GDP Shares[2]
Industry	29.6	18.2	38.6
Construction	2.1	2.9	8.0
Agriculture	7.3	2.4	8.8
Trade, procurement, and supply	8.3	3.3	10.1
Transport	1.6	12.2	9.3
Everyday services for households	1.1	1.4	0.4
Other[3]	50.0	59.5	12.0

Sources: Central Bank of Russia; Center for Economic Analysis; and authors' estimates.

[1]As of January 1, 1994.

[2]Provisional, in 1993.

[3]Derived as a residual in the first two columns; to estimate the share of these same other sectors in the GDP decomposition, it is necessary to subtract the contributions to value added of the banking sector and of the budgetary, public, and government organizations (which are also excluded from the first two columns).

A third source of doubt stems from the comparison between the path of electricity consumption and that of output. A priori, one would expect a high degree of positive correlation between these two variables. However, electricity consumption both for industry and overall declined much less than officially measured output (Chart 1).[14] Of course, the divergence between the two series partly reflects the existence of fixed costs, but its magnitude and persistence may also indicate that the actual collapse in output was not as large as the official data state, especially considering that the emerging private sector is likely to be less energy intensive than the old production apparatus. The year-on-year elasticity of electricity consumption with respect to actual output may be quite volatile, however; it depends on parameters that are hard to quantify, such as sectoral price elasticities of electricity use, ongoing changes in the output mix, and the technological scope in the short run for reducing wasteful usage and substituting one energy source for another. The buildup of large arrears on electricity bills should also be taken into account. It would therefore be difficult to go one step further and, as Dobozi and Pohl (1995) have done, estimate the bias in the output series based on electricity consumption alone.

Besides the above inconsistencies, it is clear that numerous activities cannot be captured through the traditional reporting channels, particularly in the ser-

Chart 1. Russia: Officially Measured Output Versus Electricity Consumption

(In percent)

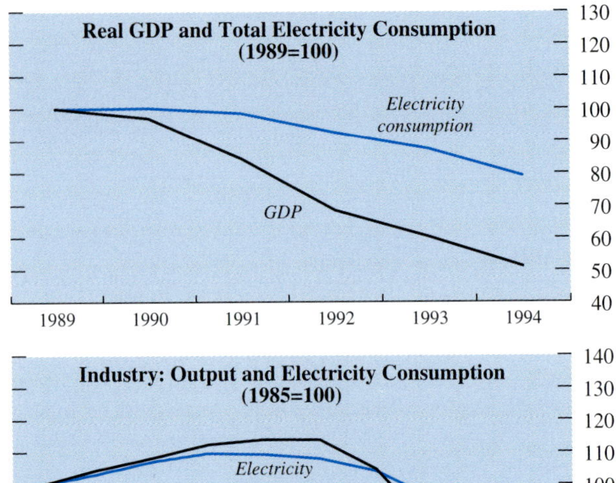

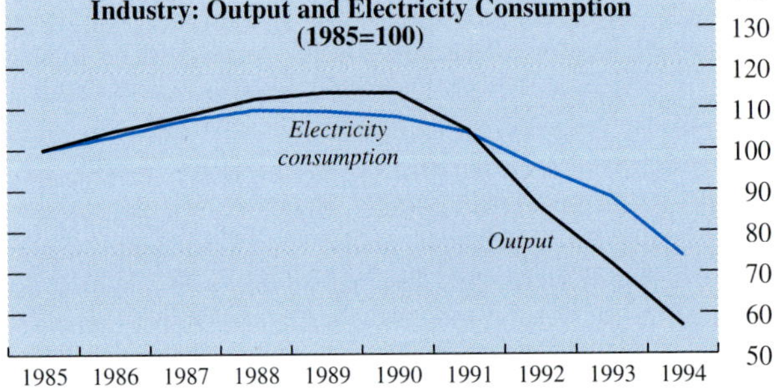

Source: Goskomstat of the Russian Federation.

vice sector.[15] Some of the areas where the problem is most acute include street trading, private taxi services, real estate services, individual translation services, tutoring, home manufacturing (such as handicrafts), small-scale private manufacturing (for example, of furniture and clothing), construction and renovation (such as provided by crews working on private housing projects), repairs of various kinds, private-practice medicine, poaching, pilfering of material inputs, such as timber or gasoline, from state-owned enterprises for private resale, small-scale smuggling (by so-called business tourists), illegal exporting of raw materials (particularly petroleum and nonferrous metals), private "security" services, and production of "moonshine" vodka.[16]

The importance of these activities is reflected in labor market statistics: according to Goskomstat, secondary employment is rising and reached 8 million

---

[14]Incidentally, the fact that the turnaround in the consumption of electricity by industrial enterprises preceded that of industrial output could be interpreted as a sign that output growth may have been overstated in the late 1980s.

[15]More than half a century ago, Clark (1939, p. 5) already deplored that "the Soviet authorities have adopted a somewhat limited and materialistic definition of national income."

[16]Ivanov and Ponomarenko (1994) indicate that thus far illegal activities are not included in official Russian GDP estimates. However, many of the occupations listed above would not be considered illegal in a market economy, even though some of them are admittedly more value additive than others.

people by mid-1994, out of a total labor force officially estimated at 75 million persons. Half of these 8 million held secondary employment on a permanent basis, of which 2.5 million were involved in "middleman trading activities." The survey data cited by Rose (1994) suggest that involvement in the second economy is probably even more widespread than Goskomstat's published estimates indicate. Another sign of the importance of this type of hidden output is the rapidly growing share in household incomes of the category of "business activities, interest and dividends, and other sources"—which accounted for 38 percent of the total by 1994—and the correlative sharp decrease in the share of wages.

While many of these activities never entered the national accounts in the first place, others apparently disappeared from the Goskomstat totals. Inspection of the deseasonalized monthly industrial output series shows very substantial declines in January 1993 and January 1994.[17] These falls are not observed for sectors such as the fuel and energy complex, where output can be monitored relatively closely, but rather for sectors such as light industry, where the extent of privatization and the nature of the production process make control more difficult. This suggests that, with the advent of a new year and the changing of tax and other rules, a number of enterprises decided to stop reporting and simply dropped out of the official statistics.[18]

As mentioned earlier, Goskomstat officials have long recognized that underrecording is a major problem. Indeed, several adjustments have started to be made by Goskomstat to the output data provided through the traditional reporting channels. Specifically, as of mid-1994, the raw numbers collected for trade, construction, and agriculture were supplemented by information from other sources (household budget surveys, customs surveys, building permits, and other survey data).[19] These adjustments added up to about 10 percent of GDP at that time. Another innovation has been the inclusion from July 1994 onward in the official monthly data on gross industrial output of an estimate for the heretofore excluded production of small enterprises. This adjustment has raised the level of that series by some 10 percent. While such efforts are most welcome, they are long overdue and apparently cover only a few sectors.

---

[17]These series are published in the monthly Goskomstat bulletins and in the quarterly reports of the Center for Economic Analysis.

[18]Another sign that some entities stopped reporting could be that nominal gross industrial output is smaller than what would be implied by real output and producer price data. As noted in Koen (1994), however, this discrepancy may also be caused by differences in sample coverage.

[19]However, it should be remembered that, while using information on building permits is sensible, unreported renovation activity would still go uncaptured, as would construction carried out in the absence of permits.

Table 4. Russia: Sales of Goods and Services
(Annual percent change)

	1991	1992	1993	1994
Retail sales				
Series based on				
old definitions	−7.2	−35.3	−0.1	−2.8
Revised series	−3.2	−3.5	1.9	3.0
Households' paid services				
Series based on				
old definitions	−20.8	−41.3	−31.0	−37.0
Revised series	−17.1	−18.0	−30.0	−36.0

Source: Goskomstat of the Russian Federation.

Alternative Real GDP Estimates

The most significant adjustments carried out so far by Goskomstat pertain to retail sales, which form the bulk of household consumption. In 1991, before revisions, they represented 83 percent of household consumption. As shown in Table 4, a drastic revision was implemented, implying that, instead of a cumulative decline of over 40 percent between 1990 and 1994, the volume of retail sales fell by only 2 percent. The revision reportedly involved three markups to the "old" series, which, for 1993, amounted to 5 percent on account of undercoverage of outlets, 20 percent for underreporting, and some 36 percent to account for street trading and supply through "hectic trade" (that is, imports by individuals in their private capacity), respectively. Paid services were also adjusted by Goskomstat. Nevertheless, the resulting cumulative 70 percent decline still seems implausibly large. The size of the revisions shown in Table 4 is of the same order of magnitude as the gap between the sum of the old retail sales and paid services series and consumption as estimated via household budget surveys.

Goskomstat, however, neither carried out the corresponding adjustments on the supply side nor compiled real GDP anew from the demand side.[20] As a result, the early estimates for real GDP continue to be used even though the evidence on expenditures calls for a re-estimation of production.[21] The exercise could be attempted by adjusting the raw output data for those sectors in which underrecording seems to be most acute, using, for example, such data as employment (including secondary employment), combined with some assumptions about productivity or even information obtained from enterprise surveys. This route is left to those who have access to the unpublished data collected by Goskomstat.

---

[20]No decomposition of real GDP changes by sectors of origin or by end uses was ever published.

[21]Official nominal GDP estimates were revised for 1992 (from Rub 15 trillion to Rub 20 trillion, and subsequently back to Rub 18.1 trillion), but, strangely enough, the revisions were not accompanied by changes in the associated real GDP numbers.

Table 5. Russia: Adjusted Real GDP at 1990 Prices
(In billions of rubles)

	1990	1991	1992	1993	1994
GDP	639.9	599.2	515.4	476.6	431.2
Consumption	444.4	396.9	360.7	350.0	338.9
Households	305.0	289.6	274.7	271.3	272.0
Goods[1]	265.0	256.5	247.5	252.2	259.8
Services[2]	40.0	33.1	27.2	19.0	12.2
Public	139.4	107.3	86.0	78.7	66.9
Gross investment	194.1	199.5	153.9	124.1	89.6
Fixed[3]	184.9	156.3	109.4	95.2	75.2
Inventory[4]	9.2	43.2	44.5	28.9	14.4
Net exports[5]	1.4	2.8	0.8	2.5	2.6

Sources: Goskomstat of the Russian Federation; and authors' estimates.

[1]Based on revised Goskomstat retail sales series (see Table 4).

[2]Based on revised Goskomstat paid services series (see Table 4).

[3]Including capital repairs.

[4]See Koen (1994) for a behavioral rationalization of stockbuilding in 1991 and 1992.

[5]Allowance is made for the underreporting of imports and exports (see International Monetary Fund (1992), (1993), and (1995) for details on the measurement of balance of payments flows).

The corrections proposed below rely solely on public information and deliberately err on the conservative side. In other words, the adjustments are of a partial nature, and, when in doubt, the smaller volume estimates were used. Moreover, no conjectures about the size and growth of the shadow economy are introduced, nor is there any speculation about the quantitative effect of improvements in the quality of output.[22] Therefore, the resulting real GDP path should be interpreted as a lower bound rather than as the most plausible estimate of actual GDP.

Starting from 1990,[23] and using that year's prices, the expenditure side of GDP was adjusted in the following way (see Table 5 for details). Household consumption was augmented by taking into account the revisions appearing in Table 4. No allowance was made for the likely increase in households' domestic production and consumption of food. Changes in public consumption were estimated on the basis of budget execution data. Changes in fixed investment were derived taking into account the rising share of capital repairs (as opposed to the installation of new capacity). Lastly, given that considerable uncertainty surrounds any estimates of stockbuilding and net exports, alternative assumptions with respect to their real rates of change were tried out. The estimates actually used involved a downward correction of the official Goskomstat data for inventory accumulation and net exports. In any event, the contribution of these two components to the rate of change of GDP was small, as they represent a relatively modest fraction of total GDP.

Based on this approach, real GDP appears to have declined significantly less than indicated by the official Goskomstat statistics. By and large, the latter overstate the annual rate of decline over the years under consideration by at least 4–7 percent (Table 6 and Chart 2); the cumulative decline in real GDP from its pretransition peak to 1994 would thus be of the order of one third, rather than one half.

The re-estimation carried out above at 1990 prices was then repeated, using prices of the previous year. This second estimation produced a series that is more directly comparable to Goskomstat's.[24] The resulting series differs only marginally from the one compiled by using 1990 prices; cumulatively, they lead virtually to the same estimate.

Quality

Notwithstanding the substantial bias distorting official real GDP statistics, there is no doubt that the total volume of gross and net output has dropped very steeply in Russia since the late 1980s. It is often posited that the welfare impact must have been of the

[22]The "Czech Economic Monitor" (1994), the "Slovak Economic Monitor" (1994), and the "Polish Economic Monitor" (1994), for example, based their alternative GDP estimates for the Czech Republic, the Slovak Republic, and Poland, respectively, on hypotheses regarding these two factors.

[23]No adjustment was attempted for the rate of change from 1989 to 1990. As most of the factors underlying the underrecording of output only became important around 1991, one would not expect the methodology followed here to produce a result very different from the official 3 percent decline.

[24]Goskomstat never published a time series for real GDP based on prices of some fixed year. The cumulatives appearing in Goskomstat documents are derived by chaining year-on-year estimates, based on prices of the previous year.

Chart 2. Russia: Alternative Estimates of Real GDP[1]

(In percent)

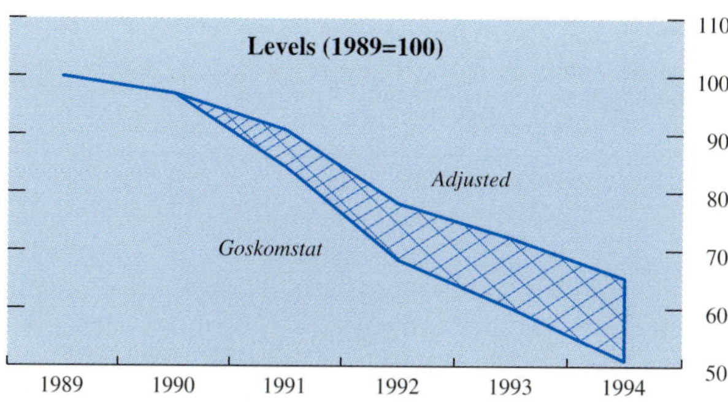

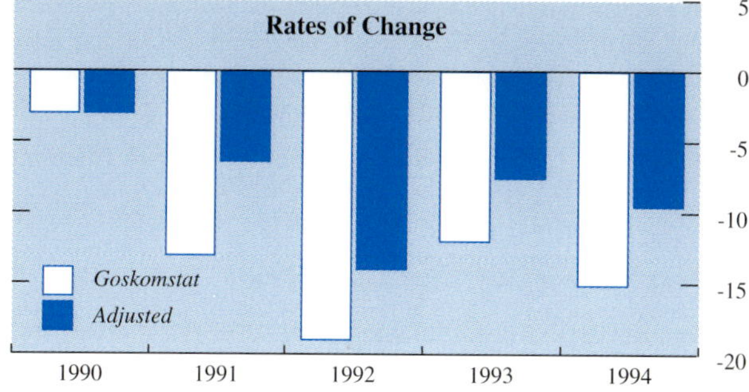

Sources: Goskomstat of the Russian Federation; and authors' estimates.

[1]No correction is made for 1990.

Table 6. Russia: Alternative Real GDP Estimates

(Annual percent change)

	1990	1991	1992	1993	1994
Goskomstat[1]	–3.0	–13.0	–19.0	–12.0	–15.0
Alternative estimates					
At prices of the					
previous year	. . .	–6.4	–14.9	–7.7	–10.6
At 1990 prices	. . .	–6.4	–14.0	–7.5	–9.5

Sources: Goskomstat of the Russian Federation; and authors' estimates.

[1]Quantities are valued at the prices of the previous year. Decimals are not published.

Table 7. Production of Selected Goods in Russia and in the United States, 1989

(Per capita)

	Russia	United States
Iron ore (kg)	726	222
Steel (kg)	630	364
Cars (units)	0.0072	0.0274
Tractors (units)	0.0159	0.0043
Fertilizers (kg)	119	94
Grain (kg)	711	1,152
Television sets (units)	0.0302	0.0592

Source: Goskomstat of the Russian Federation.

same order of magnitude as the actual decline in gross output. However, as emphasized by Winiecki (1991), for example, such an inference is misleading because it ignores the ongoing changes in the composition of output and the sharp reduction in deadweight losses associated with price liberalization and hardening budget constraints.

Machines to Make Machines

One of the characteristics of the centrally planned economy was a massive overaccumulation of capital and, therefore, a slowdown of growth despite very high investment rates. The glorification of gross industrial output, the reliance on an extensive and semi-autarkic growth strategy, the correlative use of antiquated technologies and emphasis on installation of new capacity at the expense of maintenance and distribution, and the constraints imposed by the Plan resulted in the use of more production goods per unit of consumer good than would have been necessary under more efficient arrangements. Not only were productivity levels low, but the decline in the efficiency of investment also accelerated during the second half of the 1980s, as evidenced by the rise in both the ratio of unfinished construction and uninstalled equipment to gross fixed investment and the ratio of investment to gross output.[25]

When the tyranny of plan objectives and constraints ceased, the incentives to continue with overinvestment receded, and the composition of domestic absorption changed. From 1989 to 1993, the share of fixed investment in GDP (at current prices) fell from 32 percent to 21 percent. At the same time, the output mix shifted from producer goods in favor of consumer goods (Chart 3). The steepest declines were recorded in industry, for investment goods such as locomotives, freight wagons, bulldozers, cranes, tractors, machine tools, electric motors, turbines, and steel pipes. However, a key reason for the dramatic drop observed in the production of many of these items is that they were of very poor quality or obsolete in their design. Table 7 suggests, for example, that about six times as many tractors were needed per unit of grain output in Russia as in the United States.[26] That such equipment virtually ceased to be produced should not be lamented as an output "loss"; rather, it should be interpreted as a sign that market forces were beginning

---

[25]See, for example, International Monetary Fund, World Bank, Organization for Economic Cooperation and Development, and European Bank for Reconstruction and Development (1991), and Gavrilenkov (1994a). Also striking and paradoxical is the disregard of planners for long horizons, which is obvious, for example, in the way that Russia's natural resource base was exploited.

[26]A more precise comparison would have to be based on stocks of tractors rather than on the domestically produced flow.

Chart 3. Russia: Industrial Output

(In percent)

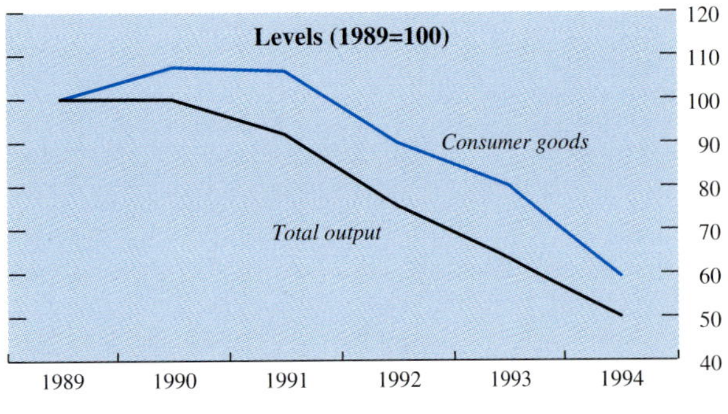

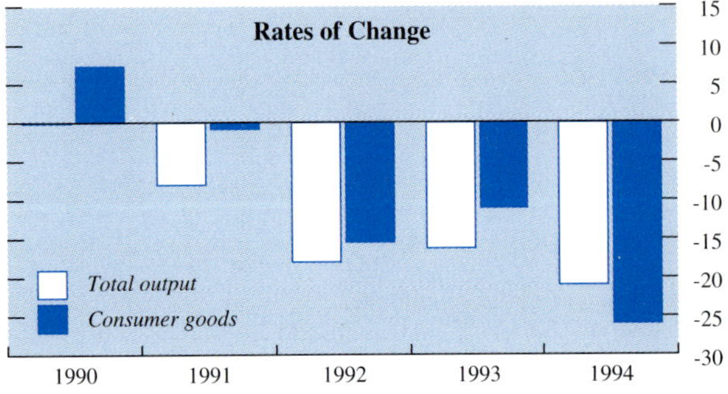

Source: Goskomstat of the Russian Federation.

Table 8. Russia: Conversion of Enterprises in the Military-Industrial Complex

(Annual percent change)

	1991	1992	1993	1994
Volume of production	−14	−18	−16	−35
Military goods	−26	−38	−30	−39
Civilian goods	−4	−7	−11	−33
Production personnel	−4	−9	−12	−16

Source: Center for Economic Analysis.

to operate. Correlatively, as can be inferred from Table 7 for the case of steel, output for some items declined from excessively high levels.

Military Output

Given the highly militarized structure of the Soviet production apparatus, a particularly important dimension of the shift in the composition of output is related to the conversion process in the military-industrial complex launched in the late 1980s. Traditionally, enterprises in the military-industrial complex produced, in addition to armaments, the bulk of civilian intermediates, such as presses for the shoe industry, spinning looms, and agro-industrial equipment, as well as the bulk of civilian final goods, such as refrigerators, ovens, vacuum cleaners, television sets, videocassette recorders, cameras, radios, tape recorders, and sewing machines. Civilian products represented some 44 percent of the output of defense enterprises in 1988.

The overall collapse in output did not spare defense enterprises (Table 8). However, the blow was cushioned by a rapid shift in production from military to civilian goods. Output declined only moderately or barely at all between 1989 and 1993 for a number of the consumer goods manufactured by defense enterprises (for example, refrigerators, vacuum cleaners, television sets, and sewing machines).[27] This shift in production, combined with drastic cuts in defense procurement, caused the share of civilian products in total output to approach 80 percent by 1993. Notably, defense enterprises not only stepped up the production of existing goods, but also attempted to diversify and innovate, for example, in the areas of electric household appliances and medical equipment.[28]

Queues and Shoddy Consumer Goods

The liberalization of internal and external trade in 1992 resulted in a dramatic expansion of consumer choice and an equally spectacular curtailment of queues.[29] Under central planning, enterprise managers had an incentive to choose the intracommodity assortment that would maximize plan fulfillment in terms of the specified physical unit of measurement rather than the one that would satisfy consumers. The death of the Plan, the liberalization of prices, and the opening up of the economy meant that a wide range of consumer goods and services that were previously unavailable or restricted to an elite were henceforth on sale in kiosks and private shops or offered by private companies. Moreover, as the real exchange rate of the ruble appreciated,[30] Russian consumers gained access to a widening array of foreign goods, which contributed to the switch from a sellers' to a buyers' market.

---

[27]However, the sharp real appreciation of the ruble in the second half of 1993—analyzed by Koen and Meyermans (1994)—contributed to substantial declines in the production of some of these items in 1994 (bottom panel of Chart 3).

[28]More detailed information and methodological comments are provided in Center for Economic Analysis (1994).

[29]Koen and Phillips (1993) analyze price liberalization at length. The economic reviews of Russia by the IMF describe the evolution of the rules governing external trade (International Monetary Fund (1992), (1993), and (1995)).

[30]Largely reflecting the massive overshooting at the time of the price jump associated with the freeing of most prices, the real exchange rate vis-à-vis the U.S. dollar on the interbank market appreciated by close to 1,000 percent between January 1992 and December 1993. In 1994, it remained within a 10 percent band around the end-1993 level.

The availability of goods continued to improve over time: while the overall retail availability coefficient (calculated as the average for selected items of the percentage of the main cities in which those items were available) was approximately 50 percent for food products and 70 percent for nonfood goods in 1992, it exceeded 90 percent by December 1994.[31] This statistic is consistent with the evidence from opinion surveys, which show a sharp decline in the time spent in queues: according to one such poll,[32] the proportion of respondents spending at least one hour a day in a queue fell from 67 percent in January 1992 to 23 percent two years later.[33] At the same time, anecdotal evidence strongly suggests that the availability of services also improved considerably.

As stressed by Lipton and Sachs (1992), among others, traditional indicators of household welfare do not capture the benefits entailed by the broadening of the consumption set and by the reduction of the time spent searching and queuing. It remains a moot point whether, as suggested by Roberts (1994), these gains exceed the measured real income losses suffered in the wake of price liberalization, but they are clearly very substantial.

Efficiency in Consumption

The former economic system was characterized not only by chronic overinvestment, a high degree of militarization, and pervasive shortages of consumer goods, but also by waste on a large scale in the consumption of intermediates and final output. These characteristics are distinct but obviously interrelated, and examples of such behavior abound in the literature (see, for instance, Grossman (1960) and Liapis and Markish (1994)). They include the deliberate destruction of producer goods, which sometimes took place when performance was measured not by output but by the consumption of an input (scrapping of unused structural steel by construction enterprises or the wanton spilling of gasoline). Another example is the accumulation of unnecessary ton-miles (actual, not written-up) hauled by trucks. More generally, the rates of breakage and spoilage in the course of the distribution process were notoriously high, while the goods received by customers often deviated considerably

from their alleged specifications, forcing end users to adapt them to their needs at considerable cost. These gross inefficiencies meant that some enterprises were actually engaged in value-subtracting activities. Declining raw output in such instances is value additive.

The rise in real interest rates and the hardening of budget constraints associated with the transition significantly increased the cost of the above-mentioned "losses." To the extent that their occurrence lessened, there was scope for consumption to decline less than gross output. Admittedly, some inefficiencies were too deeply embedded in the organization of the economy to disappear overnight. Moreover, the disruption of the traditional linkages caused by the abandonment of the old rules entailed significant but temporary coordination failures and the transitory persistence of wastage. Thus, short-run rigidities meant that the gains allowed by the move to market-based arrangements would materialize only over a period of several years.

Welfare

The earlier sections showed that output fell less in Russia than stated in the official statistics and that part of the decline was not detrimental to welfare. This concluding section tries to come closer to an overall judgment on aggregate welfare. A definitive verdict is, of course, bound to remain elusive, as some important dimensions cannot be quantified, but some of the oft-encountered misconceptions about the welfare impact of the output collapse can be dismissed.

A very crude, extremely inadequate, but frequently cited welfare indicator is the officially measured volume of gross industrial output. Many commentators in the Russian press, in line with Soviet prejudices, continue to describe the evolution of living standards over the past few years as if they were perfectly correlated with this indicator and thus assert that, on average, these standards have tumbled by more than one half (Chart 4).[34]

A more relevant production-based measure is GDP corrected for underreporting, as estimated above. On this account, aggregate welfare would have declined by no more than one third (Chart 4). However, if only because of the changes in the output mix, GDP may not be a satisfactory proxy for welfare. Another reason to prefer an absorption-based measure can be illustrated by the case of oil. A large portion of the oil produced in Russia was traditionally sent to the other states of the former Soviet Union at a price so low that

---

[31]The unavailability of items in some cities three years after price liberalization probably reflects insufficient demand or administrative restrictions on price setting, rather than persistent supply failures.

[32]New Russia Barometer III, conducted nationwide in March–April 1994 under the aegis of the Paul Lazarsfeld Society of Vienna.

[33]Residual queuing can be associated with maintained local price controls or, in a newer way, with the (most often illusory) perception of golden investment opportunities, as witnessed by the long lines to purchase the shares offered by some investment funds.

---

[34]In the process, these commentators overlook the fact that industrial output, valued at world prices, declined less than at domestic prices (see an earlier version of this paper, Gavrilenkov and Koen (1994, Section II.4)).

Chart 4. Russia: Alternative Welfare Measures

(1989=100; in real terms)

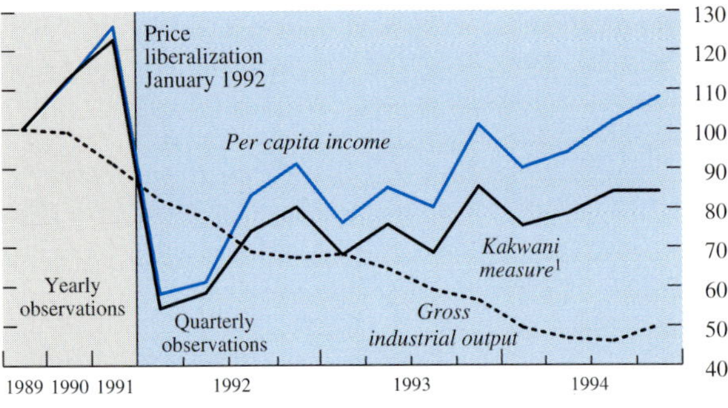

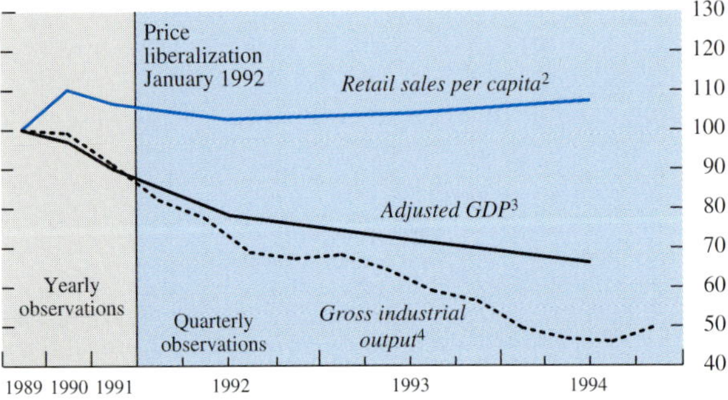

Sources: Goskomstat of the Russian Federation; Center for Economic Analysis; and authors' calculations.
[1]Defined as the product of average real per capita income and one minus the Gini coefficient.
[2]Revised yearly series, adjusted for undercoverage, underreporting, and "hectic trade" (see Table 4).
[3]Yearly series.
[4]Yearly series through 1991, quarterly series thereafter.

these shipments in effect represented a huge subsidy. The steep decline in Russian oil production since the late 1980s was accompanied by a considerable compression of these subsidized deliveries. Hence, part of the output decline was the counterpart of a cut in subsidies to foreigners, which thus did not hurt domestic living standards.[35]

Average real income per capita may be considered a better proxy for welfare than GDP. This measure suggests that, by the second half of 1994, welfare had broadly reverted to its 1989 level. It could be argued, however, that the sharp increase in income inequality registered since 1991 mitigated the recovery in average real incomes. A synthetic measure taking into account both the level of total household income and its distribution can be defined as $W = \mu(1 - G)$, where μ

is an index of average real income per capita and G is the Gini coefficient.[36] This measure, depicted as the Kakwani measure in Chart 4, increases with the aggregate income level and decreases as inequality rises. By the end of 1994, it stood at about 85 percent of its 1989 level.[37]

An alternative set of indicators could be based directly on household per capita consumption, the bulk of which is constituted by retail sales of goods. If Goskomstat's adjustments for informal trade (discussed in the first section of the paper) are taken into account, this indicator declined only moderately in 1991 and 1992 and recovered thereafter, while remaining above its 1989 level throughout the period under consideration. Sales of paid services declined much more, but they represent only a small fraction—about one tenth—of household expenditures. Aggregate private household consumption thus did not collapse. This finding is consistent with the observed increase in household ownership of consumer durables, such as cars, washing machines, and television sets (Table 9).

It could be argued, however, that the current dynamism of aggregate consumption is not sustainable because it is being paid for by the dilapidation of the capital stock, as evidenced by asset-stripping behavior or the deterioration of important segments of the infrastructure (which was never that good to begin with). In this regard, using a measure such as GDP as a proxy for welfare has the merit of including investment and thus of reflecting this trade-off. In principle, of course, welfare would be better captured by the present value of current and future consumption flows than by current consumption flows alone.

Both income- and consumption-based measures project an overly bleak image of the evolution of welfare insofar as they ignore the gains associated with wider choice and shortened searching and queuing. In addition, as emphasized by Illarionov, Layard, and Orszag (1994), services such as housing remained vastly underpriced while their consumption stayed broadly unchanged, implying that total consumption, properly defined (that is, at market-based shadow prices), declined much less than indicated by the real money income or real consumption measures described above. In this light, it

---

[35]A more complete analysis would have to encompass the changes in terms of trade and volumes exported and imported for all goods and services.

[36] One among several rationales for this measure is the following: in a society with n individuals arranged in ascending order of their incomes x_i ($x_1 \leq x_2 \leq \ldots \leq x_n$), a welfare function can be defined as $\sum_i x_i v_i$, where v_i is proportional to the number of individuals whose income is at least equal to x_i; it can then be shown that aggregate welfare equals $\mu(1 - G)$ (see Kakwani (1985) and the references therein).
[37]The Gini coefficients published by Goskomstat and by the Center for Economic Analysis differ at times, but the use of one or the other series only marginally affects the evolution of the Kakwani measure.

Table 9. Russia: Ownership of Selected Consumer Durables
(End-year; units per 100 households)

	1970	1980	1985	1990	1991	1992	1993
Television sets	52	91	103	111	112	114	115
Radios	74	92	101	99	100	102	103
Recorders	8	28	40	58	59	60	62
Refrigerators/freezers	30	89	95	95	95	95	95
Washing machines	52	76	76	77	78	79	80
Vacuum cleaners	11	32	43	51	52	52	53
Watches	433	534	547	585	595	602	614
Sewing machines	58	67	67	61	60	58	55
Cars	2	10	14	18	19	21	23
Motorcycles	8	11	15	21	22	22	23
Bicycles	50	46	51	54	55	55	55
Photo cameras	30	33	36	35	36	37	37

Source: Goskomstat of the Russian Federation (1995).

may not be unreasonable to claim that by 1994 welfare had actually improved, compared with the late 1980s.

Finally, there are a number of costs accompanying the transition, such as the deterioration in the sanitary situation, the increase in morbidity rates, the generalization of corruption, and greater uncertainty, that should be incorporated in more comprehensive welfare measures. Similarly, a number of benefits, such as the newly gained political freedoms or the reduction in pollution levels mirroring the decline in industrial production, ought also to be factored in. In some cases, it is not clear how intimately these costs or benefits are related to the output decline per se; in any event, an extended welfare analysis of this type lies beyond the scope of this paper.

Bibliography

Berg, Andrew, "Measurement and Mismeasurement of Economic Activity During Transition to the Market," in *Eastern Europe in Transition: From Recession to Growth*? World Bank Discussion Paper No. 196, ed. by Mario I. Blejer, Guillermo A. Calvo, Fabrizio Coricelli, and Alan H. Gelb (Washington: World Bank, 1993).

_______, and Jeffrey D. Sachs, "Structural Adjustment and International Trade in Eastern Europe: The Case of Poland," *Economic Policy*, No. 14 (April 1992), pp. 117–73.

Center for Economic Analysis, *Russia—1994 Economic Outlook*, No. 3 (in Russian) (Moscow: Center for Economic Analysis, September 1994).

Clark, Colin, *A Critique of Russia Statistics* (London: MacMillan, 1939).

"Czech Economic Monitor," *PlanEcon Report*, Vol. 10 (September 28, 1994).

Dobozi, Istvan, and Gerhard Pohl, "Real Output Decline in Transition Economies—Forget GDP, Try Power Consumption Data!" *Transition*, Vol.6 (January-February 1995), pp.17–8.

Ericson, Richard E., "The Soviet Statistical Debate: Khanin vs. TsSU," in *The Impoverished Superpower: Perestroika and the Soviet Military Burden*, ed. by Henry S. Rowen and Charles Wolf, Jr. (San Francisco: Institute for Contemporary Studies Press, 1989).

European Union, International Monetary Fund, Organization for Economic Cooperation and Development, United Nations, and World Bank, *System of National Accounts 1993* (Brussels/ Luxembourg, New York, Paris, and Washington, 1993).

Gavrilenkov, Evgeny (1994a), "Russia: Out of the Post-Soviet Macroeconomic Deadlock Through a Labyrinth of Reforms," *Review of Economies in Transition*, Bank of Finland, No. 3 (1994), pp. 59–80.

_______(1994b), "The Crisis of Expenditure Economy in Russia" (in Russian), *Problemy Teorii i Praktiki Upravleniya*, No. 5 (1994), pp. 28–34.

_______, and Vincent Koen, "How Large Was the Output Collapse in Russia? Alternative Estimates and Welfare Implications," IMF Working Paper, WP/94/154 (Washington: International Monetary Fund, December 1994).

Goskomstat of the Russian Federation, *The Russian Federation in Figures, 1993* (in Russian) (Moscow: Goskomstat, 1994).

_______, *Living Standards of Households in the Russian Federation* (in Russian) (Moscow: Goskomstat, 1995).

Grossman, Gregory, *Soviet Statistics of Physical Output of Industrial Commodities; Their Compilation and Quality* (Princeton, New Jersey: Princeton University Press, 1960).

_______, "The Second Economy in the U.S.S.R. and Eastern Europe: A Bibliography," Berkeley-Duke Occasional Papers on the Second Economy in the USSR, No. 21 (Bala Cynwyd, Pennsylvania: WEFA Group, July 1990).

Guzhvin, P., "Trust in Statistics" (in Russian), *Statistical Bulletin*, Goskomstat of the Russian Federation, No. 9 (1992), pp. 3–21.

Illarionov, Andrei, Richard Layard, and Peter Orszag, "The Conditions of Life," in *Economic Transformation in Russia*, ed. by Anders Åslund (London: Pinter Publishers, 1994).

International Monetary Fund, *Russian Federation*, IMF Economic Review (Washington: International Monetary Fund, 1992, 1993, and 1995).

_______, World Bank, Organization for Economic Cooperation and Development, and European Bank for Reconstruction and Development, *A Study of the Soviet Economy,* Vol. 1 (Washington: International Monetary Fund, 1991).

Ivanov, Yu., and A. Ponomarenko, "Gross Domestic Product: Definition, Estimation and Projection" (in Russian), *Ekonomist*, No. 3 (1994), pp. 11–20.

Kakwani, Nanak, "Measurement of Welfare with Applications to Australia," *Journal of Development Economics*, Vol. 18 (August 1985), pp. 429–61.

Khanin, Girsh Itsykovich, "Economic Results for Russia in the First Quarter of 1992" (in Russian), *EKO*, Nos. 6 and 7 (1992), pp. 26–38 and pp. 54–69.

Koen, Vincent, "Measuring the Transition: A User's View of National Accounts in Russia," IMF Working Paper, WP/94/6 (Washington: International Monetary Fund, January 1994).

_______, and Steven Phillips, *Price Liberalization in Russia: Behavior of Prices, Household Incomes, and Consumption During the First Year*, IMF Occasional Paper No. 104 (Washington: International Monetary Fund, June 1993).

Koen, Vincent, and Eric Meyermans, "Exchange Rate Determinants in Russia: 1992–93," IMF Working Paper,

WP/94/66 (Washington: International Monetary Fund, June 1994).

Kostinsky, Barry L., and Misha Belkindas, "Official Soviet Gross National Product Accounting," in *Measuring Soviet GNP: Problems and Solutions,* A Conference Report (Washington: Central Intelligence Agency, 1990).

Liapis, Peter S., and Yuri Markish, "Demand for Purchased Inputs Continues to Decline: Yields Yet to Be Significantly Affected," in *International Agriculture and Trade Reports, Former U.S.S.R.,* Situation and Outlook Series (Washington: U.S. Department of Agriculture, May 1994).

Lipton, David, and Jeffrey D. Sachs, "Prospects for Russia's Economic Reforms," *Brookings Papers on Economic Activity,* No. 2 (1992), pp. 213–83.

"Polish Economic Monitor," *PlanEcon Report,* Vol. 10 (November 4, 1994).

Rajewski, Zenon, "Gross Domestic Product," in *Polish Economy in 1990–1992. Experience and Conclusions,* ed. by Leszek Zienkowski (Warsaw: Research Center for Economic and Statistical Studies of the Central Statistical Office and the Polish Academy of Sciences, 1993).

Roberts, Bryan, "Welfare Change During Economic Transition: The Effects of Ending Shortages in Russia" (unpublished; Miami, Florida: University of Miami, October 1994).

Rose, Richard, "Getting by Without Government: Everyday Life in Russia," *Daedalus,* Vol. 123 (Summer 1994), pp. 41–62.

"Slovak Economic Monitor," *PlanEcon Report,* Vol. 10 (September 9, 1994).

Treml, Vladimir, "Problems with Soviet Statistics: Past and Present," in *Defense Conversion, Economic Reform, and the Outlook for the Russian and Ukrainian Economies,* ed. by Henry S. Rowen, Charles Wolf, Jr., and Jeanne Zlotnick (New York: St. Martin's Press, 1994).

United States Bureau of the Census, *Historical Statistics of the United States, Colonial Times to 1970* (Washington: U.S. Department of Commerce, Bureau of the Census, 1975).

Winiecki, Jan, "The Inevitability of a Fall in Output in the Early Stages of Transition to the Market: Theoretical Underpinnings," *Soviet Studies,* Vol. 43 (No. 4, 1991), pp. 669–76.

World Bank, *Statistical Handbook 1994: States of the Former U.S.S.R.* (Washington: World Bank, 1994).

Yurkov, Yurii, "The Statistical Mirror of the Market" (in Russian), *Ekonomika i Zhizn,* No. 35 (August 1994).

VII

Foreign Direct Investment in the World Economy

Edward M. Graham[1]

Worldwide flows of foreign direct investment began to surge about ten years ago. In the year 1984, the total flow of direct investment outward from the industrial economies (which accounted for the vast majority of total measured flows worldwide) was a substantial $49.5 billion. Subsequently, flows of foreign direct investment steadily increased each year until they peaked in 1990 at $222 billion, more than quadruple the 1984 level. Following the 1990 peak, annual flows of foreign direct investment attenuated somewhat but remained at high levels ($178 billion in 1991, $162 billion in 1992, and $175 billion in 1993).

Foreign direct investment flow is, by definition, an increase in the book value of the net worth of investments in one country held by investors of another country, where the investments are under the managerial control of the investors. Most of these investments are, in fact, subsidiaries of multinational corporations, and the investors are the parent organizations of these firms. Thus, foreign direct investment flows mainly represent the expansion of the international activities of multinational corporations. The surge of foreign direct investment that began in the mid-1980s therefore is largely a manifestation of the much discussed "globalization" of business that has taken place during the past ten years.

This paper discusses a number of facets of foreign direct investment. First, the precise nature of foreign direct investment is examined in some detail from a macroeconomic and a microeconomic perspective. Some long-term trends—where "long-term" means approximately one century—are discussed, as best as these trends can be identified given data limitations, with a special emphasis on the surge identified above. Some characteristics of foreign direct investment—and of the multinational corporations that generate it—are analyzed, including (1) the determinants of foreign direct investment as best as they are known (it shall be seen that the theory of foreign direct investment is not wholly satisfactory); (2) the effects of foreign direct investment on host (recipient) countries, including effects on economic growth; and (3) the effects on home (investor) countries. The paper concludes by discussing some of the current policy issues posed by foreign direct investment and the globalization of business.

What Is Foreign Direct Investment?

The first thing that should be said about foreign direct investment is that the term is a misnomer. Foreign direct investment is not, either in an accounting sense, whether one is talking of financial accounting or of balance of payments accounting, or in an economic sense, truly "investment." For accounting purposes, foreign direct investment takes place when the book value of the net worth of an investment controlled by investors in a country other than the country in which the investment is legally domiciled increases.[2] As noted above, in most cases, the "investment" is in fact a subsidiary of a multinational corporation.[3] The subsidiary itself is typically an ongoing business under the managerial control of the parent firm. On the balance sheet of the subsidiary, the subsidiary's net worth is simply the value of assets of the business minus the liabilities owed to entities other than the business's owners; by the fundamental financial accounting identity

$$(\text{assets}) \equiv (\text{liabilities}) + (\text{owner's equity}),$$

---

[1]The author prepared this study as a visiting scholar in the Research Department. He is Senior Fellow at the Institute for International Economics, Washington, D.C.

[2]If, as can happen, the investment is jointly owned by foreign and domestic investors, foreign direct investment corresponds only to the increase in the value of the portion of the net worth attributable to the foreign investor, including the value of any change in that portion occasioned by transfer of ownership. Thus, if an ongoing firm in some country originally under domestic ownership is sold to a foreign investor, the price paid by the foreign investor to acquire the firm is counted as foreign direct investment (this price representing, from the new owner's perspective, the value of its equity in the firm).

[3]"In most cases" must be said because there are international capital flows classified as foreign direct investment that do not involve transactions between multinational parent firms and their overseas subsidiaries, for example, purchases of residential real estate by individuals and real estate holdings by investment trusts. Worldwide, such transactions account for less than 5 percent of the total stock of foreign direct investment. Such transactions probably would be better classified in a separate category, but, at present, this is not done.

the net worth must be equal to the book value of owner's equity, which, in turn, consists of paid-in capital of the owner plus retained earnings.[4]

Thus, from a balance of payments perspective, foreign direct investment from one country to another consists (mostly) of any net increases in the paid-in capital of investors in the first country to their subsidiaries domiciled in the second country, plus any increase in the retained earnings of these subsidiaries. These increases are recorded in the long-term capital accounts of the two countries as a long-term capital outflow of the investors' country and as a long-term capital inflow of the subsidiaries' country. To count increases in retained earnings thusly might appear a bit odd, as no transaction actually takes place between the two countries. The dilemma is resolved by IMF balance of payments accounting standards by considering *all* earnings reported by the subsidiary (whether retained by the subsidiary or repatriated to the parent) as being transferred to the investors in the home country. (It should be remembered that in almost all cases the "investor" is in fact the parent organization of a multinational corporation.) The portion of these earnings retained in the subsidiary is then classified as a long-term capital flow back to the host country.

From the perspective of a subsidiary, then, foreign direct investment is a *source* of funds and not a *use* of funds. Furthermore, it is but one possible such source. Others include borrowing from local or international lenders other than the subsidiary's foreign owners and, if the foreign parent does not hold 100 percent ownership, raising equity capital from local minority shareholders. Capital expenditures of the subsidiary, which correspond roughly to the economists' concept of real investment, are *uses* of funds. It follows that foreign direct investment flows do not necessarily correspond to real capital formation generated by subsidiaries of multinational corporations.[5]

---

[4]IMF standards thus treat foreign direct investment flows as the sum of paid-in capital and retained earnings. There are substantial differences, unfortunately, in accounting standards for foreign direct investment from country to country, and not all countries follow IMF guidelines. Some countries, for example, the United States, consider any loans from the parent to the subsidiary to be paid-in capital (and, likewise, any loans from the subsidiary to the parent to be negative paid-in capital), but this practice is not universal. Not all countries count retained earnings as foreign direct investment flows—for example, Japan does not. Substantial differences among countries' definitions of what constitutes financial control result in some countries' counting as foreign direct investments what other countries' would consider to be long-term portfolio investments; for this reason, as well as for reasons of errors and omissions, total measured foreign direct investment flows outward from home countries do not equal total measured flows into host countries.

[5]Economists also include as investment any net change in the value of inventory. In what follows, this component of investment is ignored. The effect is the same if it is simply assumed that there is no net change in inventory. Also, of course, any capital that is used up during the course of a year (measured as depreciation) is, from an economic point of view, equivalent to disinvestment. In the

(In billions of dollars)

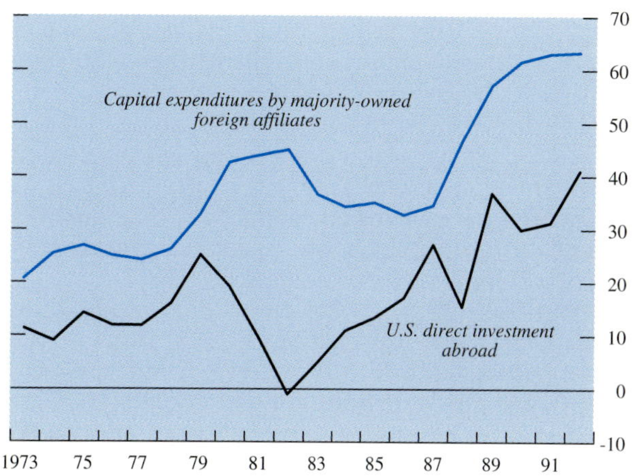

Source: U.S. Department of Commerce.

Indeed, there may be no correspondence whatsoever. Consider two polar cases. In the first, a multinational corporation acquires an ongoing firm in a country other than its home country, paying the current owners of that firm cash. In the year that this transaction takes place, the acquired firm engages in no capital investment whatsoever. The transaction represents a direct investment, but no economic investment takes place. In the second case, a subsidiary already under the control of a multinational corporation embarks upon a large capital expansion program but reports zero earnings and zero dividends in that same year, and no change takes place in the parent firm's paid-in capital; the capital expansion thus is financed via borrowing from financial lenders. No direct investment between the home and host countries is attributable to this parent-subsidiary pair, but the subsidiary has contributed to real capital formation in the host country.

An interesting question then is, How much of a discrepancy is there between measured foreign direct investment flows and economic investment? Unfortunately, global data do not exist that would enable this question to be answered. The question can be answered with respect to U.S. outward investment, because the U.S. government does keep data on the new capital expenditures of majority-owned overseas subsidiaries of U.S. firms (Chart 1).

It is immediately apparent from Chart 1 that capital expenditures of majority-owned affiliates of U.S. firms have consistently been greater than outflows of direct investment from the United States. That is,

---

discussion that follows, the term "investment" can be taken to mean either gross investment, that is, investment before depreciation, or net investment, that is, investment after depreciation.

direct investment from the United States significantly understates the economic investment worldwide (outside the United States) of U.S.-based multinational corporations.[6]

Would a similar statement hold for direct investment from other industrial countries? The answer is "probably not" because of vintage effects specific to direct investment of the United States: the average age of foreign affiliates of U.S. firms is somewhat greater than that of foreign affiliates of multinational corporations from other countries; hence, the contribution of retained earnings to U.S. direct investment outflows likely is higher than for other countries. (The qualifier "likely" is used because data limitations prevent testing of whether this last statement is really true.)

Chart 1 also suggests that new capital expenditures of majority-owned subsidiaries of U.S. firms do not move in lockstep with outflows of U.S. direct investment.[7] The likely reasons for the discrepancies are that (1) U.S. outward investment is, as already suggested, only one source of financing of the capital expenditures of foreign subsidiaries of U.S.-based firms and (2) the mix of financing is sensitive to such variables as interest rates in differing capital markets and other financial factors. Thus, following 1979, when U.S. interest rates rose relative to those elsewhere, the ratio of capital expenditures by these subsidiaries to U.S. outward direct investment fell sharply, indicating that these subsidiaries were turning to other sources of finance. Indeed, the sharp drop in U.S. direct investment abroad during the early 1980s was likely caused in part by U.S. firms borrowing funds or receiving dividends from their foreign subsidiaries in response to very high costs of raising financial capital within the United States.

All of this information simply reaffirms the opening sentence of this section, to the effect that the term "foreign direct investment" is a misnomer. Indeed, from a national income perspective—as well as from the perspective of a firm—foreign direct investment is also a source of resources for investment (where net outward direct investment implies a depletion of these resources), rather than investment itself. This is evident from the national income identity $I \equiv S - \Delta A_I$, where I is gross domestic investment, S is gross domestic savings, and ΔA_I is net change in the international assets held by domestic residents (including official reserves). Note also that $-\Delta A_I = X - M$, where X equals exports and M equals imports.[8] Foreign direct investment is just one component of ΔA_I; an increase in inward direct investment does not automatically imply an increase in I, nor does outward direct investment imply an automatic decrease in I. It has already been shown that in some cases there can be no effect. For example, in the first case above, the acquisition of a domestic firm by a foreign one, the inward direct investment flow generates a decrease in ΔA_I (implying an increase in funds available for domestic investment). But this is exactly offset by claims by domestic residents on foreigners, because the original owners of the acquired firm now hold some claim on the new owners (and this shows up in the income identity as an offsetting increase in some other component of ΔA_I).

Thus, foreign direct investment has been defined in this section with an emphasis placed on what it is not. But this is far from the end of the story. If foreign direct investment were nothing more than an international transfer of financial capital, the end of the story would in fact be close. But foreign direct investment, being a measurable manifestation of the international spread of multinational corporations, entails much more than a financial transfer. Associated with foreign direct investment are transfer of technology and other so-called intangible assets, the stuff of which long-term economic growth is largely made. These transfers, and why they take place, shall be examined shortly. Before doing so, however, it will be useful to look at some historic facts about foreign direct investment.

Foreign Direct Investment in the Long Reach of History

An unfortunate fact is that very little data pertaining to foreign direct investment exist for the years prior to World War II, and much of what data do exist are unreliable. Nonetheless, economic historians have been able to build a convincing case that foreign direct investment—and multinational corporations—played important roles in economic development at least as far back as the industrial revolution of the late nineteenth century. Indeed, the history of foreign direct investment goes back even further: the East India Company, virtually from its start a multinational corporation, was chartered in London in 1600, but little analysis of its role has been attempted.

During the late nineteenth and early twentieth centuries, large amounts of long-term financial capital flowed across national boundaries, financing projects as diverse as building the railroads that opened the

---

[6]The extent of the understatement is probably itself understated by the data in Chart 1, because these data do not account for the capital expenditures of non-majority-owned subsidiaries of U.S. firms.

[7]A simple regression of the two variables of Chart 1 on each other yields a statistically significant regression coefficient (ß) of 0.81, with an adjusted R^2 of 0.42—not a very good fit for a time series of two variables that one might expect to move in lockstep. (If the two variables did move in lockstep, one would expect the regression coefficient and the R^2 to be unitary.) Also, the intercept (α) term is significantly different from zero, indicating that the levels of the two variables are not the same.

[8]International transfers are ignored in this treatment.

American West and the construction of great tea plantations on the Indian subcontinent. Fairly reliable records of these flows exist, but it is difficult to say how much of them represented direct investment. In a pioneering study published in 1938, Cleona Lewis, working mostly with U.S. data, estimated that the vast bulk of the flows represented portfolio, rather than direct, investment, and this was accepted as fact for about four decades (Lewis (1938)). However, beginning in the middle 1970s, a number of economic historians have perused in fine detail the international accounts of the United Kingdom, by far the largest international investor nation of the period, and concluded that at least one third and perhaps more of the stock of the U.K.'s overseas investments were direct in 1914.[9] Studies of other European countries' accounts have yielded similar results.[10] By the first decade of this century, significant numbers of U.S. direct investors were active in Europe, European direct investors were active in North America, and a number of what are today's largest multinational corporations from both continents can trace their first international business activities to this era (Wilkins (1970) and (1989)). This "north-north" foreign direct investment covered a spectrum of sectors, including petroleum and other natural-resource-based industries, manufacturing, and services, especially transport (for example, railroads) and financial services (for example, insurance).

However, the bulk of foreign direct investment early in this century was "north-south" in nature, that is, the home countries were those of Europe, the United States, Canada, and Japan, and the host countries were the less-developed countries of Asia, Africa, and Latin America. This north-south foreign direct investment was heavily concentrated in resource-based industries and in transport and utilities. Thus, it is estimated that in 1914 the shares of British outward direct investment of these two sectors were 53 percent and 31 percent respectively, and that the share of both sectors combined of U.S. outward foreign direct investment was 68 percent, with manufacturing accounting for another 18 percent (Houston and Dunning (1976), and Wilkins (1970)).

World War I put a brake on the international expansion of multinational corporations, and, indeed, international business activity as a percentage of all economic activity almost surely shrank in the interwar years 1918–38. (But, again, data limitations prevent full exploration of this issue.) However, during these years, some sectors witnessed large amounts of new direct investment. These included manufacturing (this was the period, for example, when Ford and General Motors established operations in Europe, Latin America, and Asia) and, most especially, petroleum, this latter sector seeing enormous expansion in Latin America (especially Venezuela) and the Middle East. During the Great Depression years of the 1930s in particular, there was very little expansion of the international activity of multinational corporations (and, in some sectors and regions, this activity contracted), with the exception of those in the petroleum industry.

Foreign direct investment picked up sharply after World War II, especially after 1960. U.S.-based firms in the manufacturing sector especially expanded their international activities. Most of this expansion was focused on developed countries, especially those of Europe, where U.S. firms sought to establish local subsidiaries in response to the formation of the European Common Market, now the European Union (EU). As a result, between 1950 and 1970, the stock of U.S. manufacturing direct investment in Europe increased almost 15-fold, while the share of the stock of U.S. foreign direct investment in developing countries declined to less than 40 percent in 1970. By this year, the share of the stock of U.S. outward foreign direct investment in manufacturing had grown to 41 percent.

In 1970, total flows of foreign direct investment on an outward basis, as reported in IMF statistics, were slightly less than $13 billion; flows from the United States were about $7½ billion, or about 60 percent of the total; and flows from the seven largest industrial countries (the United States, Japan, Germany, France, Italy, the United Kingdom, and Canada) were a bit less than $12 billion, or about 91 percent of the total. Foreign direct investment flows from all of the industrialized countries equaled over 99 percent of the total. International data on foreign direct investment for years prior to 1970 are incomplete, but it is probable that the U.S. share of total foreign direct investment flows throughout the period 1950–70 was well over 60 percent.

Recent Trends in Foreign Direct Investment

By 1993, of the reported total outward foreign direct investment flow of over $186 billion, the U.S. share had fallen to 31 percent, the seven largest industrial countries' share to 79 percent, and the share of all industrialized countries to 94 percent. Of the 6 percent share that was not accounted for by industrial countries, the majority (3.5 percent of the total) was accounted for by Asian countries, and the remainder was spread over a number of developing countries (including but not limited to several of the major oil exporters).

Chart 2 indicates flows of foreign direct investment from the seven largest industrial countries from 1970–93, with flows from the United States and the

---

[9]The pioneering study in this regard is Houston and Dunning (1976).

[10]For a review, see Jones (1994).

Chart 2. Foreign Direct Investment Flows from the Seven Major Industrial Countries

(In billions of dollars)

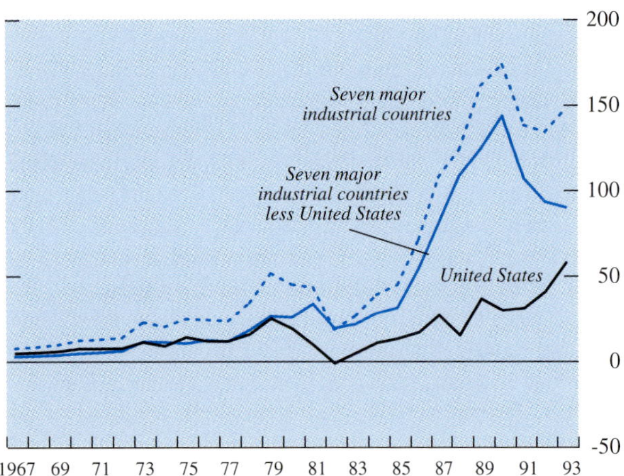

Source: International Monetary Fund.

remaining six countries separately indicated.[11] Several features stand out. First, the U.S. share of these flows was 50 percent or more from 1967 to 1979. After 1979, however, the U.S. share began to fall, reaching a low of just over 17 percent in 1990, the year of peak flows worldwide. Following 1990, however, the U.S. share rebounded sharply, reaching over 39 percent in 1993, a phenomenon examined in more detail below.

Second, total flows of foreign direct investment from the seven largest industrial countries experienced a "minisurge" during the late 1970s and early 1980s but fell sharply following 1981. From the trough year of 1982 onward, however, foreign direct investment flows increased steadily, and the growth became spectacular following 1985 until, as noted in the first section of the paper, these flows peaked in 1990. Exactly what caused this surge of foreign direct investment growth is not entirely clear. If the magnitude of the 1985–90 surge is ignored, the trends in foreign direct investment flows from the seven largest industrial countries during the past twenty-five years or so correlate quite closely with trends in national income growth (that is, these flows seem to wax and wane more or less contemporaneously with first differences in annual income), but the income elasticity of foreign direct investment flows appears to be highly unstable.[12]

What is most clear about the 1985–90 surge is that, by a number of measures, foreign direct investment became more diversified during this period. As already noted, the predominance of the seven largest industrial countries—and, within this group, the predominance of the United States—as home countries to foreign direct investment decreased. The sectoral diversity of foreign direct investment increased; in particular, the amount in the service sectors rose sharply relative to manufacturing.[13] However, by certain other measures, foreign direct investment became less diversified. In particular, the share of flows going to the industrial countries actually increased during the 1980s, and, correspondingly, the share going to the developing countries fell.

Indeed, one of the most notable features of the period was the share of foreign direct investment *received* by the United States, which became the largest host country, as well as the largest home country, to foreign direct investment. Chart 3 traces the cumulative *stocks* of foreign direct investment in the United States, as well as the stocks of U.S. direct investment abroad, from 1970 to 1993. Whereas the stock of foreign direct investment in the United States ($13.3 billion) was only 17½ percent of that of the stock of U.S. direct investment abroad ($75½ billion) in 1970, the stock of the former ($369 billion) was 96½ percent that of the latter ($382 billion) in 1989. Whereas foreign-controlled business operations accounted for a negligible portion of U.S. economic activity in 1970, they grew to account for a very substantial portion by 1989 (Graham and Krugman (1995)).

However, from 1989 to 1993, U.S. direct investment abroad grew much faster than foreign investment in the United States, so that, by the end of 1993, the stock of the former ($445½ billion) was only 81 percent of that of the latter ($548½ billion). What happened? The first thing to be noted is that some aspects of the trends are more apparent than real; in particular, data on U.S. direct investment abroad have been affected by recalibrations periodically made by the U.S. Department of Commerce (for example, the drop in the stock of U.S. direct investment abroad shown in Chart 3 as occurring in 1981 was largely the result of such an adjustment, rather than actual disinvestment by U.S. firms).

Chart 4 indicates the U.S. flows of outward foreign direct investment from 1982 through 1992, broken down by major components: new equity, retained earnings, intrafirm debt, and valuation adjustments.[14] Several points emerge from the rather confusing picture posed by the chart. First, U.S. firms largely were

---

[11]In this and subsequent charts, foreign direct investment outflows are given positive (+) signs; this is in contrast to normal balance of payments reporting, wherein capital outflows are signed negative (–) and inflows positive (+).

[12]For more on the surge of 1985–90, see Graham and Krugman (1993).

[13]Details are reported in United Nations Center on Transnational Corporations (1992).

[14]This breakdown is unfortunately not available for years prior to 1982.

Chart 3. Stocks of Foreign Direct Investment in the United States and U.S. Direct Investment Abroad

(In billions of dollars)

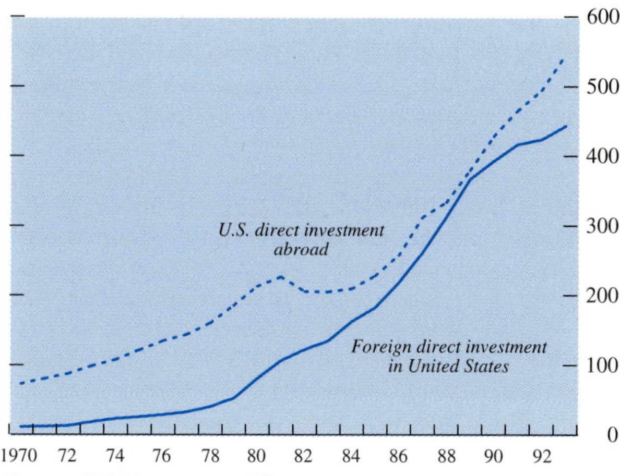

Source: U.S. Department of Commerce.

absent from the foreign direct investment surge of the mid-to-late 1980s (new equity flows were a trickle in the years 1983–90, and there was net disinvestment in 1985, 1988, and 1989), but new equity flows accelerated sharply following 1990. Second, intrafirm debt flows were negative during the U.S. high-interest years of 1982–84, lending credence to the earlier hypothesis that low U.S. foreign direct investment outflows in those years were in part a result of interest rate differentials. Third, retained earnings were strongly positive throughout most of the period. Fourth, valuation adjustments were significant (and, because these are largely generated by currency fluctuations, the effect of adding valuation adjustments to reported foreign direct investment flows is probably to mislead slightly the analyst who does not take these adjustments into account).

The Determinants of Foreign Direct Investment

Over the years, there have been many efforts to explain why firms engage in foreign direct investment. Perhaps the place to start is to note that, in a world of perfect competition, most foreign direct investment simply would not occur: multinational corporations would incur transactions costs not incurred by their domestic rivals, and these costs would drive returns to subnormal levels. It should be emphasized as well that foreign direct investment is not simply an international flow of financial capital, as might occur if arm's-length investors in capital-rich countries simply sought higher returns in capital-scarce countries: while such flow does occur, it is in the form of port-

folio investment rather than direct investment. Given these considerations, analysts have largely looked to the internal characteristics of multinational corporations in order to explain foreign direct investment.

One of the earliest studies was made by John Dunning, who examined the operations of British affiliates of U.S.-based multinational corporations relative to the British-owned rivals of these affiliates (Dunning (1958)). He found that the U.S.-owned affiliates were more productive than their local rivals, a fact that Dunning ascribed to the abilities of the former to transfer technologies and other "intangible assets" (for example, marketing and other managerial skills) from the U.S.-based parent firms to the United Kingdom and to adapt these to the British environment. But also, over time, the British firms caught up with their U.S.-owned rivals, leading Dunning to conclude that the overall effect of U.S. foreign direct investment was to raise British levels of productivity in all firms in an industry and thus generate net benefits for the British economy. Dunning's enthusiasm for foreign direct investment in the United Kingdom almost forty years ago is mirrored in the enthusiasm of many countries for foreign direct investment today.

A second pioneering study of the same epoch by Stephen Hymer explored the nature of the internal characteristics of multinational corporations that enabled them to engage in foreign direct investment, identified as "economies of scale" and "special management skills" (Hymer (1960)). Hymer was gloomier than Dunning in his assessment of multinational corporations; he argued that, while these firms were likely to be more efficient than their rivals, they would also gain market power so that the benefits of competition were lost, with the latter effect more than offsetting the former benefits. This last concern came to dominate a

Chart 4. Composition of Flows of U.S. Direct Investment Abroad

(In billions of dollars)

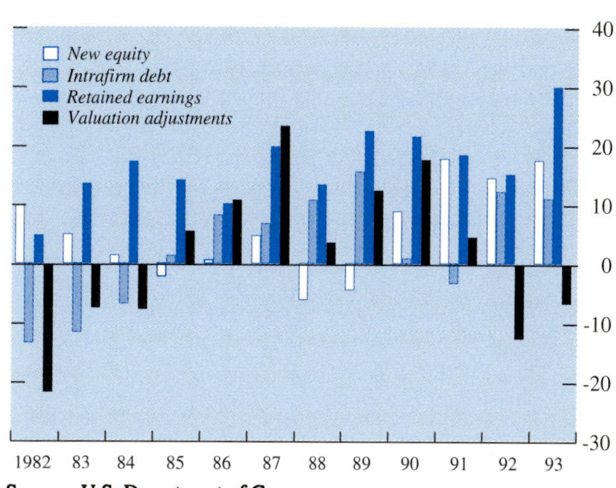

Source: U.S. Department of Commerce.

wide-ranging debate on the merits of the multinational corporations during the 1970s. At that time, it was very much in fashion, especially in developing countries, to view multinational corporations as powerful, monopolistic institutions that would corrupt governments and reduce host nations' welfare.[15] As a consequence, policies proliferated in the 1970s to restrict inward foreign direct investment and regulate closely the activities of multinational corporations. Such policies were mostly implemented by developing countries but also by some industrial countries, such as Canada.

Some analysts, while also starting from Hymer's analysis, arrived at quite different conclusions. In a series of influential articles and books, Raymond Vernon emphasized the importance of new product technology as a determinant of both international trade and investment and the role of factors specific to the home markets of firms as a determinant of how this technology gets created and diffused (Vernon (1966), (1971a), and (1971b)). Taking a somewhat different tack, Peter Buckley and Mark Casson noted that international exploitation of firm-specific advantages internationally does not require that a firm actually own and manage international operations (Buckley and Casson (1976)). Rather, the advantages could be exploited via export or licensing agreements with firms based in countries outside the home market (as, for example, many multinational corporations struck with Japanese firms during the 1960s and 1970s, when Japan severely restricted foreign direct investment inflows). Thus, to explain why operations in one country are actually owned and managed by a firm in some other country, Buckley and Casson turned to the organizational theory of the firm, as originally developed by Ronald Coase and expanded by Oliver Williamson (Coase (1937) and Williamson (1975)). According to these authors, there are economies to be realized by internalizing within a single organization production and marketing functions. These economies of internalization result, in essence, from firms' efforts to avoid the high transactions costs that are associated with attempting to achieve similar outcomes through buying and selling services in external markets. Such transactions costs include opportunity and moral hazard costs. If these economies can continue to be realized by expanding the organization to cross national boundaries, foreign direct investment occurs.

Buckley and Casson triggered a number of subsequent studies applying the organizational theory of the firm (a theory that itself has seen considerable refinement in recent years) to the multinational corporation.[16] For example, John Cantwell posits that rivalry among multinational corporations leads to more rapid development and diffusion of desirable new technologies than would occur in a world where there were no economies of internalization and where technology was transferred by licensing (Cantwell (1989)). This suggests that foreign direct investment has a positive effect on economic efficiency and growth, the conclusion first reached by Dunning. In the following sections, some of the logic and evidence for this position is examined from the perspective of both home and host countries.

Before moving to this examination, however, it should be noted that there are aspects of foreign direct investment and the multinational corporation not adequately explained by Buckley and Casson or subsequent theories based on the organizational theory of the firm. In particular, these theories cannot explain why foreign direct investment has undergone surges. There are economic theories of the determinants of foreign direct investment and the multinational corporation not based on the organizational theory of the firm, for example, ones based on the dynamics of oligopoly and on new theories of economic geography, that have some explanatory power. For reasons of space, these are not reviewed here.[17] For the moment, however, most analysts agree that explanations of foreign direct investment based on the organizational theory of the firm have more power than other genres of theory (see, for example, Graham and Krugman (1995)).

The Economic Consequences of Foreign Direct Investment for Host Countries

Foreign direct investment and multinational corporations can have both positive and negative economic effects on host countries. Positive effects come about largely through transfer of technology and other intangible assets, leading to productivity increases that improve the efficiency of resource utilization and ultimately result in higher per capita income. As has already been suggested, such effects can be direct, for example, if subsidiaries of multinational corporations are more productive than local rivals, or if they transfer technologies or other assets to local suppliers, distributors, or other firms with which the multinational corporations do business and, by doing so, enhance the productivity of these. But these effects can also come about indirectly, for example, if increased interfirm rivalry engendered within a sector by the entry of multinational corporations leads to all firms in that sector becoming more productive.

"External benefits" associated with multinational corporations can also boost productivity. For example,

---

[15]See, for example, Barnet and Muller (1974), which was for a time a best-seller in the United States.

[16]A comprehensive review can be found in Dunning (1993, Chapter 4).

[17]For a review, see Onida (1989).

a multinational corporation might employ local workers (including at technical and managerial levels), who, as a result of this employment, upgrade their own knowledge and skills and subsequently leave the multinational corporation and become employed elsewhere. To the extent that their new knowledge and skills can be utilized in their new positions, such knowledge and skills must be counted as external benefits associated with the multinational corporation, that is, benefits that are captured neither by the multinational corporation itself nor the users of its products or services. Both direct benefits, brought about by linkages between multinational corporations and local firms, and indirect benefits, whether created via increased rivalry or the generation of external benefits, are typically termed "spillover effects."

Negative economic effects can also be both direct and indirect. Direct negative effects, from a purely economic perspective, can arise from the market power of the multinational corporation and its ability to use this power to generate supranormal profits and transfer these to its shareholders, who presumably are not residents of the host country. In addition to negative economic effects, the multinational corporation might be capable of indirectly creating negative economic effects for the host country. For example, multinational corporations might be able to influence the local political process to the economic detriment of the host country's economy (for example, by inducing politicians to grant to the multinational corporation direct or indirect subsidies, such as investment incentives or protection from imports in the local market).

There is no reason why, in principle, the positive effects should be dominated by the negative effects or vice versa. This indeterminacy is perhaps why debate over multinational corporations has long been lively and subject to "sea change." As suggested in the previous section, it was the fashion during the 1970s, especially in developing countries, to view the negative effects as dominant, whereas in most of those countries today the positive effects are largely viewed as dominant. Interestingly, in the United States, where official policy had been to stress the positive aspects of foreign direct investment throughout the 1950s, 1960s, and 1970s, when foreign direct investment began rapidly to rise during the late 1980s, many politicians began to question the benefits of this influx, and some restrictive measures have in fact been passed (Graham and Krugman (1995)). Thus, to an extent, trends in official policy of the United States have moved against the overall world trend.

Given that, in principle, the economic effects of foreign direct investment can be in net positive or negative, the issue becomes an empirical one: as events actually transpire, which effects dominate? The first thing to be said on this issue is that it is truly difficult to measure the effects of foreign direct investment and multinational corporations. Does participation by multinational corporations, for example, increase or decrease firm concentration in the affected industries? Several points can be made in this regard: (1) there is an association between global industry concentration and participation by multinational corporations, but the correlation is not exact (the R^2 is far from 1.0);[18] (2) however, over time, the trends in industry concentration have been nonuniform, as concentration in industries with heavy multinational corporation participation generally fell from 1962 to 1982 (Dunning and Pearce (1985)) but rose in the later 1980s; and (3) at the level of individual countries, the trend in most such industries over the past twenty years has been for concentration to rise.[19]

However, as has been noted by numerous analysts, a rise in industry concentration does not necessarily imply an increase in monopoly power within an industry, especially at the level of individual countries. Effective competition within a country might actually be negatively correlated with domestic industrial concentration. If, for example, the concentration were to be the consequence of an opening of the country to international competition, followed by the rationalization of the domestic industry to become more efficient, domestic industrial concentration could rise even though effective competition certainly increased. Likewise, a fall in industry concentration does not necessarily imply a reduction in monopoly power; for example, a trend within an industry toward greater differentiation of products that were imperfect substitutes might lead to an increase in production of individual product varieties by just one or a small number of firms that monopolize individual market segments. Whether overall competition were to be effectively rising or falling would then depend upon the degree of intervariety competition.

In a word, while there is some information to be had in the study of firm concentration, it ultimately does not shed much light on whether multinational corporations do or do not achieve monopoly rents in host countries. To determine this, one might think that studies of firm profitability would be fruitful. But this route, too, leads to indeterminant results. This outcome is particularly true if one seeks to investigate the profitability of multinational corporations' operations in individual host countries: because multinational corporations can (and apparently do) use transfer prices to shift reported profits from one locale to another (largely for reasons of tax minimization), it is impossibly difficult to determine what really is the return of a multinational corporation in any particular

---

[18]For evidence, see Dunning (1993, pp. 428–437).
[19]Individual studies are reviewed in Dunning (1993).

location.[20] But even if one looks to the worldwide profitability of multinational corporations, one must adjust for such variables as differences in intensity of factor usage (multinational corporations, over a range of industries, tend be more capital intensive in their factor utilization than do nonmultinational rivals; hence, the former might be expected to report higher profit rates than the latter). From the many studies of the profitability of multinational corporations, the weight of the evidence seems to be that these firms are marginally more profitable than their nonmultinational rivals, but that the difference largely disappears (or becomes statistically insignificant) when factor intensity is controlled for.

Thus, the evidence on the existence, let alone the magnitude, of negative economic consequences of foreign direct investment and multinational corporations is inconclusive but tending toward dismissal of the idea that these consequences are weighty. What about the evidence for positive economic consequences?

The evidence is overwhelmingly positive with respect to direct effects. Most of this evidence is based on studies of technical efficiency. In terms of technical efficiency, a mass of empirical data supports the hypothesis that multinational corporations significantly outperform domestic rivals in host countries.[21] One major qualifying comment that must be added, however, is that most of the empirical studies on this issue have focused on labor productivity, which can be increased (without an overall increase in multifactor productivity) by substituting capital for labor. Because, as just noted, multinational corporations typically utilize more capital-intensive production methods than do their nonmultinational rivals, some of the measured differences in labor productivity might be ascribable to differing factor intensities. However, a limited number of empirical investigations suggest that the multifactor—as well as the labor—productivity of multinational corporations tends to be higher than that of nonmultinational rivals.

Likewise, numerous empirical studies confirm the presence of spillover effects from multinational corporations in host countries that create benefits to the local economy. As might be expected, the evidence is very strong that linkages between locally owned firms that act as suppliers or distributors for local affiliates of multinational corporations and these affiliates tend

to increase the efficiency of the former. However, some studies have suggested that in the manufacturing sector foreign-owned firms do not necessarily provide more technical assistance to their suppliers than do efficient locally owned firms (see, for example, Goncalves (1986)).

Similarly, there seem to be positive spillovers on competitor firms generated by the participation of multinational corporations in specific sectors. Dunning defines two categories of studies of the effects of multinational corporations upon locally owned competitor firms: those that are based on field studies and those that are based on econometric studies (Dunning (1993)). Both categories tend to support the contention that inward foreign direct investment tends to act as a stimulus to enhance the technical efficiency of local firms that must compete against multinational corporations. Two qualifying statements must be made, however. First, such studies (of both categories) have tended to examine the medium-term impact of the entry of multinational corporations on labor productivity of local rivals and have not considered the long-term impact on, say, local research and development capability. Multinational corporations have historically concentrated research and development activity in their home countries; thus, if the entry of multinational corporations causes local firms to reduce research and development (and if this research and development produces benefits captured in the local economy), some local benefit—likely long-term in nature—might be lost.[22] Second, most of the studies have been cross-sectional in nature; they show that domestic firms that must compete in sectors in which multinational corporations participate tend to have higher technical efficiencies than domestic firms that do not face such competition. These studies thus do not show whether the technical efficiencies of the domestic competitors to multinational corporations improved following the entry of the latter. A limited number of time-series studies of this issue have been conducted, with mixed results (see, for example, Globerman (1985) and Dunning (1985)).

These empirical observations are roughly consistent with a model introduced by Grossman and Helpman dealing with endogenous technological innovation and trade (Grossman and Helpman (1991, Chap. 7)).

---

[20]Interestingly, the evidence for high-profit performance for multinational corporations operating in developing countries is more mixed than for ones operating in developed countries (where, in fact, the unadjusted profit performance of multinational corporations is consistently better than that of rivals that are not multinational). However, it is likely that transfer pricing affects reported profits in developing countries more profoundly than in developed countries, so this evidence must be interpreted with caution.

[21]Individual studies are reviewed in Dunning (1993).

[22]However, Coe, Helpman, and Hoffmaister (1994) show via econometric techniques that developing countries capture considerable benefits through trade from the research and development performed in the 22 industrial country members of the Organization for Economic Cooperation and Development; because trade and foreign direct investment links between countries are correlated (see next subsection), some of the benefits ascribed by Coe, Helpman, and Hoffmaister to trade linkages might in fact be attributable to foreign direct investment linkages, consistent with the evidence reviewed here. The question then becomes, Do countries lose more in benefits if local research and development is displaced by foreign direct investment than gain from that linkage?

The formal model is a standard two-country model, in which one country is labor rich in its factor endowment and the other rich in human capital. The principal conclusion of this model is that, when technological innovation is endogenous (that is, the result of private entrepreneurs who engage in research and development as a profit-maximizing activity), and where knowledge diffuses internationally, a variant of the Heckscher-Ohlin result holds, notably that research and development takes place in the country where factor configurations make this a relatively low-cost activity (namely, the country that is rich in human capital). Under certain world factor configurations, however, the cost of manufacture of goods embodying the technology might be lower in the other country, giving firms an incentive to become multinational by manufacturing in locations other than where the research and development is performed. The labor-rich country in effect trades commodities for technology.

Overall, the evidence seems to support those who maintain that foreign direct investment tends to have net positive effects on host country economies. It would seem that, to the extent that there are negative effects associated with the monopoly power of multinational corporations, these are rather minimal and do not manifest themselves in the form of significant monopoly rents. Also, it is probably true that if foreign direct investment continues to proliferate, entry by new multinational corporations from a multitude of home countries will reduce the monopoly power of incumbent multinational corporations. The evidence that foreign direct investment does convey positive effects through technology transfer and transfer of other intangible assets, in contrast to the evidence on negative effects, is very convincing.

This last point is very important to developing countries. As is explained in the next section, inward foreign direct investment likely reduces in net the amount of international savings available to these countries. This effect, taken by itself, would reduce capital formation in these countries and their long-term growth prospects. However, this effect is likely to be more than offset by growth in productivity owing to technology transfer, such that the net effect on economic growth is positive. Furthermore, increases in growth seem to be correlated with increases in the domestic savings rates of dynamic developing countries, such that any reduction in international savings might be more than offset by increases in domestic savings.[23] The net effect would be a "virtuous circle" of increased domestic savings leading to increased domestic capital formation and, hence, additional growth. In all likelihood, the contribution of foreign direct investment to growth in developing countries is thus strongly positive. Recent empirical work by Borensztein, De Gregorio, and Lee (1994) largely supports these conclusions. Their work indicates that foreign direct investment figures importantly in the transfer of technology to developing countries and thus contributes more to growth than domestic investment. However, there is a qualifying element: this result holds only when the host country has a "minimum threshold stock of human capital," that is, it does not seem to hold for very poor countries with relatively few educated citizens. Also, their results show that foreign direct investment has the effect of increasing total investment in the economy more than one for one, suggesting complementarity between foreign direct investment and fixed domestic capital formation by domestically owned firms.

The Economic Consequences of Foreign Direct Investment for Home Countries

Concern over the effects of foreign direct investment on home countries has long been focused on employment, that is, on whether outward foreign direct investment leads to some form of job loss in the home country.[24] To the professional economist, such concern is largely misplaced, because overall levels of employment are determined by macroeconomic factors on which foreign direct investment has little bearing. The concern is more legitimate, however, if one talks about the *quality* of employment. The following questions are then relevant:

(i) Does foreign direct investment lead to sectoral reallocation of employment, such that workers are released from labor-intensive sectors in greater numbers than they can be reabsorbed at prevailing wages in other sectors, and such that the labor share of national income must fall in order for labor markets to clear? In other words, does the Stolper-Samuelson effect hold? Alternatively, does outward foreign direct investment reduce the demand for high-skill workers in the affected industries, such that these workers must seek jobs in other industries, where they are not fully compensated for the skills that they possess?[25] That is, does outward foreign direct investment cause "bad" (low-paying) jobs to be substituted for "good" (high-paying) ones?

(ii) Does outward foreign direct investment reduce capital formation at home, such that productivity (and,

---

[23]On this, see International Monetary Fund (1995, Chap. 5). As is developed earlier in this paper, multinational firms can intermediate domestic savings into domestic investment.

[24]The classic statement of these concerns is Goldfinger (1971). The concerns have more recently been reflected in the 1994 debate over the North American Free Trade Agreement in the United States, wherein H. Ross Perot echoed the views of Goldfinger, as well as in an ongoing debate in Europe over the "delocalization" effects of foreign direct investment.

[25]An underlying assumption for this to hold is that the skills are not fully transferrable or, alternatively, that they are at least in part sector specific.

hence, per capita income) grows at a lower rate than it would have, had the investment not taken place?

(iii) Does outward foreign direct investment have any effect on the rate of technological innovation in the home country?

Closely related to issue (i) is whether or not foreign direct investment and international trade are complements or substitutes, that is, whether increases in outward foreign direct investment are related to increases or decreases in exports or to increases in imports of related goods. (It is implausible that increases in foreign direct investment would be related to decreases in imports.) If, say, increases in foreign direct investment were characteristically to lead to decreases in exports (that is, foreign direct investment and exports were to be substitutes) or to increases in imports of goods or services in the same sector (that is, foreign direct investment and imports were to be complements), the case could be made that outward foreign direct investment had similar effects on the home-country economy as import liberalization in the relevant sector (as well as similar effects on labor markets, namely, that the labor share of national income could be reduced or the sectoral composition of demand for labor altered—or both—to the detriment of labor income). However, if increases in outward foreign direct investment were to lead to increases in exports (that is, foreign direct investment and exports were to be complements), it would be difficult to construct a case that foreign direct investment had harmful effects on labor, assuming that jobs in the affected sector were considered to be "good" jobs to begin with!

The issue of whether foreign direct investment and exports are substitutes or complements has been rather extensively investigated empirically, and the bulk of the evidence points toward a complementary relationship rather than a substitutive one.[26] Less research has been performed on the relationship between foreign direct investment and imports, but the available evidence suggests that this relationship, too, is complementary (Bergsten and Graham (forthcoming, App. A)). Thus, outward foreign direct investment seems to be positively associated with trade expansion. Both exports and imports seem to expand as foreign direct investment grows. It should be noted that the trade expansion is likely to be intraindustry, that is, exports and imports will tend to grow within sectors and not necessarily across sectors, suggesting that much of the trade is of differentiated products.

What are the implications for labor? Whether the effect of foreign direct investment is to reduce labor's share of national income cannot be determined from the data, but such an effect seems highly unlikely

(there is no evidence that foreign direct investment causes imports to expand in labor-intensive sectors). The effect on the sectoral composition of labor is, however, likely to be positive, because of the complementarity between foreign direct investment and exports and the evidence supporting the contention that export-generating sectors also generate "good" jobs (that is, ones that pay higher-than-average wages) in the advanced countries.

The effects of foreign direct investment on capital formation in home countries depend largely upon the international capital flows that it creates. As noted earlier, these flows effectively add to or subtract from the pool of savings available to finance capital formation. Given that $I \equiv S$, where I is domestic investment (which includes new capital investment but also net additions to inventories) and S is the total savings pool (including international sources), it follows that $\Delta I = \Delta S$, and, ignoring inventory changes, it would seem that a net increase in capital outflows from a host country will displace domestic investment on a one-to-one basis.[27] However, foreign direct investment generates a variety of international capital flows, including various payments to the parent firms of multinational corporations located in the home countries, as well as the foreign direct investment flows themselves. (Moreover, as Chart 4 indicates quite clearly for the United States, new equity outflows are only a part of U.S. foreign direct investment outflows in recent years.) In addition, foreign direct investment can affect the payment of taxes by multinational corporations to their home governments (from a national income accounting perspective, taxes are part of national savings) and, perhaps, the profitability of home operations of multinational corporations (affecting their retained earnings, which is another component of national savings).

The upshot of all of this is that it is truly difficult to assess the effect of foreign direct investment on capital formation in home countries. There is, in fact, a case to be made for asserting that in the long run outward direct investment increases the capital stock of a country, because direct investors will require that their investments have net positive present value and, hence, that future capital inflows must in magnitude exceed current outflows. But this assertion begs the question of what exactly is the counterfactual. If the alternative to foreign direct investment is additional current consumption, obviously a different consequence will follow than if the alternative is additional current investment.

A corollary would be that inward direct investment in the long run reduces the international savings of a host country. While this is almost surely true, it is not at all clear that the effect is either reduced savings

---

[26]See Bergsten and Graham (forthcoming, App. A); Blomström, Lipsey, and Kulchycky (1988); Buigues and Jacquemin (1994); Lipsey and Weiss (1981) and (1984); and Pearce (1990).

[27]For the Organization for Economic Cooperation and Development as a whole, this seems to be the case. See Feldstein (1994).

available to the host country or reduced capital formation. Indeed, at the conclusion of the previous section, the case was made that the overall effect would be increased growth and increased capital formation resulting initially from an increased efficiency of use of capital and sustained by a virtuous circle.

If the effects of foreign direct investment on domestic capital formation are, at root, indeterminant, its effects on domestic research and development activity are more clearly likely to be favorable. This result follows from the following observations.

First, there is a divergence between the total social returns generated by new technology creation and the returns appropriated by the innovator (because of spillover effects). This is a classical result, and one consequence is that private agents, left to their own devices, will tend to underfund research and development relative to what would be the socially optimal level of such funding.

Second, foreign direct investment increases the total size of the market available to the innovating firms and, hence, the appropriable returns available to them. The consequence is that they should be willing to invest more in research and development. Furthermore, as an empirical point rather than a theoretical one, firms tend to do this in their home countries, although research and development by multinational corporations (that is, research and development not performed in their home countries) has in recent years grown rapidly. The unequivocal result is that foreign direct investment should, all else being equal, increase the amount of research and development that is performed. It has also been argued that increased rivalry among multinational firms occasioned by foreign direct investment will accelerate the rate at which these firms introduce the fruits of research and development (new or improved products, or more efficient ways of producing them) to the market (Graham (1985)).

That multinational activity should boost innovation in the home country thus seems a plausible hypothesis. A contrary hypothesis can, however, be offered. For example, Porter (1990) suggests that, in some sectors, U.S.-based firms have used foreign direct investment as a means to switch from higher-cost to lower-cost areas, and that this has actually suppressed incentives to invest in product and process innovation. The question then posed is, Which of these hypotheses is, in a real world context, the dominant one on the basis of empirical evidence? Does, in fact, multinational activity boost innovation in the home country? The answer, unfortunately, is that there is a dearth of hard empirical evidence bearing on this issue. The general empirical evidence that does exist, however, tends to support the former hypothesis that outward foreign direct investment stimulates technological innovation in the home country (see, for example, Mansfield, Romeo, and Wagner (1979)). Evidence for the latter hypothesis tends to be in the form of case

studies of particular industries, and one might conclude that, while the hypothesis might ring true for certain specific cases, as a general proposition it is not on the mark.

The New Policy Environment for Foreign Direct Investment

Although multinational corporations carry out both a large portion of the world's trade and most of its direct investment, the international legal framework for trade is very detailed, whereas that for direct-investment-related activity (other than trade) is quite limited. This asymmetry has long been observed by certain scholars, who have suggested that there might be benefits to extending the multilateral trade rules to cover direct investment and allied activities.[28] Some progress was made on that front in the Uruguay Round of multilateral trade negotiations. Three of the Uruguay Round agreements have significant bearing on foreign direct investment: the Agreement on Trade-Related Investment Measures, which proscribes governmental mandating of certain performance requirements (specifically, local content and trade-balancing requirements) that were determined to be inconsistent with obligations under the General Agreement on Tariffs and Trade; the General Agreement on Trade in Services, which, inter alia, binds governments to certain right-of-establishment and national treatment standards for foreign-controlled enterprises in specified industries; and the Agreement on Trade-Related Intellectual Property, which obligates World Trade Organization (WTO) members to certain standards on intellectual property.

Despite this progress, many trade policy officials believe that more language should be incorporated into the world's multilateral trading rules pertaining to foreign direct investment, perhaps in some future multilateral agreement on investment.[29] As of the time of this writing, two very general issues in this regard were outstanding, notably (i) the venue in which such an agreement would be negotiated and (ii) the substantive content of the agreement.

On the issue of venue, the choice at the moment seems to boil down to the Organization for Economic Cooperation and Development (OECD) or the WTO. The case for the OECD as venue is that there is more consensus on substantive issues among its members, the industrial countries, than among a larger grouping and, hence, that progress could be faster, and the result

---

[28]See, for example, Kindleberger (1969) and Bergsten (1974).

[29]This was the major theme, for example, of the keynote speech of Sir Leon Brittan, Commissioner of the European Union for External Relations, before the European-American Chamber of Commerce on January 31, 1995.

more profound, in this venue than in the WTO. The case for the WTO as a venue is that almost all countries are members or prospective members and that a future multilateral agreement on investment would be effective only if a larger group of countries than the OECD member countries were to agree to abide by its rules.

On the issue of substance, there seems to be widespread consensus as to the broad substantive issues that a future multilateral agreement on investment should cover. Included in such an agreement would be principles pertaining to transparency (host and home countries' laws and policies regarding direct investment and related activities should be public knowledge and as unambiguous as possible), right of establishment, national treatment (investments, including direct investments, of foreigners should be subject to treatment under law that is no less favorable than that accorded to equivalent domestically owned investments), and investor protection (including principles pertaining to expropriation). Substantial disagreement among countries, however, lurks beneath the surface at the level of detail. In particular, how to deal with the likelihood that all nations would claim exceptions to the general principles is problematic.

There is also considerable consensus that an agreement should deal with investment measures that have the potential to distort trade flows or otherwise have effects equivalent to trade barriers. These measures would include performance requirements not currently covered by the Agreement on Trade-Related Investment Measures and perhaps also investment incentives and other subsidies granted by governments to induce foreign direct investors to locate facilities within their jurisdictions. There is much sympathy for the idea that a multilateral agreement on investment should establish procedures to settle disputes between investors and states, in order to supplement existing state-state dispute settlement procedures embodied in the WTO.

A potential model for a future investment agreement is Chapter 11 of the Agreement Establishing the North American Free Trade Association (NAFTA Chapter 11), which contains all of the elements listed above. However, some critics have noted that NAFTA Chapter 11 has done little except to codify the existing investment rules of the three NAFTA countries (Canada, Mexico, and the United States). These critics believe that, without liberalization of existing investment restrictions, negotiation of a multilateral agreement would be a sterile exercise. Other critics, however, believe that NAFTA already goes too far and that, in particular, the investor-state dispute settlement mechanisms in NAFTA Chapter 11 encroach unduly upon national government sovereignty.

These difficulties notwithstanding, it was agreed at the meeting of the OECD countries at the ministerial level in May 1995 to begin negotiations on an invest-

ment agreement. The WTO will likely consider any new investment initiative before its ministerial-level meeting to be held in Singapore in December 1996. Thus, by the time that the WTO meeting is held, there might be some progress within the OECD.

The view of this author on the issue of venue is that, in light of the timing of the two ministerial meetings, substance might actually be allowed to drive venue. If substantive progress is being made at the OECD, meaning progress toward liberalization, it would then be advisable to allow the OECD effort to continue without a parallel effort being launched at the WTO. Then, at some later time, the fruits of the OECD work could be the basis for negotiations at the WTO. If no such progress is made at the OECD, by contrast, it would seem advisable that the whole effort be allowed to migrate to the WTO. As has been noted by a number of trade policy experts, oftentimes trade liberalization is more easily achieved in a "big package" than in a small one. The reason is that political constituencies in favor of liberalization can be counted on more reliably to provide political support for a big package than a small one, whereas often a small package galvanizes opposition from special interests more effectively than the liberalization constituency.[30] Thus, failure to achieve liberalization at the OECD might not necessarily imply automatic failure at the WTO.

If neither the OECD nor the WTO proves to be fertile ground for a multilateral agreement on investment, there are other possible venues. Prime among these would be the Bretton Woods Institutions, the World Bank or the IMF. The World Bank already contains much expertise in the field of direct investment policy, notably within the International Center for the Settlement of Investment Disputes (ICSID) and the Multilateral Investment Guarantee Agency (MIGA). The ICSID was created to facilitate settlements of disputes between investor firms and host countries. At present, 130 nations are signatories to the ICSID. However, the ICSID has not been frequently used as a facility actually to settle investment disputes. But the ICSID could become much more active in the future if it were used, as envisaged, as the principal arbitral body for the settlement of investment disputes under Chapter 11, Part B of NAFTA.

The MIGA is an institution designed to supplement and perhaps eventually supplant national investment insurance programs. The MIGA was designed to encourage foreign direct investment specifically in developing economies. Like the ICSID, the MIGA to date appears to be somewhat underutilized. In 1994, 147 countries were signatories to the MIGA, but only

---

[30]For example, in the United States, the political forces in favor of liberalization seemed more prepared to fight for passage of the Uruguay Round legislation than for other trade-liberalizing legislation in recent times. See Schott (1994).

about one hundred contracts were outstanding, with contingent liabilities of about $1 billion. However, the demand for MIGA guarantees has been rising, especially for insurance associated with investment in the formerly socialist countries.

The main advantage of the World Bank thus is that many of the facilities that might be attached to a multilateral investment agreement already exist within it. If the venue chosen for such an agreement were to be the World Bank's sister organization, the IMF, these facilities would be located close by. The advantage of the WTO is that trade and investment policy issues are complementary and, thus, it would be desirable for the secretariats associated with a new investment agreement to work closely with the existing WTO staff. However, the overriding objective would be to achieve the best possible agreement; if choice of venue were to affect outcome, the venue that enabled this objective to be achieved should be the one chosen.

Bibliography

Barnet, Richard J., and Ronald E. Muller, *Global Reach: The Power of the Multinational Corporations* (New York: Simon and Schuster, 1974).

Bergsten, C. Fred, "Coming Investment Wars?" *Foreign Affairs*, Vol. 53, (October 1974), pp. 135–52.

Bergsten, C. Fred, and Edward M. Graham, "Global Corporations and National Governments: Are Changes Needed in the International Economic and Political Order in Light of the Globalization of Business?" (Washington: Institute for International Economics, forthcoming).

Blomström, Magnus, Robert E. Lipsey, and Ksenia Kulchycky, "U.S. and Swedish Direct Investment and Exports," in *Trade Policy Issues and Empirical Analysis,* ed. by Robert E. Baldwin (Chicago: University of Chicago Press for the National Bureau of Economic Research, 1988).

Borensztein, Eduardo, José De Gregorio, and Jong-Wha Lee, "How Does Foreign Direct Investment Affect Economic Growth?" IMF Working Paper, WP/94/110 (Washington: International Monetary Fund, September 1994).

Buckley, Peter J., and Mark C. Casson, *The Future of the Multinational Enterprise* (London: MacMillan,1976).

Buigues, Pierre, and Alexis Jacquemin, "Foreign Direct Investment and Exports to the European Community," in *Does Ownership Matter: Japanese Multinationals in Europe*, ed. by Mark Mason and Dennis Encarnation (Oxford and New York: Oxford University Press, 1994).

Cantwell, John A., *Technological Innovation and Multinational Corporations* (New York: Basil Blackwell, 1989).

Coe, David T., Elhanan Helpman, and Alexander W. Hoffmaister, "North-South Research and Development Spillovers," IMF Working Paper, WP/94/144 (Washington: International Monetary Fund, December 1994).

Coase, Ronald H., "The Nature of the Firm," *Economica* (New Series), Vol. 4 (November 1937), pp. 386–405.

Dunning, John H., *American Investment in British Manufacturing Industry* (London: Allen & Unwin, 1958).

_____, "The United Kingdom," in *Multinational Enterprises, Economic Structure and International Competitiveness,* ed. by John H. Dunning (New York: Wiley, 1985).

_____, *Multinational Enterprises and the Global Economy* (Wokingham, England: Addison-Wesley, 1993).

_____, and Robert D. Pearce, *The World's Largest Industrial Enterprises, 1962–1983* (New York: St. Martin's Press, 1985).

Feldstein, Martin, "The Effects of Outbound Foreign Direct Investment on the Domestic Capital Stock," NBER Working Paper No. 4668 (Cambridge, Massachusetts: National Bureau of Economic Research, March 1994).

Globerman, Steven, "Canada," in *Multinational Enterprises, Economic Structure and International Competitiveness*, ed. by John H. Dunning (New York: Wiley, 1985).

Goldfinger, Nat, "A Labor View of Foreign Investment and Trade Issues," in Commission on International Trade and Investment Policy, *United States International Economic Policy in an Interdependent World*, Vol. 1 (Washington: U.S. Government Printing Office, 1971).

Goncalves, Reinaldo, "Technical Spillovers and Manpower Training," *Journal of Economic Development*, Vol. 11 (July 1986), pp. 119–32.

Graham, Edward M., "Intra-industry Direct Foreign Investment, Market Structure, Firm Rivalry and Technological Performance," in *Multinationals as Mutual Invaders: Intra-Industry Direct Foreign Investment*, ed. by Asim Erdilek (New York: St. Martin's Press, 1985).

_____, and Paul R. Krugman, "The Surge of Foreign Direct Investment in the 1980s," in *Foreign Direct Investment*, ed. by Kenneth Froot (Chicago: The University of Chicago Press for the National Bureau of Economic Research, 1993).

Graham, Edward M., and Paul R. Krugman, *Foreign Direct Investment in the United States*, 3rd ed. (Washington: Institute for International Economics, 1995).

Grossman, Gene M., and Elhanan Helpman, *Innovation and Growth in the Global Economy* (Cambridge, Massachusetts: MIT Press, 1991).

Houston, Tom, and John H. Dunning, *U.K. Industry Abroad* (London: Financial Times Books, 1976).

Hymer, Stephen H., "The International Operations of National Firms" (Ph.D. diss., Department of Economics, Massachusetts Institute of Technology, 1960; reprint, Cambridge, Massachusetts and London: MIT Press, 1976).

International Monetary Fund, *World Economic Outlook*, World Economic and Financial Surveys (Washington: International Monetary Fund, May 1995).

Jones, Geoffrey, "The Making of Global Enterprise," *Business History*, Vol. 36 (January 1994), pp. 1–17.

Kindleberger, Charles P., *American Business Abroad* (New Haven and London: Yale University Press, 1969).

Lewis, Cleona, *America's Stake in International Investments* (Washington: Brookings Institution, 1938).

Lipsey, Robert E., and Merle Y. Weiss, "Foreign Production and Exports in Manufacturing Industries," *Review of Economics and Statistics*, Vol. 63 (November 1981), pp. 488–94.

______, "Foreign Production and Exports of Individual Firms," *Review of Economics and Statistics*, Vol. 66 (May 1984), pp. 304–8.

Mansfield, Edwin, Anthony Romeo, and Samuel Wagner, "Foreign Trade and U.S. Research and Development," *Review of Economics and Statistics*, Vol. 61 (February 1979), pp. 49–57.

Onida, Fabrizio, "Multinational Firms, International Competition, and Oligopolistic Rivalry: Theoretical Trends," *Rivista di Politica Economica*, Vol. 79 (September 1989), pp. 83–140.

Pearce, Robert D., "Overseas Production and Exporting Performance: Some Further Investigations," University of Reading Discussion Papers in International Investment and Business Studies, No. 136 (Reading, England: University of Reading, Department of Economics, 1990).

Porter, Michael E., *The Competitive Advantage of Nations* (New York: Free Press, 1990).

Schott, Jeffrey J., *The Uruguay Round: An Assessment* (Washington: Institute for International Economics, 1994).

United Nations Center on Transnational Corporations, *World Investment Report* (New York: United Nations, 1992).

Vernon, Raymond, "International Investment and International Trade in the Product Cycle," *Quarterly Journal of Economics*, Volume 80 (May 1966), pp. 190–207.

______ (1971a), *Sovereignty at Bay: The Multinational Spread of U.S. Enterprises* (New York: Basic Books, 1971).

______ (1971b), "The Location of Economic Activity" in *Economic Analysis and the Multinational Enterprise*, ed. by John H. Dunning (London: Allen & Unwin, 1974).

Wilkins, Mira, *The Emergence of Multinational Enterprise: American Business Abroad from the Colonial Era to 1914* (Cambridge, Massachusetts: Harvard University Press, 1970).

______ , *The History of Foreign Investment in the United States to 1914* (Cambridge, Massachusetts and London: Harvard University Press, 1989).

Williamson, Oliver E., *Markets and Hierarchies, Analysis and Antitrust Implications: A Study in the Economics of Internal Organization* (New York: Free Press, 1975).

World Economic and Financial Surveys

This series (ISSN 0258-7440) contains biannual, annual, and periodic studies covering monetary and financial issues of importance to the global economy. The core elements of the series are the *World Economic Outlook* report, usually published in May and October, and the annual report on *International Capital Markets*. Other studies assess international trade policy, private market and official financing for developing countries, exchange and payments systems, export credit policies, and issues raised in the *World Economic Outlook*.

World Economic Outlook: A Survey by the Staff of the International Monetary Fund

The *World Economic Outlook,* published twice a year in English, French, Spanish, and Arabic, presents IMF staff economists' analyses of global economic developments during the near and medium term. Chapters give an overview of the world economy; consider issues affecting industrial countries, developing countries, and economies in transition to the market; and address topics of pressing current interest.

ISSN 0256-6877.
$34.00 (academic rate: $23.00; paper).
1995 (May). ISBN 1-55775-468-3. **Stock #WEO-195.**
1994 (May). ISBN 1-55775-381-4. **Stock #WEO-194.**
1994 (Oct.). ISBN 1-55775-385-7. **Stock #WEO-294.**

International Capital Markets: Developments, Prospects, and Policy Issues

This annual report reviews developments in international capital markets, including recent bond market turbulence and the role of hedge funds, supervision of banks and nonbanks and the regulation of derivatives, structural changes in government securities markets, and recent developments in private market financing for developing countries

$20.00 (academic rate: $12.00; paper).
1995 ISBN 1-55775-516-7. **Stock #WEO-695.**
1994. ISBN 1-55775-426-8. **Stock #WEO-694.**

Staff Studies for the World Economic Outlook

by the IMF's Research Department

These studies, supporting analyses and scenarios of the *World Economic Outlook,* provide a detailed examination of theory and evidence on major issues currently affecting the global economy.
$20.00 (academic rate: $12.00; paper).
1995. ISBN 1-55775-499-3. **Stock #WEO-395.**
1993. ISBN 1-55775-337-7. **Stock #WEO-393.**

Issues in International Exchange and Payments Systems

by a Staff Team from the IMF's Monetary and Exchange Affairs Department

The global trend toward liberalization in countries' international exchange and payments systems has been widespread in both industrial and developing countries and most dramatic in Central and Eastern Europe. Countries in general have brought their exchange systems more in line with market principles and moved toward more flexible exchange rate arrangements in recent years.
$20.00 (academic rate: $12.00; paper).
1995. ISBN 1-55775-480-2. **Stock #WEO-895.**

Private Market Financing for Developing Countries

by a Staff Team from the IMF's Policy Development and Review Department

This study surveys recent trends in private market financing for developing countries, including flows to developing countries through banking and securities markets; the restoration of access to voluntary market financing for some developing countries; and the status of commercial bank debt in low-income countries.
$20.00 (academic rate: $12.00; paper).
1995. ISBN 1-55775-456-X. **Stock #WEO-994.**
1993. ISBN 1-55775-361-X. **Stock #WEO-993.**

International Trade Policies

by a Staff Team led by Naheed Kirmani

The study reviews major issues and developments in trade and their implications for the work of the IMF. Volume I, *The Uruguay Round and Beyond: Principal Issues*, gives and overview of the principal issues and developments in the world trading system. Volume II, *The Uruguay Round and Beyond: Background Papers*, presents detailed background papers on selected trade and trade-related issues. This study updates previous studies published under the title *Issues and Developments in International Trade Policy*.
$20.00 (academic rate: $12.00; paper).
1994. *Volume I. The Uruguay Round and Beyond: Principal Issues*
ISBN 1-55775-469-1. **Stock #WEO-1094.**
1994. *Volume II. The Uruguay Round and Beyond: Background Papers*
ISBN 1-55775-457-8. **Stock #WEO-1494.**
1992. ISBN 1-55775-311-1. **Stock #WEO-1092.**

Official Financing for Developing Countries

by a Staff Team from the IMF's Policy Development and Review Department led by Michael Kuhn

This study provides information on official financing for developing countries, with the focus on low- and lower-middle-income countries. It updates and replaces *Multilateral Official Debt Rescheduling: Recent Experience* and reviews developments in direct financing by official and multilateral sources.
$20.00 (academic rate: $12.00; paper)
1994. ISBN 1-55775-378-4. **Stock #WEO-1394.**

Officially Supported Export Credits: Recent Developments and Prospects

by Michael G. Kuhn, Balazs Horvath, Christopher J. Jarvis

This study examines export credit and cover policies in major industrial countries.
$20.00 (academic rate: $12.00; paper).
1995. ISBN 1-55775-448-9. **Stock #WEO-595.**